François Mitterrand

François Mitterrand
A Political Odyssey

Denis MacShane

UNIVERSE BOOKS
New York

to my mother

Published in the United States of America in 1983
by Universe Books
381 Park Avenue South, New York, N.Y. 10016

© 1982 by Denis MacShane

83 84 85 86 87 / 10 9 8 7 6 5 4 3 2 1

Printed in the United States of America

Library of Congress Cataloging in Publication Data

MacShane, Denis.
    François Mitterrand, a political odyssey.

    Includes index.
    1. Mitterrand, François, 1916–   . 2. France
—Politics and government—20th century.
3. France—Presidents—Biography. I. Title.
DC407.M5M32   1983   944.083'092'4 [B]
82-23793   ISBN 0-87663-418-8

093268

Contents

Preface

This account of François Mitterrand does not claim to be either exhaustive or definitive. Its purpose is to provide an accessible account of its subject and the emergence of the Socialist government of France.

The chief source for this book has been the words written and spoken of François Mitterrand by himself. He has written ten books: *Aux Frontières de l'Union Française* (Julliard 1953), *Présence française et Abandon* (Plon 1957), *La Chine au Defi* (Julliard 1963), *Le Coup d'Etat Permanent* (Plon 1965), *Ma Part de verité* (Fayard 1969), *Un Socialisme du possible* (Le Seuil 1970), *La Rose au Poing* (Flammarion 1973), *La Paille et le Grain* (Flammarion 1975), *L'Abeille et l'Architecte* (Flammarion 1978), and *Ici et Maintenant* (Fayard 1980). In addition there are two volumes of his speeches, writing and journalism: *Politique* (Fayard 1977) and *Politique 2* (Fayard 1981). I am grateful to all his publishers for permission to quote from his books.

There are several biographies of Mitterrand published in French. Roland Cayrol's *François Mitterrand 1945–1967* (Fondation Nationale des Sciences Politiques 1968) is indispensable for Mitterrand's early political career. Franz-Olivier Giesbert's *François Mitterrand ou la tentation de l'histoire* (Editions du Seuil 1978) is more journalistic but also succeeds in presenting a rounded picture of the man. My short sketch owes a lot to Giesbert. Finally there is Charles Moulin's *Mitterrand intime* (Albin Michel 1982) which is written by a close family friend of Mitterrand and is particularly good on the first half of his life. Every senior French politician of the Left has written a book or books setting out his personal beliefs and policies. The arrival of the French Left in power has been enormously helped by the publishing laws that obtain in France, which oblige even the smallest bookshop to carry the latest political works. In any small newsagent in French towns you will see on display the latest books by Mitterrand or Georges Marchais or Régis Debray or Jean Ellenstein. Compared with the British and North American practice where the political theory, biography, programmes and journalism of the Left are only to be found widely available in a handful of obscure radical bookshops, French books about Socialist ideas and practice are as easily obtainable as a Simenon thriller. There is a price to be paid for this. The cosiness of the Paris publishing scene and the small, incestuous circle of writers, academics, publishers, critics, and television interviewers tends to be self-limiting; and, as Régis Debray noted in his *Teachers, Writers, Celebrities: The Intellectuals of Modern France* (Verso 1981), more effort appears to be put into securing television interviews about a book than in writing the work in the first place. Debray, as one of the most interviewed, profiled authors (his rating became even higher when Mitterrand took him into the Elysée as an adviser on Latin America) on the French Left, knows what he is talking about. But coming from Britain, one finds the widespread availability of left-wing books, in quantity as well as quality, highly admirable. Both the Socialist and Communist Parties have their publishing houses with a wide range of titles. The major French publishers also bring out a succession of political books each year. It cuts both ways. There are many right-wing books as well. Giscard d'Estaing's *Démocratie Française* (Fayard 1976) sold two million copies and already right-wing authors are zeroing in on the Mitterrand government. Another major difference between French political publishing and the British or American tradition is the speed with which French publishers bring out books. The period between the delivery of a manuscript and its appearance on sale can be as short as six weeks compared with the nine to eighteen months across the Channel or Atlantic. This means that books in France play a part in topical political debate. In a plural democracy, right-wing ideas deserve their place in the public forum (and even if they do not deserve a place they usually succeed in buying it) but one of the main claims of Socialist discourse is that its ideas are clearer, more logical, more compelling and ultimately more attractive than those of the Right. In most capitalist democracies the ideas of the Left are restricted either by not being published or by attaining only a limited distribution in book form. In France, notwithstanding the lack of access to television and radio, the Left were lucky to have a publishing tradition that especially after 1968 helped to spread Socialist thought.

The profusion of books about the French Left or by its leaders makes the job of anyone trying to write about the subject much easier. There are also some excellent books in English on French politics since 1945. Two good all-round introductions are *Contemporary France: Politics and Society since 1945* (Routledge and Kegan Paul 1979) by D.L. Hanley, A.P. Kerr and N.H. Waites which has an excellent bibliography, and Vincent Wright's *The Government and Politics of France* (Hutchinson 1978). P.M. Williams's *Crisis and Compromise* (Longmans 1964) covers the Fourth Republic particularly well, and his *French Politicians and Elections 1951–1969* (CUP 1971) is very good on Mitterrand's presidential bid in 1965 and the electoral dominance of de Gaulle. J.R. Frears's *France in the Giscard Presidency* (George Allen and Unwin 1981) handles the period 1974–1981 in a clear and fair way. On the French Left there is R.W. Johnson's extremely enjoyable *The Long March of the French Left* (Macmillan 1981) which takes the story up to 1980. It is a scrupulous book, but written with great verve. *The Left in France* (Macmillan 1982) by Neil Nugent and David Lowe takes the story up to May 1981 and is essential reading for those who want to understand the structure and organization of all the component elements of the French Left.

Two general books are well worth reading. John Ardagh's *The New France* (3rd edition, Penguin 1977), although it has little about politics, gives a wonderful idea of how France has changed since 1945. For the period before that, and to understand Mitterrand and the French Left, one has to go back to the nineteenth century. Theodore Zeldin's *France 1848–1945* (OUP 1973) is quite simply one of the finest books on France in English.

Clearly much has been gleaned from French newspapers, especially *Le Monde, Le Matin* and *Le Nouvel Observateur* but it would be churlish not to acknowledge the debt that the British public, at least, owes to the correspondents that national newspapers have in France. In the quality newspapers and weekly journals, British journalists excel themselves in reporting France. By turn tender and sharp about a country they all clearly love, the corps of Paris 'corrs' provides the best coverage of any foreign country that is available in the British media.

Many people have discussed Mitterrand and the French Left with me or have read drafts of this book. I should like to thank Layla Assouline, Mark Cousins, Nadia Gerstenkorn, Collin Gonze, Michel le Merle, Fabrice Le Quintrec, David Lowe, Colin MacCabe, Hélène Pour, Deborah Smith and Joan Smith for their comments and help. Thanks also to Christopher Wilson for suggesting over a *kir* in the midsummer sunshine of Provence that my enthusiasm over the great Socialist victory of May 1981 should be turned into a book that would explain Mitterrand and his political history to people who had little idea of either.

Finally, a note on language. I have tried as far as possible not to use French words and expressions except where it is absolutely unavoidable; for example, *autogestion* (literally self-management but it embraces concepts about workers' control, community participation and democratic planning that cannot be rendered in a single English word). Sometimes this has led to English versions that will appear clumsy and unsatisfactory to the student of French. But this is a small price to pay to avoid leaving the quotation in the original. I believe that the importance of French politics extends far beyond those of us in Britain lucky enough to have had French teachers good enough to instil in us the rudiments of the language. Therefore I have tried to write this book so that someone who could not even begin to conjugate *être* will feel at home.

By the same token, I have tried in most cases to avoid the French habit of using initials and I have spelt out parties' names in full English translation. Clumsy as this will seem to any student of French politics, I have done it quite deliberately. The transfer of French acronyms is acceptable if you are sufficiently conversant with them to remember what each stands for in the text. In one recent book on French politics written in English the author listed seventy-nine abbreviations he proposed to use in his text. Ten of them began with the letter U (UDF, UDR, UDSR, UEC, UFE, UGSD, UNEF, UNR, UNR-RP, URP). This is part of the process of making politics a mysterious world into which only the initialated, as it were, may enter.

Paris – Geneva, March 1982

1
May 1981

You are either for the exploiters or the exploited.

To be in Paris on the early evening of 10 May, 1981 was to be present at one of the symbolic dates of French history. Like much contemporary history it was witnessed for the most part on television. In a small apartment in a working-class district of Paris, I watched with a handful of friends as the television channels waited until 8 p.m. when they could announce the result of the presidential contest between the incumbent, Valéry Giscard d'Estaing and his Socialist challenger, François Mitterrand. In Paris, the polls closed at 8 p.m., in the provinces at 6 p.m., and the millions of greyish-white slips of paper bearing the name of Giscard or Mitterrand were now being counted.

The television programmes had hired teams of pollsters and the results of their surveys, fed into computers, would give the result, accurate to a few decimal points, the moment the polls closed in Paris. The face of Jean-Pierre Elkabbach, then France's leading political interviewer and a man widely thought to have pro-Giscard sympathies, gave little away as he kept talking up to 8 p.m. But when the moment came to announce who would be France's next President, his mouth could not avoid the grimace. His features disappeared to be replaced by a computerized outline of the face of François Mitterrand with the text that he was now President of the French Republic blinking on and off at the bottom of the screen.

The group of workers, intellectuals and Socialist Party activists I was with exploded with joy. There was an almost physical pleasure being shared by these French men and women at Mitterrand's victory. Few could remember a Socialist government holding office in France. Most had worked patiently for the Socialist Party in campaigns during the 1970s. Some had come to it from other parties. Even those who professed themselves apolitical took pleasure in seeing Giscard removed.

The image of France that was carefully projected overseas, an image of continued growth despite the energy crisis, of Concorde and high-speed trains, of culture, fine cuisine and the topless pleasures of the *Côte d'Azur* was not how my companions perceived their country under its twenty-third year of unbroken conservative rule. If you were without a job, rising unemployment made it unlikely you would get one. If you were a union militant, you faced the sack. If you were an immigrant, you faced police harassment. If you were a student, your university faced closure. If you were a broadcasting journalist, there were so many questions you could not put to a government minister. If you were a woman, abortion and contraception, despite some legal reforms, were difficult to obtain.

This was a very different France from that portrayed in most magazines, or the France seen by hundreds of thousands of holidaymakers enjoying its physical beauty. An OECD (Organization for Economic Co-operation and Development) survey on how different nations perceived their countries' social attitudes in the 1980s showed that 26% of French people considered their society to be unjust compared with 17% in Great Britain. More interestingly, 49% of French people considered themselves to be 'egalitarians' compared with 18% in Great Britain. To be an immigrant, a union activist, or unemployed in Britain or the United States was probably little different from in France but the long, long reign of the Right, the sheer lack of alternation of government, meant that in the eyes of my friends, Mitterrand's victory would somehow put these problems right.

After the announcement of Mitterrand's victory I caught the Metro to the Socialist Party's handsome headquarters, a stone's throw from the National Assembly. In the tented courtyard champagne was being served to guests. It was a crowded, excited evening with masses of Parisians chanting outside the narrow front door while inside the lights of television cameras made a warm night unbearably hot. Party leaders like Lionel Jospin, Laurent Fabius, and Gaston Deferre wandered about vaguely shaking hands, trying to give purposeful interviews but all with a look of wonderment that the Socialist Party had finally won. In one corner, a tiny television set occasionally showed the scenes outside a small hotel in the middle of France. This was *Le Vieux Morvan* in Château-Chinon in the heart of Mitterrand's constituency. There the new President had awaited the result. Suddenly, the television presenters broke off their studio interviews in Paris to go over to Château-Chinon. Mitterrand, a small, rather portly sixty-four-year-old, appeared to read out a short message of victory. The profound emotion that must have been in his heart and mind did not show in his face.

Leaving the Socialist Party headquarters I walked down the Boulevard St Germain. As I neared the junction with the Boulevard St Michel, the very heart of the Latin Quarter, the crowds became more dense. Cars were streaming down the road, sounding their horns, their passengers waving red roses and flags, on over the Seine towards the Bastille, that great rendezvous for those in France who have wished to demonstrate against authority since that glorious day, 14 July 1789. In anticipation of Mitterrand's victory, the Socialists had made preparations for a celebration in the Place de la Bastille. Lionel Jospin, the Party's First Secretary, had urged Mitterrand supporters to go there during his many broadcast interviews after the victory announcement. By now the crowds were converging. Cars were being parked three deep as drivers could proceed no further and left their vehicles. The usually grim-faced Paris policemen smiled and ignored these massive breaches of traffic regulations.

In the Place de la Bastille itself it was impossible to move. How many were there and how many came and went? Half a million? One million? It was impossible to tell. From nearby Metro stations, from streets leading into the square came a procession of people. Sometimes in groups of two and three, sometimes long columns marching behind Socialist Party or trade-union banners. On a giant stage, singers and actors and writers and politicians addressed and entertained the crowd. On a smaller scale there were similar scenes in the other main cities of France but the momentous, shared experience of political achievement and pleasure in the Place de la Bastille in Paris was something that none of the younger participants had ever encountered before. For the older people there, the only comparison was with the celebrations after Paris was liberated in the war. Mitterrand's victory they saw as a new liberation for France. A few seconds after midnight there was a cloudburst and Paris was showered with a heavy rainstorm. It did nothing to slow down the celebrations, which continued throughout the night.

The rest of the world woke up the next morning to find that the figure of Giscard had gone. Diplomats and journalists rushed to telex their descriptions of the man who would be President of France until 1988. The outline facts were well-known. Mitterrand had been a public figure for more than thirty years and there were files thick with newspaper cuttings about him. He had been a wartime resistance leader. He had held office in eleven governments in the Fourth Republic. He had opposed de Gaulle in the 1965 presidential election and from 1971 had been leader of the Socialist Party. He had signed the Common Programme with the French Communist Party and formed, with them and the Left Radical Movement, the Union of the Left. He had come close to victory in the 1974 presidential elections and again in 1978 in the legislative elections.

It was possible to fill in some details. He had been happily married for nearly forty years with two grown-up sons. He had homes in Paris and in south-west France. He had been a practising Catholic until 1960 but by 1975 had confessed he was no longer a believer. He was a passionate countryman. His homes were full of books and he loved his country's literature. To quote another political bibliophile, Michael Foot: 'Men of power have no time to read; yet the men who do not read are unfit for power.' Mitterrand was more than a reader. He had published ten books and there were two fat volumes of his collected speeches, articles and essays on sale. He had made many journeys to Florence to research a biography of the Medici prince, Lorenzo the Magnificent. Was it there, in the style of renaissance politics,

4

that one should look for the real Mitterrand?

A quick glimpse at his political career certainly suggested elements of flexibility and expediency that Machiavelli would appreciate. His political development ranged from support of the Algerian war whilst a Fourth Republic minister to invocations of Marx as Socialist Party leader twenty years later. Was he an opportunist who was converted to Socialism because it represented the best route to power? Or was he always an idealist whose French sense of republican democracy hardened into an understanding of the need for profound economic and social change if France were to live up to its motto and become a free, equal, and fraternal society? What was his real attitude towards Communism and the French Communist Party? Which would be the more important factor in shaping his foreign policy – his frequent denunciations of Soviet treatment of dissidents, the Russian invasion of Afghanistan and the Kremlin's grip on East Europe, or his equally firm condemnations of the role of the CIA in Chile and Greece and Washington's continued support for dictatorial regimes in Latin America?

There are three full-length French biographies of Mitterrand and innumerable profiles. But there is no settled opinion on his political character. The adjective that keeps appearing as France's most experienced political writers try to grapple with his personality is 'enigmatic'. He has been described as 'pathologically shy', yet capable of 'an astonishing spontaneity which he cannot control'. Often wounded by insults, he can produce the most hurtful, cruel political assaults on others. He is said to have an almost 'feminine capacity' for political seduction 'only equalled by his caustic coldness'. 'The man,' wrote one observer, 'is complicated and protects himself by his complexity.'

Now he is President, the Mitterrand that was available to friends and political associates, who would allow journalists to observe him as he made conversation with his constituents in a café, has gone. The Socialist Party leader has become the President of all France. His actions now count more than his words and the judgements applied to him will be different from those applied in the past. In this book I have tried to trace Mitterrand's life and politics, in the hope that it will provide some guidance to how and why he acts during the years of his

5

presidency. This can only be a provisional account as we shall have to wait some years before being able to make a balanced judgement of his role in French history. And to do justice to the richness of the intellectual, cultural, country-loving sides of his character as well as the drama of much of his political life, the qualities of a novelist are needed. Balzac would do nicely, while the only English writer secure enough in his handling of political character to be able to cope with Mitterrand would have been Disraeli.

It is fashionable to see 1968 as the turning point in the post-war history of the French Left. The excitement of the May-time political earthquake, the whiff of revolution hanging over the ripped-up cobblestones of the Latin Quarter, and the delightful imagination of the students' slogans have proved irresistible to political commentators, especially those from outside France. One cannot count the number of books written on May, 1968. But as far as I have been able to discover no one has written a book on the Congress of Epinay in 1971. Yet from this congress emerged the modern French Socialist Party with François Mitterrand at its head. Students on the streets may shake a government, striking workers will frighten it into concessions or push it into repression, but it is only a widely based party that can, within the electoral framework of democracy, actually replace a government. This is the connection between the Congress of Epinay and the Socialist victory of 1981. Organization is a more durable political instrument than spontaneity. Demonstrating in the streets may be important, winning a parliamentary majority or a presidency is indispensable. But you cannot just win an electoral majority for its own sake. You have to have objectives and policies ready to put into practice that will bring about the changes which people join the party to see implemented. Mitterrand stuck to a definite set of Socialist policies drawn up with the Communist Party in 1972. He went out and argued for these policies in public and did not give the impression that they were there only on paper, ready to be ditched or watered down on taking office. So the history of Mitterrand, the Socialist Party and the French Left in recent years has an importance for all Western democracies where Socialists are seeking power through the ballot box and working out what to do with it once they have got it. In this book Mitterrand's life has been set against a general, if simplified, explanation of French politics and especially the French Left.

The very word 'left' used as a political adjective we owe to France. In a debate in the French National Assembly a few weeks after the 1789 revolution the supporters of a strong king with the power to veto laws sat on the right-hand side of the session chairman, while those in favour of a strong parliament that would control and supervise the executive placed themselves on the left. Thus the Left and the Right were born, political descriptions that have spread well beyond France. In the history of the French revolution we also find many of the contradictions that the Left in France, and elsewhere, have still to resolve today. The commitment to individual liberty against the need for effective state power. Intense patriotism side by side with an appeal to peoples in other lands. Support for the resolution of conflicts through the rule of law alongside the spirit of revolution, barricades and direct action.

Marx and Lenin took many of their political categories and examples from the history of the French Left; their writings are littered with references to Bonapartism, the Thermidor, the Paris Commune. The history of the French Left has been absorbed by Socialists, even if often unconsciously, all over the world. Establishment figures have constantly stated that the Left is just a figure of speech, that instead of Socialism or the Left we should talk about Socialisms and the Lefts. Few go so far as the great nineteenth-century French politician, Adolphe Thiers, who, although a staunch republican, saw the republic as an expression of bourgeois interests, and said in 1877, the last year of his life: 'We no longer talk of Socialism and that is a good thing. We have rid ourselves of Socialism.'

In his book *French Democracy* (1976), the then French President, Giscard d'Estaing, claimed that there were not two Frances but four. Mitterrand has preferred a definition which divides his country into two camps, 'the exploited and the exploiters'. Others have seen religion or region as more important in understanding French political views. Certainly the French Left has never been solely composed of the industrial working class. It was not until after the Second World War that the effects of mass industrialization were fully realized in France; and Britain in 1900 had fewer people living and working on the land than France in 1950. The Left's involvement with French peasants goes back to the middle of the nineteenth century when the taxes demanded by the Paris government were bearing very heavily on the newly enfranchised peasantry. Today both Socialists and Communists draw considerable support from sections of the small farmers of France, especially the wine-growing areas of the south and south-west.

The wish that the Left as a political idea would dissolve away may be expressed by commentators in many different democracies. But as the French essayist Emile Alain noted: 'When someone asks me if the divisions between parties of the Left and Right, between left-wingers and right-wingers, still have a meaning the first thought that strikes me is that the person who asked the question is definitely not part of the Left.'

The Left therefore has been present in French history for nearly two hundred years, yet it has hardly ever been in power. This century we have seen only the two years of the Popular Front government in 1936. After the war Socialists and Communists participated in a coalition government with Christian Democrats, which was at first presided over by General de Gaulle. In 1956, the Socialist leader Guy Mollet became Prime Minister for two years but his period of office is mainly remembered for such hardly left-wing activities as the Suez adventure and the savage conduct of the Algerian war. In fact, the Left had to wait until 1981 for the arrival of a President and an absolute majority in the National Assembly. Nearly two hundred years of theorizing, of hope, and the history of past failures now sit on the shoulders of Mitterrand and his government as both the French people and the whole world wait to see if the French Left, having secured political power, can effect the changes which they have been so eloquently demanding for so many years.

Mitterrand's own writings are stuffed with references to French history and those who have analysed his career refer back to the grandees of the history of the French Left to work out in whose footsteps he is following. Mitterrand is sensitive to the fact that French history is marked by the decisive involvement of the masses at key moments, matched by the intervention of the military, usually to repress a popular revolt and make France safe again for its bourgeoisie. In 1830, the overthrow of the Bourbon monarchy was followed by the French army being used to break strikes. The 1848 revolt dislodged forever the French monarchy but the new French President declared himself Emperor in 1851 and 10,000 opponents to the new imperial regime were deported. The Paris Commune of 1871, another the the key moments in the French Left's collective memory, ended in the massacre of 20,000 Parisians and the deportation of 38,000 of what the *Figaro* described at the time as 'democratic vermin'.

Still those who believed in the democratic republican ideals, the right of workers to form unions and strike, in press freedom, the need for an education system free of religious control, battled on. Many French political thinkers and activists contributed to the left-wing groups which came together in 1905 to form France's Socialist Party, SFIO. SFIO stands for *Section Française de l'Internationale Ouvrière* – French Section of the Workers' International. The International referred to in this title was the Second International founded in Paris in 1889 to replace the First International launched by Karl Marx in 1864. It was under the prompting of the Second International that the French Left came together to form the SFIO, the acronym by which the party was known until 1969.

The two main SFIO leaders at the time of the party's birth were Jules Guesde and Jean Jaurès and in their personalities one can see the two main strands of the French Left. Guesde (1845–1922) worked to introduce Marx's ideas into French politics. In 1879 he founded the French Workers' Party based on class struggle and the socialization of the means of production. Guesde was dogmatic, authoritarian and ran his party in a highly centralized manner. Jean Jaurès (1859–1914) was a brilliant intellectual and orator who was elected a deputy at the age of twenty-five. Not unlike Mitterrand, he came to Socialism late in life and declared that Socialists should be ready to make alliances with other parties and work through parliamentary legislation to achieve change.

The constitution of the SFIO in 1905 seemed to suggest that

Guesde's ideas had captured the party. It stated: 'The Socialist Party, while seeking to achieve the reforms currently demanded by the working class, is not a party of reform but a party of class struggle and revolution.' But Jaurès' superior political abilities imposed themselves on the party after 1905. He called for an 'open' Socialism whose ultimate aim was the conquest of power by the working class but which accepted that methods other than a revolutionary seizure of power or the syndicalist general strike should be used. 1914 settled the careers of both men. Jaurès, a pacifist, was assassinated in July 1914, while Guesde was swept along by the patriotic tide and entered the government as an enthusiastic prosecutor of war aims.

The distinction between Guesde's Marxist, flinty, class-struggle idea of Socialism and Jaurès' more humanist, all-embracing vision was further underlined in 1920 when the SFIO split and French Communism was born. The occasion was the instruction from the Third International, founded by Lenin in 1919, calling upon Socialist parties everywhere to adhere to the Third International, accept its twenty-one conditions for membership and introduce a highly centralized Bolshevik system of party organization as well as align the party's foreign policy along the lines dictated from Moscow. The 1920 Congress of Tours saw SFIO delegates, by a majority of 3–1, vote to join the Third International while the majority of Socialist deputies, led by Léon Blum, rejected adherence to Moscow. Blum (the third great figure in SFIO history after Jaurès and Guesde) told the congress that the instructions from the Third International were based on a massive error which was 'to make generalizations for Socialists in all countries, on the basis of a certain number of ideas drawn from the specific and localized experience of the Russian revolution'.

The 1920 Congress of Tours was the beginning of the great split in the French Left which endures until today. Mitterrand's political life has been dominated by that fissure and its after-effects, from his first efforts to be selected a member of the National Assembly in 1946 when he found his most doughty opponents were the Communists, to the day in midsummer 1981 when he announced that there would be four Communist ministers in his government.

To readers who live across the Channel or across the Atlantic it is difficult to convey the immense presence of the Communist Party in French politics and society. Perhaps the best way is to pay a visit to the annual Communist festival, the *Fête de L'Humanité*, held every September. In a huge patch of open space to the north of Paris one million visitors come to see the French Communist Party on display. There are stalls from nearly every region of France. One can spend hours walking from stand to stand each with the name of a different region, town or commune on it. But as one criss-crosses the alleys in the midst of the strolling crowd one is suddenly struck by the number of stands devoted to the stomach and the paucity of stands offering a political message. Four out of five of the regional stands offer the food and wine of the French provinces. They compete with each other in offering regional specialities and tempting the passers-by with fragrant smells and the best bottles from local vineyards.

Of course politics and the concerns of the French Communist Party are present. There are bookstalls, seminars, stands run by Communist Parties from all over the world; one is given leaflets on all sorts of issues or asked to sign petitions, and the high spot of the *Fête de L'Humanité* is the speech from the Party leader in front of a crowd one hundred thousand strong. But the point about all the food and the family atmosphere is this: the French Communist Party is more than a relentless band of committed political activists with a narrow vision of how to apply Soviet-style Communism to France. It is a society within a society able to look after all the needs of those who care to join it. Finding a job, joining a sports club, looking for a friend, cultural events and political education are all encompassed within the Communist Party. It has a cultural, social and intellectual existence that goes beyond policy-making and vote-gathering. Its roots were implanted as a result of its activities in the resistance during the war. Socialist and Radical Party governments were discredited by their actions in the years leading up to 1939, while a majority of Socialist deputies had voted to suspend the National Assembly and invest Marshal Pétain with almost dictatorial powers in 1940. The Communists were no less opportunistic before the Nazi invasion of Russia in 1941 obliterated the Stalin-

Hitler pact and made fighting Germans an international Communist priority. But of their bravery during the war there is no question. After the liberation people flocked to join the Communist Party, imbued with the spirit that was to be found everywhere in Europe betwen 1944 and 1947 of seeking to build a more just, egalitarian, caring society and to avoid the possibility of going back to the economic and political solutions of the pre-war era.

In 1946, Communist Party membership stood at 800,000 and in the National Assembly election the Party received 28% of the vote. The Communist Party has maintained a considerable, if never quite as large a presence ever since. As we shall see later the behaviour of French Socialists contributed in no small measure to sustaining the Communist Party's continuing massive existence, but to understand the French Left one must take into consideration this large, well-rooted Communist Party which has no equivalent, save for Italy, in other democratic countries.

The trade-union movement in France is also strange by the practices and standards of English-speaking countries. There are no independent, autonomous craft or industrial unions organizing, say, steelworkers in one union and transport workers in another. Instead there are general confederations which may have industrial or craft sections but are strictly subordinate to the confederation. Workers in an aerospace factory may belong to any of the three main union confederations and as there are no closed-shop or union-membership agreements in France the multiplicity of unions in each workplace renders them less effective. Although the French working class has erupted into history books with great strikes and demonstrations there has been a lack of the steady, detailed, development of organization which is necessary to build permanently based mass-membership trade unionism. Only about one in six workers belongs to a union. There are few national collective agreements. French employers have treated unions with an indifference bordering on contempt, and proportionate to the country's wealth French workers have lower pay and fewer fringe benefits than workers in comparative countries.

The French employers' hostility to trade unions keeps alive the sentiment and language of class struggle which is missing in those countries where unions have rights of representation and access to employers and government. In turn French unions have always been more explicitly political in their rhetoric, though they never tried to create their own party in the way the British trade-union movement gave birth to the Labour Party. The main French confederation, the CGT (*Confédération Générale du Travail* – General Confederation of Labour) was founded in 1895. A key text for French trade unionism was the Charter of Amiens adopted in 1906. This incorporated many of the anarchist trends common in nineteenth-century working-class organizations in France. In particular, they rejected adherence to any political party and stressed that in addition to seeking wage increases the job of trade unionism was to 'prepare for total emancipation, which can only be achieved by the expropriation of capital . . . the method of action [should be] the general strike and . . . the union, which is currently a base for resistance will in the future be the basic group for organizing production and distribution and provide the basis for social reorganization.'

The idea of revolutionary syndicalism, and the union providing the future organization of society following the general strike which would overthrow capitalism, retained a powerful hold in French unions. The CGT split after 1920 and a fission between Socialists and Communists occurred. A new Communist version of the CGT was set up. After the war the by now unified CGT split again when a group of right-wingers and ultra-leftists walked out and formed another confederation. This unusual alliance was caused by the increasing Communist control of the CGT, and since 1947 the CGT has been firmly under Communist Party influence, even domination. Although some Socialist Party members sit on the Executive Committee nearly all the CGT's full-time officials are Communist Party members. The General Secretary and his deputy sit on the Communist Party's Political Bureau and in its domestic and international politics the CGT has faithfully followed the Communist Party line, albeit with some time lags.

Teachers are in their own union as are supervisory staff and junior managers. In 1919, the General Confederation of Christian Workers was founded. This became an effective force in the 1960s when it removed the reference to 'Christian' and became the CFDT, *Confédération Française Democratique du Travail* – French Democratic Labour Confederation – and adopted the more radical, leftist policies associated with workers' control. There still remains a small Christian union on the margin of the French labour movement. The CFDT played an active part in the 1968 events when ten million workers went on strike and in the 1970s was closely involved with one wing of Mitterrand's Socialist Party.

The crucial point about the SFIO and later the Socialist Party is that it has never had an organized link with French trade unions. Neither cash nor personnel have flowed from unions to party and the evolution of Socialist policy and electoral tactics have not been dependent upon or shaped by the attitudes of the French unions. If a French trade union's general secretary wants to contribute to a policy debate at a Socialist Party congress he must join as an individual member and hope he is elected as a rank and file delegate.

So Mitterrand and the Socialist Party have developed without having to pay the kind of attention that their sister parties in West Germany, Sweden and, above all, Britain are obliged to pay to organized labour. Whether this is a positive or negative attribute is perhaps a question to be answered in a few years' time but it is essential to get clear in one's mind the separation of French trade unionism from the Socialist Party and the very different history, organization and role of unions in France before the Mitterrand story begins.

This book is a politician's life story. It is called a political odyssey but its destination is not yet determined. To find out where he will take France and to see whether he has the ability and will to master the forces both inside and outside France that can determine the country's future, irrespective of who sits in the Elysée, we have to examine his past actions, speeches and writings. Not only is an examination of Mitterrand's life helpful in working out what he will do in the future, but it may also be of interest to those in Britain and elsewhere engaged in debate about the nature and practice of democratic Socialism, social democracy, labourism or Socialism.

2
A Catholic Upbringing

The Bible nourished my childhood.

François Maurice Adrien Marie Mitterrand was born on 26 October 1916, the same year as Harold Wilson and Edward Heath. He was born in the family home in Jarnac, a small town of 5,000 inhabitants not far from Cognac in the south-west of France. It was stolid, bourgeois Catholic France, a long way from Paris. The French countryside recurs again and again in Mitterrand's life, and in his writing and speeches. Weekends were always spent in his constituency to the west of Dijon, while the Mitterrand summer home is in the Landes, on the Atlantic coast south of Bordeaux. He has a passion for walking, sometimes with friends, often alone, and despite having been a professional Paris politician since 1945, he knows the names of trees, shrubs and birds as if he had always lived in the countryside.

Jarnac, his birthplace, flickered briefly into French history in the sixteenth century as the site of a famous victory by the Catholic forces led by the Duke of Anjou over the Protestant forces under the Prince of Condé. It has hardly been touched by war since. Mitterrand was born a few weeks before the end of the battle of Verdun, the most costly of the First World War's abattoir battles which left 750,000 French and German soldiers dead on the battlefield.

The experiences of having been both a child of the First World War, which cost so many French lives, and a soldier crushed in the humiliating defeat of 1940 have left their mark on Mitterrand: his sense of a Socialist France does not include a France without a means of defence strong enough in his eyes to avoid the bloodshed of 1914–18 or the degradation of 1940. He was the fifth of eight children and grew up in a tightly knit Catholic family. His father, Joseph, was the stationmaster at the important town of Angoulême. It was a good, well-established job to have, even though it meant that Joseph Mitterrand could only return to Jarnac for holidays.

When he was at home, Joseph Mitterrand was a solitary figure, accessible to his children but, at the same time, distant. He buried himself in his books and went for long walks. An active Catholic who acted as a stretcher-bearer at Lourdes and was a pillar of the lay Catholic Society of St Vincent de Paul, he was, according to his son, trapped between the right-wing atmosphere that automatically went with the provincial Catholic life of the period and his rejection of the 'arrogances and injustices of the right'. Much later François Mitterrand was to write: 'My father knew he was living at the end of an era and was silently angry at the antiquated rites and the formalized misunderstandings that went with the final days of the period.'

Mitterrand's mother, Yvonne, was also a devout Catholic. Her dowry for the marriage had been the house in Jarnac together with a summer home set in 250 acres which were looked after by three tenant farmers. From his wife's father Joseph inherited a vinegar-making business in which he took little interest even though he was successful enough with it to become President of the Union of Vinegar-Makers of France. Yvonne filled her life with God and the children. She got up at five o'clock, went to mass, visited poor people in the town and looked after her house and eight children. There were rosaries to be said, a short daily meditation, a reading of holy texts. But religion was not all. In the evenings she would read the classics of French literature – Balzac, Lamartine and Chateaubriand. Pious as she was, she did not force the Catholic Church down the throats of her children. It was her God; the children could make up their minds as they grew up.

Mitterrand reports happy memories of his childhood. Life followed the rhythm of the seasons in provincial France. There were excursions and long walks, lengthy, silent games of chess with his grandfather. At dinner there were rarely fewer than twelve people and no one was allowed to speak ill of others or to discuss money. The local priests and other guests, sometimes foreigners, were regularly invited. The Mitterrand children were sent to England to improve their English, though little trace of this is left – Mitterrand is a poor linguist and when, on occasion, he refers to England or the United States in his writings, he shows little real understanding or sympathy for the Anglo-Saxon philosophy or way of life.

There was some talk of politics. At the beginning of the century his uncle had been active in the Sillon movement, one of the forerunners of Christian Democracy. There were the problems of the French franc and of German reparations; new and frightening figures like Lenin and Mussolini were much discussed in the newspapers. His mother kept a diary in which she recorded her visits, the books she read and the political events of the day. The talk was that of the average, well-informed, interested and concerned French family. But there was no political commitment as such.

At the age of nine, Mitterrand was sent away to boarding school run by priests of the Diocese of Angoulême. But he says he keeps a memory of 'kindly and peaceful teachers. There was no brainwashing. I left school with enough freedom to use my freedom.' It was a hard academic regime aimed at getting boys through the all-important French *baccalauréat* examination, which is the essential passport to university or entry into any of the professions in France. He was a loner, refusing to join the school scouts or any other of the school associations though he was goalkeeper in the school football team. This aloofness, his style of being apart even from his close associates, has stayed with him all his life. It is normal for colleagues in political parties, and especially on the Left, to address each other using the French second person singular, *tu*. Never Mitterrand who, except for a handful of close personal friends, always uses the more formal, distancing second person plural, *vous*. At the same time, he has a circle of personal friends which he has kept over the years. Some of these friends date back to student and wartime days. They testify to his generosity, his habit of spontaneous present-giving – usually a book – or the impromptu visits he makes to hospital bedsides. There is an extremely emotional Mitterrand, impulsive even, which he tries to keep tightly under control in his public and political life but which expresses itself in this capacity for warm and loyal personal friendships.

He was often sick at school, including one long spell in bed recovering from peritonitis. Apart from one serious illness in the 1950s he has led a healthy life as an adult and was still playing tennis in his sixties. The periods of childhood illness reinforced his pleasure in reading. At home he would spend hours without moving as he worked his way eagerly through a book. He read philosophy, the French classics as well as the newly acclaimed young novelist Henry de Montherlant. He was still a devout Catholic, praying every night before going to bed. At one stage in his teens he even thought about becoming a priest. He did well in his lessons, especially French, Latin and philosophy, though he had problems with English, physics and mathematics. It would not be unfair to say that Mitterrand disdains the technical detail of economics, and in 1974 he paid the penalty when the brilliant former Finance Minister, Giscard d'Estaing, won the presidential election because, in part, he was seen to be the better economic technician. In the television debate between the two men, Giscard's mastery of statistics and economic concepts seemed to swamp Mitterrand, who was clearly ill at ease in the world of economics. At school and later at university, the world of politics and the need for a mastery of economics was irrelevant to the intellectual life Mitterrand was leading. His school reports were good, describing him as a hard and intelligent worker, though one teacher complained that he was sometimes unclear in his dissertations.

Mitterrand left his sheltered provincial background for university in Paris in 1934. He came to a Paris racked by demonstrations and street clashes between rival political groups. There was little unity on the Left with the French Communists denouncing their Socialist opponents as 'social-fascist' and equating social democracy with fascism.

The crisis in world capitalism had hit France hard. Between

1931 and 1935, steel production went down by 40% and unemployment nearly doubled. The 245,000 cars produced in 1929 had slumped to 165,000 in 1935 while real wages dropped by a quarter between 1930 and 1935. Governments lacked all cohesion – five came and went in a period of eighteen months in 1933–4. Anti-Semitic, nationalist groupings sprung up ready to spread the message of Hitler and Mussolini to France. Sixteen people were shot dead in a Paris demonstration in 1934. The policy of the French Communist Party in this period was dictated by Comintern from Moscow. Partly in response to his own struggle for internal control of the Communist Party of the Soviet Union, Stalin had issued orders in 1928 that Communist Parties were to treat Socialist, Social Democratic and Labour Parties as organizations of bourgeois reformism, objectively no better than the conservative or even fascist parties with which they were struggling. The Communist term of abuse 'social-fascist' was applied to the rest of the Left and in the key period leading up to Hitler's arrival in power in 1933 the German Communists spent more time attacking the German Social Democratic Party than the Nazis. This policy was abruptly changed after Hitler took over and instead Moscow ordered Western Communist Parties to seek electoral alliances with other left-wing parties. In France, the Communist Party launched a call for a 'Popular Front' against the Right and to defend France from fascism; to begin with there developed a 'unity pact' between Socialists (SFIO) and Communists followed by a common electoral programme between Communists, Socialists (SFIO) and the Radical Party in January 1936.

In May 1936, the Popular Front parties won the election and Léon Blum, leader of the Socialists, became Prime Minister. The Communists refused to enter the government though they supported it in the National Assembly. A wave of strikes broke out and the Renault factories were occupied. The strikes spread to other sectors and soon France was gripped by what was more or less a rank and file general strike. Blum promised new laws providing for a forty-hour week and paid holidays and pressed the employers to make other concessions. The leader of the French Communist Party, Maurice Thorez, toured the country urging the strikers to return to work. 'It is all very well to start a

19

strike,' he said, 'but you must also know how to end one.' Despite the social advances made by the Popular Front government, French capital remained unbowed. In the electoral programme drawn up between the Socialists, Communists and Radicals, there had been no commitment to a radical restructuring of French industry, and, in particular, there was no programme of nationalization. Public ownership, argued the French Communist Party, was irrelevant in a capitalist society and would, in any case, alienate middle-class voters whose support was necessary at the polls. The unwillingness to harness the wave of mass enthusiasm that followed the Popular Front victory in May 1936, meant that apart from the economic benefits conceded by the employers there was no institutional change in France leading to a shift of power in the direction of the people the Popular Front claimed to represent. Blum himself only lasted twelve months in office, and after the fall of the Popular Front government many of the concessions made by the employers in the hot summer of 1936 were clawed back. None the less, the memory of the Popular Front and the important symbolic advances of the forty-hour week and the introduction of paid holidays held good and were to be an important reference point for both Socialists and Communists in determining their handling of political relationships in the decades after 1936.

Save for May 1968, the middle years of the 1930s were the most intense political period lived through by French people this century. It was a period that largely passed by the young student Mitterrand. Writing many years afterwards, Mitterrand claimed to have shared the joy of the night of the election in 1936 which marked the beginning of a 'new era of deliverance for the French people'. Yet apart from attending some meetings as a curious spectator, there is no evidence from the period that Mitterrand involved himself in any political activities or even took part in the numerous demonstrations in Paris between 1934 and 1938. He says that the Socialist students 'intimidated' him.

He had arrived in Paris in 1934 very much the provincial student, dressed in plus fours and white socks. He shared a house with fellow students from the French provinces. It was run by priests, but they turned a tolerant eye to the comings and goings of the students. Not that Mitterrand led a spectacularly exciting student life. His modest allowance meant he could only go to the pictures twice a month. Then, as now, student life in Paris meant enjoying the pleasure of strolling in the Latin Quarter and long discussions over a coffee. Under French law the customer has the right to stay as long as he likes in a café once a drink is ordered, an obligation that can make proprietors furious but is invaluable to students who want to spend an evening talking in the midst of some of the most lively streets in Europe.

What did they discuss? Literature, above all. Unlike English or American students who are given a framework of lectures, seminars, classes or tutorials with an obligation to produce regular written work, the French student is left to his own devices provided he can get through an annual test at the end of each year. There are lectures but attendance is not compulsory. Mitterrand did not bother to follow any lectures after the first few weeks though he never had any difficulty in passing his examinations and was awarded degrees in law and political science in 1938. He read widely, learning by heart passages of Stendhal and Pascal.

André Gide was one of his heroes and Mitterrand followed closely the evolution of Gide, who seemed to keep pace with all that was most advanced in the first thirty years of the twentieth century. Gide was attracted to Soviet Communism during the 1920s but in 1936 published *Return from the USSR* which was severely critical of the inequalities in Stalin's Russia as well as the blind faith which the Russian people were obliged to place in Stalin himself.

He was fascinated by Julien Benda, whose book *The Betrayal of the Intellectuals* shook France and the rest of Europe when it appeared in 1927. Benda criticized the drift of intellectuals towards the political excitement to be found in the extremism of Communism and fascism. The intellectual's job was to defend reason, to promote the virtue of thought rather than action. Benda was, however, prepared to argue his case in public, and although a champion of the French enlightenment he rejected political neutrality. Benda came out strongly against Hitler and Mussolini and would appear on anti-fascist platforms while maintaining an anti-Marxist position. As well as going to hear Benda speak, Mitterrand attended anti-Nazi meetings to listen to Léon Blum and André Malraux but he recalled: 'The friends I made while a student were more interested in music and literature than in politics. Thanks to them, I discovered Erik Satie, Honegger and Stravinsky before Doumergue and Daladier*. The *New French Review* and surrealism opened up a world for us that was unknown rather than forbidden.' It was the writer that was being formed during that period rather than the future politician. Mitterrand contributed to the ephemeral reviews that came and went in student Paris. He wrote an ironic piece about the celebration of the fiftieth anniversary of Victor Hugo's death.

If a personal philosophy can be discerned from what Mitterrand wrote during his student days, it would revolve around the idea of the necessity and importance of individual effort. To a sister he wrote: 'Everything comes down to this: to win or to lose. One never stays motionless. Because to stop moving is to begin losing.' Already Mitterrand is developing a rich elegant prose style and already there is the careful choice of words which leaves traces of ambiguity rather than precision and clarity in the reader's mind. Mitterrand uses the most studied language of any practising French politician and even his most severe political critics agree that he could have made a career as a writer had he so wished. He still devours French novels and has written poetry about which he is sufficiently confident to allow its publication.

If Mitterrand's student friends do not recall him marching in demonstrations, putting up posters, handing out leaflets or joining a political party or organization, it was impossible to avoid all political commitment. Ever since the Dreyfus† case, the whole of French society seemed to cleave naturally in two whenever a major public issue arose.

*Gaston Doumergue was President of France, 1924–31 and Edouard Daladier was Prime Minister of France, 1938–40.

†Captain Alfred Dreyfus, a brilliant Jewish army officer, was wrongly accused of passing secrets to the Germans and imprisoned in 1894. It quickly became clear he was innocent but the army and government refused to reopen the case. A campaign led by Emile Zola finally led to his pardon in 1899, but it took another seven years of bitter campaigning before he was reinstated in 1906. The Dreyfus case divided France into two camps.

Those who had supported Captain Dreyfus – the Socialists, the Radicals, the intellectuals, would always form ranks against the establishment – the army, the Church, and right-wing politicians. Dreyfus was rehabilitated in 1906 but everyone in France would still, in the 1930s, know whether to place himself in the pro- or anti-Dreyfus camp. It was a kind of reflex self-identification that went beyond political allegiance. To be, even retrospectively, for or against Dreyfus was to indicate an idea of what kind of country France should be. It was to oppose *la Patrie* (the fatherland) to *les Droits de l'homme* (the rights of man).

It was the section of French society and the establishment that had refused to give justice to Dreyfus that lined up behind Mussolini when he invaded Ethiopia in 1935. One of Mitterrand's professors, Gaston Jèze, acted as an adviser to the Ethiopian government when the invasion was brought before the World Court in The Hague. Right-wing students tried to break up Jèze's lectures and even attack the professor in the street. The legal faculty was divided. One was for Jèze or against him. There was no opting out. It was a miniature Dreyfus case for the students. Mitterrand was firmly on Jèze's side. All his life Mitterrand stayed a champion of individual liberty. Two examples are worth mentioning. In 1950 he outraged the French right wing when he offered a safe conduct to Félix Houphouët-Boigny, leader of the black community in the Ivory Coast, who was being hunted by the French police. In 1975 he offended his fellow Socialist leader, Helmut Schmidt, by supporting the campaign against the *Berufsverbot* law which the West German authorities were using to dismiss civil servants suspected of having Communist sympathies. One of his first actions on becoming President was to abolish the State Security Court which General de Gaulle had set up in 1962 for what were, in effect, political trials.

Apart from showing in a fairly generalized way his sympathy for the left causes of the period, Mitterrand stayed away from active political involvement. He explicitly refused an invitation to join the extreme right-wing *Action Française* even though one of its prominent adherents was a family friend. None the less, as his student days went by, it was more and more difficult for Mitterrand to avoid confronting political issues. He was never an activist but he could not remain aloof. For the question of the Spanish civil war was also dividing France. Mitterrand, of course, detested Franco. The news from Germany of Hitler's persecution of the Jews equally demanded that sides be taken. After all, one of the most significant aspects of the Dreyfus case had been the revelation of deep-rooted anti-Semitism in the French establishment. But it was Hitler's annexation of Austria in 1938 that moved Mitterrand, aged twenty-one, to publish his first political text. In the *Revue Montalembert*, a small journal produced by the students in the house where Mitterrand lived, he attacked the weakness of the French and British governments that had given Hitler such an easy triumph.

> Forgetting the fact that the righteous must be stronger than the strong if they want to be involved in world affairs, the victorious countries from the Great War rested on their laurels and went to sleep in the cardboard castle of the post-war treaties. And each time yesterday's defeated man struck out or destroyed or burnt something, claiming necessity and proclaiming his good intentions for the future, we said to him: 'So far, but no farther.' In the life of a people as well as that of an individual, each withdrawal is a battle lost. A strategic withdrawal always masks a defeat, and the explanations which try to diminish the failure, or reveal the causes, or avoid the responsibility do not alter the fact that with his first defeat man pronounces his own condemnation. What is chastity once violated? What is strength of will if it bends? What is liberty if it is given away?

The angry, if flowery, comment of the twenty-one-year-old Mitterrand ends with a prophetic image. 'Looking at the triumphant arrival of the god of Bayreuth [i.e. Wagner] in the land of Mozart, I know the sacrilege that is being prepared and despite myself I feel a sense of shame as if I were in some way responsible.' The young and still very Catholic Mitterrand – he went to mass every Sunday and was active in the Society of St Vincent de Paul – was finally coming to terms with his personal need or personal obligation to involve himself in politics.

3
Resistance Leader

Here's a war for you. We'll observe. We will accept the strongest, the survivors, and they will succeed us. But first prove yourself.

The war began and ended badly for Mitterrand. Doing his compulsory military service along with three million other anonymous French soldiers in September 1939, he found himself in May 1945 without a proper job and very little clear idea of his future. Yet the war years were clearly the most decisive period of Mitterrand's life. For it was between 1940 and 1945 that a shy Catholic intellectual was transformed into a brilliant organizer and acknowledged leader. It was during the war that Mitterrand met and failed to get on with de Gaulle, the beginning of a relationship that haunted Mitterrand all his life and that still affects how he sees the presidency of France. It was in this period that he developed the capacity for relying on his own judgement and relishing both the responsibility and the authority that go with the making and executing of important decisions which affect other people. Finally it was in the war years that he learnt to work with, but keep his distance from, the French Communist Party. Mitterrand survived being badly wounded, escaped three times from German prison camps, became an important resist ance leader, flitting between London, North Africa and France, evading the Gestapo all the time, and at the age of twenty-seven found himself occupying a ministerial seat in the temporary administration set up following the liberation of Paris in August 1944.

In September 1938, the newly graduated Mitterrand was called up for compulsory military service. The army plays a role in French domestic life which is sometimes difficult to appreciate for those brought up on Anglo-Saxon ideas of the separate and subordinate role that the army should play in a political democracy. The key dates of French history – from the revolutionary columns that defended the gains of 1789 to de Gaulle's hurried, secret meeting with army commanders in 1968 that promised him enough support to repel the workers and students threatening to topple his government – have involved its army. The army has thrown up many of France's national leaders – Napoléon, Pétain and de Gaulle, while its involvement in the Dreyfus case or the Algerian putsch in 1958 that led to de Gaulle's return to power traumatized the nation and showed the French army's readiness to involve itself in social and political matters. Its willingness to do this may be a function of its lack of success as a military machine. Waterloo, Sedan, 1940, Indo-China, Algeria; the French army has known more defeats than victories, with its moments of glory at the end of the First and Second World Wars being displaced by the helping and very necessary hand of British and American troops.

With his family background (his youngest brother, Jacques, enrolled in the French military academy of St Cyr and went on to become a general and the commander of the French air force in the 1970s), as well as his university degrees, Mitterrand would normally have expected to become an officer when he began his military service. Instead Mitterrand rejected officer training – he said he simply did not want to become an officer and gave no further reason – and was enrolled in the ranks. Mitterrand did his peacetime service conscientiously enough though it was always possible to slip away to see old friends in Paris at the weekend. He was a sergeant when France declared war on Germany on 1 September 1939 and spent the winter manning a section of the Maginot Line digging anti-tank ditches in the bitter cold of the

Ardennes. The Maginot Line running from Switzerland to Belgium, and behind it, the biggest of Europe's armies, was thought to guarantee the protection of France. The shock and failure of May 1940, as the German army crushed the French army, was seen not just as a military defeat but a condemnation of the corrupt, hierarchical and politically decadent Third Republic in operation since 1870. Mitterrand had a foreboding of what was to come, writing to his closest friend, Georges Dayan, in the winter of 1940: 'Are they putting us through a test from which will emerge our qualities of resistance, aggression and vitality? As if they were telling us, "Here's a war for you. We'll keep an eye on you. We will accept the strongest, the survivors and they will succeed us. But first prove yourself."' Mitterrand lacked the traditional deference an NCO is supposed to have for his officers and he appeared on a disciplinary charge for failing to offer them due respect. French officers, he felt, were admirers of the Third Reich who had no interest for the men under their command. Later he described his feelings: 'I went through the phoney war and could not care less about a system and an order which was foreign to me. What I had seen of the dying Third Republic taught me that there was nothing in it either to love or to hope for.'

The Third Republic died on 10 May 1940, when the Germany army broke through the French defences. Mitterrand was in charge of a munition dump and was badly wounded by shrapnel, traces of which are still in his body. He was dumped on a cart and for two days lay helpless as his comrades pulled him along in the midst of the retreating French soldiers and fleeing civilians. As they dived for cover when the Luftwaffe straffed the roads Mitterrand could only look up at the sky unable to move. He reached a French military hospital where his wounds were treated and there he was taken prisoner by the German army. Nearly two million French soldiers went into captivity. The collapse of the French government, the return of Marshal Pétain on 16 June 1940 and the BBC broadcast by the then unknown General de Gaulle two days later swept over the convalescing Mitterrand's head. He was sent off to a prisoner-of-war camp, Stalag 9A, where he found anarchy prevailing amongst the prisoners. As they squabbled and even fought over the meagre rations provided by the Germans, their degraded state seemed to mirror the collapse of France. With a group of others, Mitterrand helped restore order and discipline amongst the 40,000 prisoners. Classes were started and lectures organized. Mitterrand took up Greek and began work on a book, never finished for publication, called the *Seven Hills of Paris.* 'Being obliged to live with a mass of people,' he wrote, 'one gets to know solitude.'

Pétain was negotiating with the Germans and de Gaulle was broadcasting from another country, but it seemed to the prisoners of war around Mitterrand that both men represented in their different ways the old, now dead, France. In the camps, however, the French spirit refused to be crushed. On the stroke of midnight on 13 July, Mitterrand recalls, a strange sound could be heard in many different parts of Germany – the sound of 1,800,000 Frenchmen singing the Marseillaise. 'The disputes and the quarrels faded away. There was only a people coming together to celebrate their glory and their past and to throw down a challenge to the conqueror. The guards walked nervously up and down the camp corridors while the Prussian officers shouted for silence; the Marseillaise that became stronger and stronger conveyed in itself our future liberation.'

In March 1941 came his first escape attempt. Together with a priest, his escape companion, Mitterrand made careful preparations. They saved up a store of food and with the help of a potato stencil made false papers. They decided their best course was to head for the Swiss border nearly 400 miles to the south. They made a rough map of Germany and set off. Colditz, wooden horses, intricate tunnels and relentlessly watchful guards belong rather to the film world of prisoner-of-war camps than reality. In the giant sized camps for the 1,800,000 French POWs it was not a major problem to find an unwatched fence to climb over – the difficulty came in having the logistical back-up, enough food, false papers, a map, and sufficient determination not to be put off by the difficulty of trekking through hundreds of miles of enemy territory. For twenty-two days Mitterrand and his comrade marched steadily southwards, moving by night and sleeping by day in woods under the scanty cover of a shared blanket. And then their guard dropped. Three miles from the Swiss border, they decided to risk walking near a village in daylight. Suspicious villagers called the police and the two Frenchmen were taken back to prison.

Six months later he tried again. With two companions he got out of the camp and made his way across Germany on trains posing as a foreign worker. He managed to cross into occupied France, and exhausted, booked into a cheap hotel in Metz, a few miles from the German border. This time it was the receptionist who betrayed him and once again Mitterrand was hauled back to captivity. The Germans now rated him a very irritating prisoner indeed and decided that he would have to be transferred east to Poland where escape could reasonably be considered to be impossible. He was being kept in a camp in Lorraine near to where he had been picked up. On 10 December 1941, Mitterrand took a decision that might easily have cost his life. He had been told of a reliable café a few miles from the camp whose proprietor would look after any escaped French prisoner. Mitterrand grabbed at his last chance for freedom. Throwing away both calculation and preparation he climbed over the main gate early one morning. The guards opened fire but with luck, helped by the pre-dawn darkness, none of the bullets touched him. He ran off, chased by German soldiers. They were only a few hundred yards behind when he arrived at the café in which he had been promised shelter. It was shut and as the shouts of the pursuing Germans got closer Mitterrand came close to despair. Suddenly he heard a noise – it was the iron shutter covering the entrance being rolled back. Like a mouse arriving at its hole, Mitterrand scuttled under the shutter to the astonishment of the young waitress sleepily opening the café for the morning trade. He was hidden for two days and then passed down an escape route mainly organized around Communist railway workers, already by then in the forefront of the resistance. On Christmas Eve, 1941, he knocked on the door of the family home in Jarnac for the strangest if most joyful Christmas reunion that the Mitterrand family had ever known.

Jarnac was in occupied France, which meant probable execution if Mitterrand was recaptured. He crossed into Vichy France, living semi-openly in St Tropez and in the Jura, far from the attentions of German troops. With the establishment of Marshal Pétain's government in Vichy in July 1940, Hitler agreed to leave two-fifths of France free of German troops. It was a sop that right-wing French politicians took eagerly and they governed Vichy France in the interests of their German overlords. The history of French collaboration with the Germans is now being increasingly exposed. One of Mitterrand's early acts as President was to permit the transmission of Marcel Ophuls' film *The Sorrow and the Pity* depicting the widespread wartime collaboration. The film was made for television in 1969 but banned by the Pompidou and Giscard governments. The film shows how France adjusted itself to the 1940 defeat and quickly came to live with the occupier. By his usual brutal standards, Hitler handled the occupation of France with some sensitivity. In addition to leaving Vichy France to its own devices, he sent officials and military commanders to run occupied France who sought, within the limits of military necessity, to encourage a feeling of normality inside the country. Most of Paris's intellectual stars and artists stayed at work. Some, like Sartre, Cocteau, Genet and Picasso produced their best work under the occupation. Paris publishing houses were producing more books under the Germans than were their British or American equivalents. Box-office receipts trebled. When allied bombers attacked the Renault factories which were making tanks for the German army and killed 500 people there was a march by 300,000 Parisians to commemorate the victims. Few raised questions about French workers producing arms for Hitler. Pre-war fascist leaders came into their own, setting up political parties which supported Nazism and which enrolled scores of thousands of French people. There were thousands of volunteers for the French division of the Waffen SS which fought on the Eastern front while a specially created French militia acted as an indigenous Gestapo. As part of Vichy France's so-called 'national revolution' laws were passed against Jews, trade unions were dissolved and the famous republican slogan was replaced by a call to 'Work, Family, Fatherland'. It was, as David Pryce-Jones has written: 'the hour for scapegoats, alibis and recrimination, conspiracy and above all, self-preservation'.

For nearly three years Mitterrand lived in Vichy and occupied France (in November 1942 the Germans occupied the whole of France but left day-to-day administration in the hands of the

Vichy politicians and civil servants) at first quite openly; he even worked for a period as an official in the Vichy department dealing with servicing French prisoners of war; and then clandestinely when he moved full-time into resistance work. To begin with, Mitterrand moved freely around Paris and the rest of France and in 1943 denounced Vichy politicians at a public meeting organized to gather support for the regime. He stood on a chair and told the speaker that he did not represent France. Fellow resistance members provided a protective shield as he was hustled out of the hall. Months later, the incident was referred to in a Free French broadcast from London. Mitterrand was praised for having shown 'an essential fighting spirit'.

After the war Mitterrand was decorated with the *Légion d'Honneur* and other resistance rewards but it was the *Francisque*, a Vichy decoration, that he received in 1943 that was to cause controversy right through his life. The decoration, which was handed out routinely to civil servants, was accepted by Mitterrand who said he was acting on the advice of Free French leaders in London who had told those active in the resistance to accept such awards the better to improve their cover. Mitterrand's award was gazetted while he was in London on a secret mission to de Gaulle's headquarters. After the war he was bitterly attacked by both Communist and right-wing opponents for having accepted the Vichy award. Even as late as the 1981 presidential election attempts were made to stir up controversy over the Vichy decoration.

This can be ascribed only to the desperation of his opponents willing to use any weapon to wound but, as we shall see, Mitterrand sometimes displays a certain ambivalence in some difficult and potentially damaging political situations which lays open his actions to more than one interpretation. There is no reason to doubt the Mitterrand explanation of the Vichy decoration but, on the other hand, his decision to allow his name to go forward was not something which he was compelled to do.

Of his work in the resistance there can, however, be no doubt. After the German occupation of Vichy France Mitterrand stopped working directly for the government and instead, set up a society to support prisoners of war and deported people. In an exchange system which Mitterrand publicly denounced, the

French administration agreed to deport three Frenchmen to work in Germany for every prisoner of war released. It was under this scheme that Georges Marchais, leader of the French Communists in the 1970s and their candidate in the 1981 election, was to be sent to work in a Messerschmitt factory in Germany. Using his officially approved prisoners' aid society as a front, Mitterrand built up a resistance network all over France. He was a painstaking organizer. One of his comrades spoke of his 'fabulous self-control'. Yet he could be careless and was to be seen in Paris wearing a suit he had obtained while on a secret mission to London or smoking English cigarettes made with Virginia tobacco – unobtainable in wartime France.

The resistance movement in France was a diffuse affair. Each town would have several resistance groups based on different political parties, trade unions, churches, or simply groups of friends who could trust each other. Often they were as opposed to each other as to the Germans. They came and went, were infiltrated or simply stopped activity when a key member moved to another part of the country. De Gaulle struggled to unify the resistance movement but never fully succeeded.

As Henri Michel, France's leading resistance historian, has noted, even to arrange a circle of friends who would meet weekly to talk about how much they disliked the German occupation was an act of resistance that raised morale and carried risks if a pro-Vichy Frenchman happened to overhear the conversation. Formal military engagements such as ambushes or assaults on German military installations, were the exception rather than the rule for the resistance though in the period before the Allied invasion in June 1944 and during the fighting to liberate France the armed resistance fighters made a notable contribution behind German lines. Resistance activities ranged from small-scale sabotage to the clandestine publication of hundreds of newspapers and journals opposed to the German occupation and Vichy collaboration. Another important task was helping support escaped prisoners and prisoners still inside Germany. Mitterrand's group, known after his pseudonym as the 'Morland' group, was involved in this task, which included making false papers which were smuggled into prisoner-of-war camps. A favourite trick was to send in portraits of Marshal Pétain with false identity papers and escape maps hidden between the Marshal's picture and the frame. Direct attacks on German soldiers were far outnumbered by the killing of French collaborators. German reprisals either in reaction to an assault on themselves or against their French helpers were harsh. Forty thousand people were arrested in 1943 and several members of Mitterrand's own group were tortured and killed. Mitterrand refused to permit counter-reprisals. In one case when there was overwhelming circumstantial evidence that a member of his group was a Gestapo informer (a fact confirmed by a Gestapo agent after the liberation) Mitterrand refused to have the man executed for want of conclusive proof.

In November 1943, Mitterrand went to London to make contact with the Free French forces. It was an unhappy experience. He refused to sign a loyalty oath to General de Gaulle and, in return, the Free French left him alone in a lodging house with no money, nor even, he complained, a change of shirt. They wanted him to merge his resistance movement with a similar one based on prisoners of war which was headed by de Gaulle's nephew. Mitterrand was unhappy with the proposal, not just because de Gaulle's nephew seemed to lack the necessary organizational ability but politically he leant towards a kind of right wing mysticism blaming France's misfortunes on Socialists, freemasons and Jews. Instead, Mitterrand flew to Algiers to meet de Gaulle himself. From the very first moment they locked horns. De Gaulle reproached Mitterrand for having come to Algiers on a British aeroplane. Mitterrand replied, 'I didn't think to check whose plane it was before getting on board.' De Gaulle told Mitterrand to combine his resistance group with the one run by de Gaulle's nephew. Mitterrand politely refused and the interview ended coldly. From that first meeting dated the hostility between Mitterrand and de Gaulle. After de Gaulle died, Mitterrand was among the first to acknowledge de Gaulle's place in French history and his contribution to keeping the spirit of France alive in 1940. But if de Gaulle's death lent enchantment to his former enemy's memory, Mitterrand was a bitter and intractable opponent of de Gaulle's politics during his lifetime. In 1958, at what is for a politician the relatively early age of forty-one, Mitterrand went into an anti-Gaullist wilderness that lasted twenty-three years. He was a virulent, at times even a violent critic of de Gaulle during the Gaullist presidency. Unlike Socialist intellectuals such as André Malraux, one of Mitterrand's heroes of the 1930s, who became magnetized by de Gaulle's personality and was de Gaulle's Minister of Culture between 1958–69, Mitterrand never gave way to the magic of de Gaulle's haughty presence and personal authority. For Mitterrand who had been wounded, who had spent eighteen months suffering in a German POW camp and who now faced each day the possibility of torture and execution as the organizer of a resistance movement in occupied France, de Gaulle was a general, a representative of hierarchical right-wing France that had led to the defeat of 1940. Now he was ensconced in London and Algeria, squabbling with other exiled military chieftains for the right to be considered the leader of the French people.

After the war Mitterrand said that the Gaullist history books ignored 'the real story of the struggles against the enemy and identify service for de Gaulle with service for France while the service for France that did not add to de Gaulle's glory was considered to be negligible if not actually suspect'. De Gaulle, in return, was ready to smear Mitterrand. In 1946 he told Pierre Mendès-France: 'Beware of Mitterrand. Deep down he's a Communist.'

Mitterrand was advised to leave Algiers in 1943 as accidents had been known to happen to those who did not fall in with de Gaulle's wishes. He stayed for a while with the French-American singer Josephine Baker in Marrakesh. With her help Mitterrand found himself on a plane taking General Montgomery back to Britain. Montgomery welcomed the unknown Frenchman without asking for his papers or a travel document and offered him tea on the way back. He dropped Mitterrand off in Glasgow because the arrival of someone without documentation in London would have caused too many difficulties for the security sevices. The young Mitterrand found himself on the tarmac in Glasgow waving at Montgomery as the plane took off for London. A few weeks later a motor torpedo boat took him back to France.

In March 1944, there was a merger between the three main resistance organizations based on helping escaped prisoners of war. In addition to Mitterrand's group there was the one led by de Gaulle's nephew and a third was organized by Communists. Mitterrand's group was the largest and most effective. Mitterrand emerged as leader of the unified group with both de Gaulle's nephew and the Communists serving under him. It was in the resistance that Mitterrand first came to know and work with Communists. 'From that period date friendships that the years have not diminished,' he wrote. 'Amongst other benefits that I owe them is that they taught me not to shut my eyes if I wanted to avoid being crushed by their formidable machine. It was difficult to maintain the right balance between watchfulness that allowed you to do nothing and over-confidence that allowed them to do anything. I still have difficulty in finding that balance.' He teased his Communist colleagues about their closeness to Moscow, the Stalin-Hitler pact and the behaviour of the French Communist Party between the invasion of France in 1940 and Hitler's assault on Russia in 1941. It is a period that even now few French Communists care to remember.

The Party stayed aloof from offering support against the Nazi invasion of Poland and the entry of France into the war. With the collapse of France, the Party applied to the German authorities for permission to relaunch *L'Humanité*, the Communist newspaper. The Communist-dominated CGT union supported the ideals of the Vichy regime. Not all the Party's leaders supported the line and there were strikes by Communist miners early in 1941. Once Hitler invaded Russia, everything fell into place. French Communists played a leading role in the resistance, ready to make the most heroic sacrifices in the fight against the Germans.

On 19 August 1944, Mitterrand took part in his last action as a resistance leader when he stormed and occupied the General Commissariat of Prisoners of War in Paris. He had been nominated by de Gaulle as the temporary Secretary General in charge of prisoners of war and deportees. The fifteen Secretary Generals formed an *ad hoc* government to run France until de Gaulle arrived to set up a more permanent administration. At the age of twenty-seven Mitterrand attended his first Cabinet meeting in newly liberated Paris. He even saved de Gaulle's life when the general nearly fell from an open window from which he was saluting the crowd. A sudden surge in the crowded room behind de Gaulle sent him off-balance and he was about to fall when Mitterrand grabbed his arm and pulled him back. Despite this personal service (though Mitterrand says that de Gaulle did not see who had saved him) de Gaulle soon dispensed with Mitterrand when it came to forming a permanent government. He was offered a post as the senior civil servant to run the ministry handling prisoners of war but declined.

He celebrated his twenty-eighth birthday in October 1944 without a real job and without a clear idea of what to do. In the many pieces he wrote for the paper *Libres*, the journal of the Federation of Ex-Prisoners of War, he adopted an insistent, at times strident style attacking the establishment, denouncing the hack politicians of the Third Republic who were now trying to return to public life, and was careful to look after his constituency. He called for a better deal for the POWs and deportees. In a pamphlet, *Prisoners of War in Front of Politics*, he offered an almost Marxist gloss on the significance of the words 'fraternity' and 'liberty'.

> In 1848 we marched under the banner proclaiming 'fraternity' yet during that period children under the age of twelve worked fourteen hours a day in the mines. It is useful to note that when we talk of 'liberty' we should remember that 'liberty' does not consist of the right of the middle classes to read whatever newspaper they want. Or rather, it does consist of that but a lot more besides. The first liberty is to have enough to eat.

Although he joined with other left-wing resistance leaders to stop a Communist takeover of the unified resistance movement that emerged early in 1945, Mitterrand had, by the end of the war, located himself politically. Between the two great camps in French politics and society, Mitterrand had chosen that of the Left. As his ministerial career was to show, that did not mean he was to act as a committed Socialist from 1945 onwards. He was to shift his position this way and that as the years passed; the spectrum of French politics formed and dissolved so rapidly that individuals considered firmly on the Left one day were denounced as compromising centrists the next. Mitterrand was

36

like other politicians. The competing demands of career and principle, of party advantage and ideological purity are to be seen throughout his public life.

In situating Mitterrand on the Left as early as 1945 one is acknowledging the division of France into two great camps. There is a steady and unbroken, if on occasion indistinct, line that began with the surging masses of the 1789 revolution, proceeds through the 1848 overthrow of the Bourbon monarchy, is nearly broken with the repression of the Communards in 1870, re-establishes itself in the Dreyfus case and again in the Popular Front of 1936 and resistance movement during the war and emerges triumphant in 1981. It is based on a belief in man's ability to emancipate himself through his own efforts, whether in the philosophical sense arising from the eighteenth-century Enlightenment or in the economic sense arising from nineteenth-century Socialist thought. From 1945 onwards Mitterrand, even if he was often at odds with sections of the French Left and even if he was placed, and indeed would have placed himself, as being much more of the Centre than of the Left, none the less belonged to and helped carry forward that tradition.

4
The Youngest Minister

I am not a maniacal anti-Communist.

In 1947, aged thirty, Mitterrand became a minister, the youngest person to hold ministerial office in France in a hundred years. Over the next ten years he was to be in and out of eleven of the many governments in France's Fourth Republic which lasted from 1946 to 1958. It was a period that was to give French politics a bad name. Compared with the solid stability of the two-party system in Britain and the United States, the amoeba-like French political system was derided both inside France and internationally. Under the Fourth Republic, the deputies in the National Assembly were elected by a system of proportional representation: this allowed any number of parties, pressure groups, local interest associations of individuals to stand and contributed greatly to the parliamentary chaos of the period. It led to a government of men, not parties.

In the immediate aftermath of the war political unity rather than division appeared successfully to glue together politicians of quite separate ideologies. What could be called the spirit of the resistance, a sense of shared objectives based on equality, sacrifice and comradeship, combined with an ardent desire for social and economic change, was the key factor that held together

38

French politics in the two years following the war's end. De Gaulle presided over a tripartite government consisting of three broad parties – the Socialist SFIO, the French Communist Party and the Christian Democrat Popular Republican Movement. Although de Gaulle left the government early in 1946, the tripartism continued to hold force until May 1947. During those two and half years, economic and social changes were made which can be compared with those introduced by Clement Attlee's reforming Labour government in Britain. The tri-partite government, first under de Gaulle then under Léon Blum and Paul Ramadier, pushed through the nationalization of the coal, electricity and gas industries, the Bank of France and the four main deposit banks, the Renault car firm, more than thirty insurance companies and part of the aviation industry. The state controlled a quarter of all investment directly and nearly half indirectly through the nationalized banks. It passed reforming laws providing for social security benefits, pensions, and gave increased workplace power to the unions. A press freedom and distribution law, introduced in 1944 at a time of anger against the mainly collaborationist newspapers, has made the French press (though not its television and radio) the most plural in Europe and ensures that newsagents have to carry newspapers and magazines reflecting all political viewpoints. One in ten workers was a direct employee of the state. When Mitterrand's nationalization proposals came under right-wing fire in the 1970s, he took pleasure in pointing out that it was de Gaulle who carried through the single biggest set of nationalizations ever undertaken by a West European government and, in addition, de Gaulle took so much into public ownership with the full support and political involvement of the French Communist Party.

At the same time France committed itself to interventionist economic planning and the reform of administrative structures. A brilliant young team of planners under Jean Monnet began reorganizing France's industrial and agricultural infrastructure with such success that the destroyed France of 1945 became the world's fourth industrial power by the 1970s. The political chaos of the Fourth Republic tends to obscure the successes of French administrative and economic planning. De Gaulle was to pick up the credit for the new, powerful France that he presided over in the 1960s but the basic work was done by French administrators working at times almost independently of, or at least without reference to, the politicians in government. Some ministers, like Robert Schumann, who held office in successive governments were able to develop decisive and important policies but the planners and administrators played an equal, if not more important role, than their titular political heads. In France there is not that strict cleavage between politicians, civil servants and outside experts that exists in Britain, and to a lesser extent, the United States. Politicians like Giscard d'Estaing or Michel Rocard began life as civil servants working for the all-powerful Finance Inspectorate. Giscard plucked Raymond Barre from an economic professorship to be Prime Minister. Mitterrand's Foreign Minister, Claude Cheysson, was a high-powered Common Market official before being called back to Paris by Mitterrand. In fact Mitterrand is the first post-war President who has been nothing other than a professional politician all his life.

When the war ended Mitterrand was working as a journalist on the newspaper of the veterans' association and was also editorial director of a publishing house. He resumed his legal studies but was not called to the Bar until 1957, the year he was appointed Justice Minister! His heart was already set on politics. In 1945 he warned against the idea that a democratic country could be governed without parties. The French people, he wrote, justifiably condemned the system of parties that had brought defeat in 1940 but experience suggested that single-party government was even worse. Political parties were necessary, he concluded. But which party to join? The Socialist SFIO, already in government, was aggressively cultivating a quasi-Marxist image. Its new young leader, Guy Mollet, was urging the party on to full-blooded Socialism. Mitterrand told friends at the time: 'I would be suffocated inside SFIO.' The Radical Party, which might have attracted Mitterrand since it considered itself left of centre without explicitly embracing Socialist beliefs, was hopelessly compromised as the party that had signed the Munich agreement in 1938. The newly launched Popular Republican Movement, although formed by leading resistance figures was already taking on a right-wing hue. Instead Mitterrand joined the Democratic and Socialist Union of the Resistance whose title describes its origins. It came into being as an organized party after non-Communist left-wingers had resisted an attempt by the Communist Party to take over the resistance movement which by early 1945 was more or less unified. Its policies were unclear, which suited Mitterrand, whose own political philosophy was unformed. It was also a small party with never more than twenty deputies in the National Assembly (France's parliament) during the Fourth Republic. Until 1971 Mitterrand was always to stay with small left-wing parties. (Party is perhaps too kind a term. None of the parties Mitterrand was to be associated with in the first decades of his political life had a mass membership or an organization at the base. They were rather the political alliances of Paris politicians. Political grouplets might be a more accurate description.) His taste for leadership and position, already whetted by his resistance activities, would be more easily achieved in small parties than in the mainstream SFIO.

Mitterrand was defeated in his first attempt to become a deputy in June 1946. A new election called a few months later after the narrow approval in a referendum for the Fourth Republic's constitution which gave considerable power to the National Assembly and to its deputies but very little to the executive and none to the President provided Mitterrand with his opportunity. He was offered the chance to fight the Nièvre constituency in central France. It is a rural constituency which apart from a short period after 1958 has always supported Mitterrand. He nearly missed being allowed to stand at all as he arrived with his nomination papers at 11 p.m. on the last day when they could be handed in. The Prefect refused to accept them so late in the evening and Mitterrand had to make frantic calls to influential friends in Paris before the Prefect was told to including Mitterrand on the polling list.

He tirelessly worked his way around the widespread constituency, often getting lost and amusing the villagers with his pre-war car which always seemed to be breaking down. It was a curious election with four parties standing – the SFIO, the Communists, the Christian Democrats and Mitterrand. Mitterrand's main competition was from the SFIO and the Communists. His manifesto was deliberately contrived as anti-Communist, anti-nationalization and anti-bureaucracy. Even with the most charitable interpretation, it was a campaign of almost undiluted opportunism. But it worked and Mitterrand, having just celebrated his thirtieth birthday, found himself at the Palais Bourbon, the imposing building on the left bank of the Seine which houses the French National Assembly.

His election victory on 10 November 1946 also closely followed the second anniversary of his marriage. Mitterrand had had one serious love-affair before the war but had released the woman from her obligations when he was captured and imprisoned by the Germans. In February 1944, he was in the Paris apartment of a young woman, Christine Gouze, who acted as a letter-drop for his resistance group. On the piano there stood a photograph of a pretty young girl. According to Mitterrand's biographer Franz-Olivier Giesbert, the following conversation took place:

'Who's that?' Mitterrand asked as he stopped to look hard at the photo.

'My sister Danielle,' replied Christine Gouze.

'How old is she?'

'Nineteen.'

'What does she do now?'

'She is getting ready for her exams back home in Burgundy.'

'I'm going to marry her.'

And that is exactly what happened. The young Danielle was brought to Paris for a secret dinner with Mitterrand. At first she found nothing in common with the stocky resistance fighter disguised with a moustache and a hat pulled over his eyes. But Mitterrand's charm and personality soon changed her mind and a few months later, having only seen each other three times, they were married. Danielle Mitterrand comes from a staunch Socialist family. Her father, a teacher, had been dismissed from his job by the Vichy regime and had gone to live at their summer house in Cluny. This he turned into a safe house for local resistance members. Danielle still keeps the pin-box given to her by a woman resistance hero who had stayed at the Gouze house and who was later tortured and killed by the Gestapo. For the three months between meeting Mitterrand and marrying him, Danielle was herself working in the underground, nursing resistance fighters at a casualty station in the Burgundy woods.

Just as her family background is very different from that of Mitterrand so too her personality is in marked contrast to his. She has kept out of the political limelight and Mitterrand has always refused to parade her as a political, vote-gathering wife. Whether in Paris or staying in the countryside she has always succeeded in organizing a zone of contentment for themselves. She inherited her family's committed Socialism and was known to criticize Mitterrand's association with centrists and right-wingers during the Fourth Republic. They have two sons, a journalist and a young politician who, to his father's joy, was elected a Socialist deputy in the 1981 legislative elections. Another child died soon after he was born in 1945.

The year 1947 opened well for Mitterrand. In January, the Prime Minister Paul Ramadier made him Minister for War Veterans. Ramadier was trying to broaden his tripartite government. Mitterrand was known as a successful representative of the interests of prisoners of war, resistance members and veterans. He was also an effective polemical journalist. Ramadier reasoned that to have Mitterrand in the government obliged him to support it rather than lead critics against it. Despite the success in pushing through economic and social reform measures the tripartite government had done so at the expense of the living standards of the working class. The real wages of workers fell by nearly half between 1944 and 1947. Communist leaders, including the deputy Prime Minister Maurice Thorez, exercised tough labour discipline. Thorez regularly visited coal pits to tell miners that their habit of presenting phoney sick-notes when they wanted a day off had to stop. What resources France had were directed into rebuilding the productive capacity of industry rather than social consumption. But this industrial growth also led to the re-emergence of a French bourgeoisie looking as sleek as it did in pre-war or Vichy years. Class consciousness did not disappear as a result of tripartism but working-class demands were kept in check by Communist involvement in the government. The Communist Party was the most popular at the polls, gaining 28% of the vote compared with the Socialists' 18%. It was the largest membership party with nearly one million adherents.

Mitterrand was to find out straight away how powerful was the influence and involvement of the Communist Party. He arrived at his ministry to find the way barred by striking pickets. His predecessor had tried to dissolve a ministerial car pool which had been turned into a private transport undertaking by Communist activists in order to carry militants from meeting to meeting. In response the Communist trade union within the ministry had called a strike. Mitterrand found his ministry occupied and pickets camping in his office. Mitterrand's response was hard and uncompromising. He ordered the dismissal of leading strikers and announced their replacement with heads of local ex-prisoner of war groups. 'I will not be a minister under these conditions,' he said. The union and the Communist Party backed off and Mitterrand had made his name within hours of entering office because of his decisive, even abrupt, handling of the strike and occupation. A few days later he attended his first Cabinet meeting where Maurice Thorez told the 'baby' of the cabinet: 'There are some things which have to be done when one is in government and you have done well.'

Thorez' participation in the government was not to last much longer. By the beginning of 1947, the consensus between the allies based on the Yalta agreement was breaking down. Locating the blame for the start of the cold war is as much a question of ideology as of history. The United States ended the war as the world's most powerful economy. Two-thirds of the world's industrial capacity and three-quarters of the world's invested capital were within American borders. It was the leading military power with 400 naval and air bases and it had the atomic bomb. Most important of all it had the dollars essential to post-war reconstruction. America was ready to put those dollars to use but not if European governments contained Communists. Stalin's Russia also had need of American capital if it was to rebuild without squeezing its people's productive capacity almost beyond endurance. The Red Army's occupation of East Europe was followed too by the dismantling of liberal democratic structures in East European countries and the absorption of Socialist and peasant parties into a single-party political system. In Greece, a civil war raged between Communist-led resistance fighters and right-wingers seeking the re-establishment of the monarchy. In March 1947 came the announcement of the Truman Doctrine when the American President declared that the United States would support anyone fighting Communism. The threat of the military stick was followed in June 1947 by the economic carrot in the shape of the Marshall Plan which offered massive dollar credits to help rebuild Europe, provided the economic framework of countries accepting Marshall Aid was based on the market economy: Marshall Aid was only available to rebuild capitalism, not to introduce Socialism.

In France, Communist members of the government had been placed in an impossible position. Government leaders, including the Socialists, wanted them out of office in order to placate Washington and guarantee American credit. Communist ministers were supporting policies contrary to all their stated principles. They found themselves voting for the government's colonial Indo-China policy whilst Communist deputies abstained. In March 1947 there was a Cabinet row with Communists opposing the lifting of parliamentary immunity of black deputies accused of anti-colonial riots in Madagascar. Worse was the growing gulf between the Communist Party leadership and its industrial base. A strike at Renault in April was widely supported despite being denounced by both the Party and the Communist-dominated CGT union. Previously such industrial action had been weathered and Communist discipline had forced workers to pick up their tools. The Renault strike was different as workers made clear that two and a half years of worsening living standards was too much. Nationalization plus Communist participation in government had not improved the Renault worker's life in a tangible way. The Party decision to back the strikers and thus to defy the government wage freeze gave Ramadier the formal excuse to ask for the resignation of Thorez and the other Communist ministers.

Thorez led his colleagues out of government and into a political ghetto – in terms of holding any of the levers of governmental power – that lasted thirty-four years. Unlike Communist Parties in Britain or the United States with negligible membership and barely any following at the polls, the French Communist Party has always had a mass base. In 1947, nearly one French voter in three had supported it. There was, and is, a flourishing Communist social and cultural structure which, coupled with control of local councils and domination in certain industries – mines, railways, automobiles, printing – meant that one could live almost all of one's life within a Communist environment. It was like being a member of a Church with the added piquancy of being a member of a Church militant, always under persecution by those in power. In the period following the break up of tripartism it seemed as if the fight between the French Communists and their opponents was pitched at the level of a religious war such was the intensity with which it was fought.

On leaving the government, the French Communist Party reverted to a hard rock-like Stalinism. Thorez was a close personal friend of Stalin, having lived in Moscow during the war, and was to spend two and a half years there convalescing after a stroke in 1950. He never questioned any of Stalin's decisions and supported the Moscow line. When Yugoslavia's Tito or Poland's Gomulka or Czechoslovakia's Slansky were denounded by Stalin Thorez echoed him. His venom quickly turned against his former Socialist colleagues whom he now described as 'lackeys of American imperialism' while in the National Assembly he compared them to Goering and Goebbels. De Gaulle launched his own political party in the summer of 1947 and made it clear that its ideological thrust was a vehement anti-Communism. The Socialists, nervous of being outflanked by de Gaulle whose new party obtained nearly 40% in the municipal elections, and smarting under Communist insults, began bitterly criticizing the Communists. The SFIO Congress in 1947 was described as an orgy of anti-Communist invective and its leader, Guy Mollet, hitherto considered a committed leftist, became almost fanatical in his attacks on Communists.

The political bitterness was made worse by the wave of strikes that broke out in the autumn of 1947. The economic causes of the strikes were plain enough. Price rises were far outstripping wage increases (in the second half of 1947 prices went up 51% while wages only increased by 19%) and there were desperate food shortages which had led to food riots. In September, Stalin had called a meeting of Communist Parties in Warsaw which launched Cominform and called for a political offensive against the United States. The French Communist Party had been accused of being too reformist and its representatives promised that they would be more resolutely anti-American on return to France. The hardening political attitudes matched the desire by the working class for a better deal. A general strike was ordered in Marseilles followed by strikes in the north of France and the Paris region. By mid-November 1947, 3 million workers were on strike and the country was paralysed.

To the Right and to the Socialists in government, it was an attempt at a Communist takeover. Few could forget that most of the Communist resistance fighters had kept their weapons. Rumours of secret Communist arms caches swept the country. Eighty thousand reservists were called up and several divisions of the French army were brought back from Germany. Armed riot-police were sent in to break up picket lines. Workers responded by occupying prefects' offices and blowing up railway lines. The government, while remaining a Socialist-Christian Democrat coalition, had a new right-wing Premier, Robert Schumann. Mitterrand voted in the Cabinet for the use of troops to break the strike. After three weeks, the trade-union confederation, CGT, weakened by a walk-out of members objecting to both the general strike call and the effective Communist control of the confederation, called off the strike. The American government meanwhile had announced an aid package of $600 million and Communist denunciations of American imperialism were contrasted with what to a hungry France appeared to be open-handed generosity.

The anti-Communist offensive continued. Communists were removed from leading positions on boards of nationalized industries or dismissed from the civil service. Communist union leaders and militants were victimized in factories. It was described as a 'foreign' party and Thorez lost the support of most French patriots when he said that French workers would not resist if the Red Army occupied Paris. The French government, still a coalition of politicians who liked to call themselves the 'Third Force' to distance themselves from the Communist Party and de Gaulle, moved steadily to the right, joining NATO, and in the autumn of 1948, going on the offensive against miners with a series of decrees ordering 10% of the workforce to be sacked and further victimization of union or Communist militants. The strike that ensued was crushed by 40,000 troops transferred from

Germany especially for the purpose. Soldiers opened fire on miners and when the strike was over four workers had been killed, 2,000 were in prison and 6,000 had been sacked. The guiding spirits in this attack on the miners had been the Ministers of Industry and the Interior, both of them SFIO Socialists.

In July 1948, Mitterrand became Information Minister. His main job was to oversee French radio, though he remains proud of having presided over the start of television transmissions in France. He made one important technical mistake when he settled upon a broadcasting system based on 819 lines as opposed to the 615 lines used elsewhere in Europe. This meant that the French television industry could not develop an export capability. It is a long-forgotten debate but the French insistence on 819 lines, which they argued, probably correctly, gave better definition, underlined that curious French national pride in sticking by their own way of doing things even when it meant being badly out of step with the rest of the world. As Information Minister Mitterrand exercised a firm editorial control. Each day there was a conference at noon where, together with representatives of the Interior and Industry ministries he gave orders to the head of French radio. He was criticized by Communists, Gaullists and Socialists each of whom, in turn, charged the radio output with being too right-wing, too left-wing or, in the case of the Socialists, too Communist. Mitterrand shrugged off the complaints. 'Radio,' he told the National Assembly, 'makes policy every day and its policy is the defence of the French national interests.' As the government, he added, represented the popular will, it had every right to oversee what was being broadcast. It sounds shocking to British or American ears used to a firm distance kept between government and broadcasting. Unconsciously Mitterrand was doing no more than echoing the famous syllogism of Lord Reith, the first Director General of the BBC and the man usually associated with establishing the BBC's reputation for independence. Seeking to justify the BBC's refusal to give airtime to trade unionists during Britain's 1926 general strike Reith said that as the BBC was for the people and the people were for the government it therefore followed that the BBC was for the government. Mitterrand the Information Minister was simply following Reith's logic to its conclusion.

French radio, and later television, has never been able to shake off the state's tutelage.

In 1948 Mitterrand intervened to transfer a radio journalist for including what the Minister claimed was Communist propaganda in a documentary programme. On the other hand, the producer for France's main political magazine programme which regularly invited politicians of all colours to broadcast has said that he never once received an order from Mitterrand to interview or not to interview any particular person.

Mitterrand left the government in 1949 not because of any sudden political shift but because his ministerial seat was needed by a new Prime Minister. Being a minister or even Prime Minister in the Fourth Republic was rather like being a square on a Rubik cube. You were turned this way and that, never knowing in whose Cabinet you would be sitting in a few months' time nor beside whom you would find yourself. Mitterrand enjoyed the game. He was young and he looked up to the older politicians who shuffled in and out of office. He remembers them all with fondness and is grateful at being allowed to start his political education at so high a level at such a young age. He was known to be efficient and got on well with his colleagues. It was a period for making friends.

The only ideology discernible from this first period in office is that of anti-Communism. Mitterrand told a Communist journalist at the time: 'I am not a maniacal anti-Communist, even though such a position would be justified because the Communists are heaping mud on me. In my own constituency their smears about the Vichy decoration I was awarded are unspeakably foul because they know I fought alongside them in the resistance. It is true that I want to defeat the Communists. But through the ballot box. I do not mean to use administrative methods against them. I will never send a Communist to prison.'

The rupture of the French Left in 1947 and the unleashing of the cold war that followed, both internationally and inside France, were the most important events in the young minister's life. Although he sat in the Cabinets of the time that took anti-Communist measures, Mitterrand, much later, was to bring the French Communist Party in from the icy cold to which it had been consigned, or to which it had consigned itself, in 1947. The entry of French Communists into Mitterrand's government in the summer of 1981 brought public criticism from America's Vice President, George Bush. But 1981 was no longer 1947 and France no longer depended on American dollars for survival. Even right-wing politicians in France attacked Bush for presuming to interfere in France's internal affairs. During the 1960s and 1970s Mitterrand pondered the question of what role should French Communism have and what did Socialism in France mean if it did not include or, at least, involve the millions of French people who voted Communist? It is a question still not completely resolved but at least President Mitterrand has the experience and the memory of his first years in office to remind him of what can go wrong.

5
Colonial Problems

I was bequeathed a colonial policy which on good days was based on paternalism and, on bad days, repression.

The bulk of Mitterrand's ministerial life in the Fourth Republic was spent dealing with colonial affairs. He struggled to reform, humanize and introduce some justice into French colonial policy. He did so against a background of venomous opposition both from the Right, who accused him of selling off the empire, and from the Communists, who placed on his shoulders the responsibility for the tortures and repression carried out by the French army. He failed because he was never able to accept that the French possessions overseas had a right to determine their own existence – a right laid down in the 1789 Declaration of the Rights of Man which underpinned the whole of the left tradition in France. As the surge for national independence gathered strength, France was forced to concede that right to Vietnam (1954), to Tunisia (1955), and to Morocco (1956) but as late as 1957, at a time when he no longer held ministerial office, Mitterrand told the National Assembly that Algeria had to remain French and suggested creating a Federal Republic consisting of France, Algeria and the remaining French possessions in Africa.

Like the Colonial Ministers under Clement Attlee's 1945–51 Labour government who never dreamt of granting independence to Britain's African colonies and actually encouraged white settlers to emigrate there, Mitterrand was unable to make the philosophical breakthrough to a complete understanding of the need for and support for the right to national independence. It was Engels, after all, who cited Algeria as an example of the benefits of colonializing civilization. Before the arrival of the French in 1830, Engels pointed out, Algeria had been nothing more than an undefined geographical area loosely under Ottoman tutelage and peopled with disease-ridden warring tribes. With the French came education, medical services and economic development and prosperity. It was Marx perhaps who made the more prescient point when he wrote that no country will find peace with itself while its armies occupy another country.

The dismantling of the French empire and the independence of French colonies dominated French politics from 1945 until de Gaulle cut the Gordian knot by conceding Algeria's independence in 1962. Today France still hangs on to a few overseas territories and early in his presidency Mitterrand was embarrassed by a rising in the Pacific island of New Caledonia, still in French hands because of its immensely valuable nickel deposits.

After the war France tried to shed its imperial image and, sensitive to the United Nations' call for national self-determination, removed the words 'empire' and 'colonies' from its official political vocabulary. Instead under the Fourth Republic constitution there came into existence the 'French Union' which covered the colonies and protectorates that formerly constituted the French empire. There were Overseas Territories such as the countries in French-speaking black Africa and Overseas Departments like Algeria or the Caribbean Islands of Martinique and Guadeloupe. They had the right to elect deputies to the National Assembly in Paris though on a disproportionate basis – eighty-three deputies to represent the 62 million inhabitants of the 'French Union' outside of France, against 544 deputies for the 50 million inhabitants of metropolitan France. The deputies were elected in each department or territory by two electoral colleges, one for the whites and one for the natives, with the former having a majority of votes despite their numerical inferiority. Algeria was treated somewhat separately with its own Algerian Assembly. Half of the 120 seats were reserved for the 900,000 strong white minority and elections for the remaining sixty seats to represent the 8 million Algerians were fixed in favour of representatives who supported continued union with France. The failure of the Algerian Assembly to act as an effective conduit for nationalist aspirations was one of the reasons that led Algerian nationalists to go underground and launch the 1954 insurrection.

Although he was not to become a Minister with responsibility for Overseas Territories until 1950, Mitterrand had already stated his position on colonial questions in an article he wrote in 1945. He put forward the classic liberal defence that the European colonizer brings peace, progress and economic development to the natives. But, he went on: 'the arrival of the Declaration of the Rights of Man or the smoke from a factory chimney are not seen by local people as necessarily welcome gifts'. If Mitterrand was ready to acknowledge faulty logic in the justification for having an empire he was not prepared to give it up. 'We need our colonies. To abandon them is to abandon ourselves. Let us change our methods if they are harmful. Let us avoid exaggerating our virtues but don't let's dwell on our faults. Our policy is imperfect and mixes good and bad, heroism and greed, generosity and stupidity. But who has done a better job?'

After he left the government in 1949 Mitterrand went on a long trip through French Africa visiting Senegal, Niger, Liberia, Dahomey and French West Africa. He travelled slowly, calling on French officials and joining in big-game hunts. He observed with humour the behaviour of the wives of senior French administrators and noted that although Liberia was a free country its economy was controlled by the Firestone Rubber company. 'I saw corrupt and lazy officials still operating at a pace where a reply to a letter could take three months. But I also saw the great love for France for having sent her teachers, doctors and engineers.'

In July 1950, he was invited to join the government by the new Prime Minister, René Pleven, who was General Secretary of the party to which Mitterrand belonged, the Democratic and Socialist Union of the Resistance. Mitterrand asked for and was given the Ministry for Overseas Territories which put him in charge of the colonies he had just visited. Another minister looked after Indo-China, the Foreign Minister was responsible for Tunisia and Morocco, while the Minister of the Interior had responsibility for Algeria. The only time Mitterrand saw the other three ministers who shared with him responsibility for the 'French Union' was at the weekly Cabinet meeting. Government business was regulated according to a strict protocol which placed the problems raised by the older ministries at the top of the agenda and left to the bottom any items concerning the newest ministry created only in 1946, that of Overseas Territories, occupied by Mitterrand. It meant that he rarely got the chance to discuss policy in the Cabinet and was left to his own devices in deciding what to do with the French possessions in West and Equatorial Africa.

This division of French colonial responsibilities amongst so many government departments reinforced the lack of cohesion in policy. Beyond a kind of 'what we have we hold' philosophy there was no forward-looking development of an overall policy. The lack of effective political control consequently gave much greater power to the Governor-Generals, Residents and military commanders in the French colonies. The history of French decolonialization was often made by arbitrary acts of French administrators or officers acting on their own accord without reference to the French government, or, if they did communicate with Paris, with the Minister simply endorsing the action concerned, often involving quite severe repression, without reference to his government colleagues.

Mitterrand tried to shake up both the politics and the administration of the Overseas Territories for which he was responsible. He made contact with Léopold Senghor, leader of the blacks in Senegal and well known as a writer and poet. Senghor was a deputy in the National Assembly like Félix Houphouët-Boigny who was leader of the blacks in the Ivory Coast. But unlike Senghor who preached moderation, Houphouët-Boigny was regarded as a dangerous radical.

In 1946 Houphouët-Boigny founded the Democratic African Rally. This loosely grouped the black deputies who believed in national independence for their countries. As a political group within the National Assembly, it was allied to the French Communist Party. Mitterrand decided to try and woo the Democratic African Rally away from the Communists and towards his own party, the Democratic and Socialist Union of the Resistance. His first invitation to Houphouët-Boigny to visit him in the ministry caused a stir because Houphouët-Boigny was in hiding following certain policy statements by the Democratic African Rally. Mitterrand needed the support of both the Prime Minister and the President to obtain safe-conducts for the black leader. Mitterrand offered Houphouët-Boigny his full support in the search for black rights and promised that he would do away with special privileges for the white minority. But if Houphouët-Boigny wanted to resume his political activities, he would first have to acknowledge the authority of the 'French Union'. The tactic of incorporation worked, to the fury of the right-wing deputies who organized a petition accusing Mitterrand of having delivered 'black Africa to international Communism'. In fact the reverse was the case. Mitterrand's encouragement of the Democratic African Rally led their leaders to send missions all over French black Africa ordering their local sections to enter into talks with local French administrators. Mitterrand sent out instructions from Paris that the colonial civil servants were to co-operate with black leaders and try to reach agreement with them on local problems. He backed this new policy with the removal of hard-line or unsympathetic colonial administrators, and sent out personal missions from the ministry to underline his commitment to co operation and an increase in black rights. On a ministerial visit to Abidjan, Mitterrand invited Houphouët-Boigny to accompany him to the French Club. The governor protested, saying Houphouët-Boigny was an enemy of France while his chief aide told another black leader, later to be President of Chad: 'The moment the Minister has gone, I'm going to kick your arse out of here.' Both men were recalled to Paris. Mitterrand's policy of rapprochement slowly brought the black African deputies away from the French Communist Party towards his own party. During his year in office Mitterrand swung French African policy away from simplistic colonial repression towards a more subtle incorporation. In a book published in 1953, *At the Frontiers of the French Union*, Mitterrand was to be seen still arguing for French hegemony over African territories. He criticized the lack of a clear policy but called for a union of French-speaking countries, proposing that they gain a measure of internal autonomy; military, economic and diplomatic policies would still be shaped in Paris. The French colonies in West and Equatorial Africa finally achieved independence in the early 1960s but economically and diplomatically most have chosen to remain close to France. They also achieved their independence without recourse to the kind of bloody uprising that was necessary in Kenya before Britain's hold in East Africa could be loosened. Many of the French-speaking African leaders who attended Mitterrand's investiture as President in 1981 were men whom he had met and encouraged in their political activities while Minister for Overseas Territories. To French colonialists of the time however, he was a traitor. At a meeting in the Ivory Coast the local white representatives told him: 'You are handing Africa to the blacks and sacrificing us. Your policy is anti-French.'

The complaints in Paris against Mitterrand's liberal African policy also increased and when a new government was formed after the election in June 1951, Mitterrand was left out of it. These breaks in his ministerial career during the Fourth Republic gave him time to think about policy. After Africa, the greatest colonial problem faced by France was Indo-China where the Vietminh led by Ho Chi Minh were waging a successful war of national liberation against French troops. After the evacuation of Vietnam by Japanese troops in 1945 Ho Chi Minh had proclaimed the country's independence, though his influence was restricted to the northern half of Vietnam. The French Prime Minister of the time, the Socialist Léon Blum, unsuccessfully argued for a negotiated independence with Ho Chi Minh. Instead in March 1946 French troops reoccupied Vietnam and installed a puppet emperor Bao-Dai in Saigon. In November 1946 a French battleship, acting without approval from Paris, shelled Hanoi causing several thousand civilian deaths. In return Ho Chi Minh ordered attacks on French installations and a full-scale war broke out. France tried to pretend that the fighting was a localized internal quarrel and in 1949 gave the 'emperor'

Bao-Dai the right to form an administration, have an army and send diplomatic representatives to neighbouring South-East Asian states. As the United States was to discover fifteen years later, placing hope on Saigon-based regimes was a waste of men and resources. More and more French troops were sucked into Vietnam which, after the outbreak of the Korean war, was justified by the French Right as part of the Western stand against Communist advances in Asia.

Apart from the French Communist Party which backed the Vietminh, the strongest critic of French policy in Indo-China was Pierre Mendès-France whose political life was to become interlocked with that of Mitterrand. A brilliant and persuasive speaker who was renowned for his bleak honesty, Mendès-France had been a deputy for the Radical Party since 1932. He had served in the Popular Front government of 1936 and with the Free French during the war. Although he had been briefly a member of the government in 1945 he had since then stayed aloof from the governmental musical chairs played by other politicians. Mitterrand and Mendès-France had got to know each other due to their collaboration with the new weekly journal *L'Express* which, with its support for progressive policies and its championing of Mendès-France, soon established itself as the most influential and lively political journal in France. Mitterrand supported Mendès-France's thesis that France had to get out of Indo-China where the costly war was increasingly straining the French economy and, when the National Assembly refused to ratify Mendès-France's nomination as Prime Minister in June 1953, Mitterrand wrote angrily that the defeat was to be blamed on the arrival of French McCarthyism. Mendès France, declared Mitterrand, would change the style of French politics through a renewal of parliamentary life. In a brief period in government in 1953 Mitterrand had shocked his Cabinet colleagues by suggesting face-to-face negotiations with Ho Chi Minh and Mao Tse-tung. His call in the National Assembly for a French withdrawal was greeted with cries of 'defeatist' from the right. In fact, the political arguments for getting out of Indo-China that Mendès-France and Mitterrand advanced were not to carry the day until the humiliating defeat for the French army at Dien Bien Phu in May 1954. This finally persuaded a majority of deputies to vote

in Mendès-France as Prime Minister. He immediately negotiated a treaty with Ho Chi Minh which led to the creation of
North Vietnam. The free elections which were meant to be held
throughout the country in 1955 never took place after Ngo Dinh
Diem deposed the emperor and declared South Vietnam to be a
separate, independent state. It was to be another twenty years
and a kind of cruel action replay involving the United States
instead of France before Vietnam was united and independent.
In the 1960s Mitterrand was a forceful critic of the United States'
presence in Vietnam.

By the time he entered Mendès-France's government
Mitterrand had further strengthened his reputation as being, in
terms of the politics of the period, a supporter of reform and
cautious evolution on colonial questions. Briefly a minister in a
government that only lasted for five weeks early in 1952,
Mitterrand put forward a plan to provide Tunisia with its own
internal government and a genuinely representative assembly. It
was welcomed by Tunisian nationalists and condemned by the
local French population. The succeeding government opted for
repression, arresting Habib Bourguiba and other Tunisian
nationalist leaders. Two hundred Tunisians died as the French
army put down demonstrations called to protest against
Bourguiba's arrest. A year later Mitterrand was once again in
government as Minister for the Council of Europe, but the
problems in North Africa dominated the agenda. In August
1953, the chief French administrator of Morocco deposed the
Sultan Mohamed V who was considered the leader of the
Moroccan nationalists. In 1947, the Sultan had called for an
independent Morocco and French policy towards him had
wavered between repression and incorporation. The decision to
depose him was taken in secret between the French Prime
Minister, Joseph Laniel, and the French administration in
Morocco. Mitterrand forcibly protested against the lack of consultation with the Cabinet and threatened to resign. A few days
later a known hard-liner was installed by Laniel as chief
administrator in Tunisia. Again the Prime Minister had not
consulted with his colleagues in the government. The Cabinet
was told that it 'cannot involve itself in what happens in every
French village, and Tunis is only a village'. Mitterrand resigned

in protest, not, as he wrote in *L'Express* explaining his resignation, because he had stopped believing in a policy of firmness or in the necessity to uphold national prestige, but both had to be subordinated to an evolutionary policy 'which will develop against us if it develops without us'. This resignation was the only time during the Fourth Republic that Mitterrand left a government of his own volition and on a point of principle. This resignation further increased the Right's dislike of him, particularly as it came at a time when France was rocked by a strike of 4 million public employees. Mitterrand enhanced his reputation on the Left as a politician ready to resign in support of a progressive policy. He was able to throw himself wholeheartedly into support for Mendès-France and was rewarded with the important post of Minister of the Interior when Mendès-France formed a government in June 1954.

The short period (June 1954 to February 1955) of Mendès-France's premiership is looked upon as the brightest moment during the Fourth Republic, when France appeared to have found both the men and the measures which were coherent, progressive and could lead to some political stability. Although a left-wing member of the Radical Party, Mendès-France ignored party allegiances when it came to forming his government. He had categorically rejected Communist involvement in his government, even telling the National Assembly that he would rather be ratified as Prime Minister without the support of Communist deputies. Nor did he find a place for Guy Mollet, the leader of the Socialist Party, SFIO, in the Cabinet. His disdain for allies on the Left not only helped keep the life of his administration fairly short, it also meant that in the years ahead neither Socialists nor Communists would acknowledge his claim to be the leader or spokesman of the Left in France. Despite near-universal recognition (even Winston Churchill praised him) of his administrative ability, his intellectual integrity and social far-sightedness, the refusal of Mendès-France to base himself on a party and thus to ensure organizational support for his policies contributed to his downfall and his failure to re-emerge as a substantial politician. The necessity for a party and the need to work with all the forces on the Left was not lost on Mitterrand.

Mendès-France started well. He went straight to Geneva and

negotiated an end to the war in Indo-China withdrawing France from Laos and Cambodia as well as Vietnam. Afterwards he went to Tunisia to restore Habib Bourguiba as the nationalist leader; this was followed by the granting of internal autonomy, which in 1955 led to full independence for Tunisia. Algeria was left to Mitterrand. On the surface the three departments of Algeria seemed quiet enough. The white minority was confident that its control of power could not be challenged. The elections to the Algerian Assembly in 1948 and 1951 had been fixed so that after 1951 Algerian nationalists were not represented. With most of their leaders arrested, exiled, driven underground and otherwise harassed there were few Algerian nationalists for Mitterrand to deal with. He wanted to apply fully a reform proposed in 1947 which abolished French control of Algerian villages and would allow universal suffrage for the Algerian Assembly. But Algeria was not like French-speaking black Africa where the white settlers were clearly an alien minority without much clout in metropolitan France. The 900,000 French in Algeria felt as if they were living in and were an integral part of France. They had a tightly-knit block of deputies in the National Assembly. By voting with the right wing these deputies could easily unseat the Mendès-France government. Mitterrand, by now considered something of an expert on the shifting alliances and voting intentions of the various groups of deputies, considered it important to keep the Algerian deputies as sweet as possible.

In a trip he made to Algeria in October 1954, he played up to the French, speaking glowingly of the role of France overseas, investing one of the die-hard white leaders with the Legion of Honour and pointedly ignoring nationalist demonstrations. Before boarding the aircraft taking him back to Paris Mitterrand told journalists: 'Algeria is prosperous and calm. I return full of optimism.'

A week later Ben Bella, one of the leaders of the Algerian nationalists, ordered the first wave of bomb and incendiary attacks that launched the Algerian war of independence. Mitterrand's response was to send several thousand extra troops to Algeria to root out what he told the National Assembly were 'criminals who have sought refuge in the mountains and carry out actions in the name of a cause which is not their own'. He went on: 'Algeria is France. And who amongst us would hesitate to use all the means necessary to safeguard France?' Two days before Mitterrand addressed the National Assembly, the Communist newspaper *L'Humanité* had given details of the torture carried out against Algerian nationalists by the French police. Mitterrand made no reference to these revelations when he addressed the National Assembly. The widespread use of torture was to reach its height later on in the Algerian war but Mitterrand cannot, nor in later years did he seek to, avoid responsibility for the behaviour of the French security forces during his period as Minister of the Interior. Mitterrand the liberal reformist was far from sight when he told the National Assembly that the nationalists' action rendered inconceivable any sort of talks with them. 'There can be only one form of negotiation: war.' Mitterrand's rhetoric was aimed at reassuring the Algerian deputies whose votes were so vital. Privately he did not believe that the attacks represented a widely supported uprising but publicly he had to be seen to be taking measures to calm the French population in Alger and Oran.

He decided to dissolve the grandiloquently named Movement for the Triumph of Democratic Liberties, which was the main nationalist grouping in Algeria. Local French administrators blamed the movement for the attacks but they were in fact organized by a small group called the Revolutionary Committee of Unity and Action which became the nucleus of the National Liberation Front. In agreeing to suppress the movement, Mitterrand drove its members underground and into the arms of those who launched the attacks. Up to then the movement had tried to work legally, organizing demonstrations and strikes in support of the nationalist cause. Dissolved, its leaders gave up the hope for a negotiated path to independence and joined the insurrection.

Mitterrand flew to Algeria to praise French soldiers as 'pacifiers' and watched warplanes laden with napalm take off to 'pacify' mountain villages. He was never a complete hawk and angered local military chieftains by refusing permission for certain of the military operations the army wanted to carry out. As he told the National Assembly: 'The army is not there to carry out repression but to bring back peace, order and confidence in France.' In the same debate he said: 'If Algerians are French it is our role to ask ourselves if the conditions of existence offered to them are really acceptable. That is not always the case. Agreement and peace in Algeria are not separable from equality and prosperity.' He also ordered an investigation into the methods used by the police in Algeria.

At the start of 1955 Mitterrand decided to sugar the military pill by putting forward a programme of reforms aimed at increasing the rights of the indigenous Algerians. Some women were to be given the vote, Algerians could hold office in the local communes, there would be agricultural reform giving Algerians access to non-cultivated land and there would be major investment aimed at improving water supplies and land reclamation. More alarming in the eyes of the whites was Mitterrand's proposal to unite the Algerian police with the metropolitan police and increase the direct control exercised by his Paris-based Ministry of the Interior. He also wanted to change the administrators in Algeria and replace them with people he trusted. The promise of reforms and insertion of more liberal administrators who had worked in black Africa was Mitterrand's answer to the Algerian problem. For the group of deputies who represented the French settlers in the National Assembly, it was all too much. In addition, they were against Mendès-France's choice for Governor-General of Algeria, the apparently left-inclined Jacques Soustelle. (Soustelle was later to become a notorious pro-colonialist hard-liner on Algeria.)

Mendès-France had other political problems. His campaign against alcoholism and his appeals for French people to consume less wine and more milk had been widely ridiculed and, perhaps more importantly, had alienated the large number of deputies whose votes came from wine-growing regions. The evening after the explosions which effectively signalled the beginning of the Algerian war, he had broadcast to the nation, but his theme was the perils of alcohol rather than the problems of Algeria. Acrimonious divisions over the proposed Common European Defence force and the re-armament of West Germany further destabilized the already shaky coalition of parties and groups who had voted him into office seven months previously. After a long and bitter debate in the National Assembly the Mendès-France government was voted down. The 'ultras' of Algeria had won their first head.

A year later, in February 1956, Mitterrand returned to the government as Minister of Justice. The Prime Minister was the Socialist Guy Mollet and under him the Algerian war was waged with relentless and increasing savagery. Torture, murder and vicious repression summed up Mollet's policy. Mitterrand sat in the Cabinet and said little. One of his colleagues, Gaston Deferre, claimed that Mitterrand always took the moderate side in any Cabinet debate on Algeria and personally stopped the execution of several imprisoned Algerians whom hard-line Cabinet members wanted to see guillotined. Unlike Mendès-France, who resigned from the Mollet government in protest at the Algerian policy, Mitterrand stayed in. He was busy on other projects as Justice Minister and if he disagreed with Mollet on Algeria, at least his presence in the government might serve as a modest restraint on the worst of the excesses.

Once before, Mitterrand had resigned in principle and his protest had not altered government policy. Now he stayed within the government and his presence did not alter government policy either. If his political conscience was bothered it did not extend to resignation though colleagues and civil servants reported him as much more moody, irritable and withdrawn during his time as Minister of Justice. After he left the government in June 1957, the last time he was to hold office until 1981, Mitterand returned to his theme of reform and the need for compromise and co-operation with native Algerians. But Algeria was still to remain French. He was unable to perceive Algeria as a state with a right to determine its own future. For the whole length of his career as a minister responsible for the shrinking remains of the French overseas territories Mitterrand was constantly under attack by the Right for 'selling off' the empire. It was difficult for him to understand that reformist and liberal as his policies might be, in fact they were radical by the standards of the day, his political approach was still essentially colonialist. Hindsight makes such harsh judgements easy. The democratic desire not to give way to force, especially when that force takes the form of bomb attacks against civilians, the denunciation of people who take up arms in the name of politics as 'criminal terrorists' is not peculiar to France or Mitterrand. Current problems in, say, the Middle East or Northern Ireland suggest that politicians who consider themselves Socialist and democratic are often still incapable of developing sufficient imagination to find political solutions when offered the alternative of a military option which commands more support from the press and the public. It was to be another five years after Mitterrand had ceased holding office before French public opinion had swung sufficiently against the Algerian war to permit French withdrawal. Mitterrand was unable to be ahead of his time.

6
De Gaulle Takes Power

The presence of General de Gaulle means that
from now on, despite himself, violent minorities
will be able successfully to begin attacking
democracy without facing any punishment.

The arrival in power of General de Gaulle in the summer of 1958 was a decisive turning point not only for post-war France but for François Mitterrand's personal career. While other left-wing politicians were trying to scramble aboard the Gaullist band-waggon, Mitterrand scornfully attacked the process that had brought de Gaulle to power and publicly committed himself to outright opposition to the new regime. As a result, he lost his seat in the Gaullist landslide in the 1958 elections. The politician who had mastered the intricacies of Fourth Republic politics, who had held two great offices of state as Interior and Justice Minister and who was even whispered as a possible Prime Minister, found himself at the age of forty-one, if not on the political scrapheap, very much in the political wilderness. Before seeing how this came about we must retrace certain steps in Mitterrand's career and in the development of French politics leading up to 1958.

By 1958 Mitterrand was more than a man who had successfully held several ministerial portfolios. He was an accomplished politician who was President of his party, the Democratic and Socialist Union of the Resistance, and was acknowledged as one of the leaders of the Left in France. He had painstakingly built up his political power base starting from the period when he was leader of the group of sixteen deputies belonging to his party in the National Assembly. He used his position as Minister for Overseas Territories to win over the black deputies of the Democratic African Rally to support his own party. With that success behind him, he proceeded to take over the party machine installing a personal friend as General Secretary. At the annual Congress his speeches leant to the left, to the pleasure of rank and file delegates. At the 1951 Congress he told them: 'We accept resolutely and clearly the socialization of means of production. If we don't, we are not Socialist and should remove the word from the party title.' By 1953 he had succeeded in replacing René Pleven as party leader. It was a modest revenge, for Pleven had dropped Mitterrand from the 1951 government because of pressure from right-wing deputies opposed to Mitterrand's African policy. Years later Pleven commented: 'Mitterrand had a taste for and was a consummate artist in operating the party machine. He enjoyed it and dedicated the necessary time to make it work.' Mitterrand was to use, and to refine, the same techniques of controlling the party machine through the judicious insertion of completely faithful friends into key posts when the time came to rebuild and consolidate his hold on the leadership of the Socialist Party.

The same political artistry was evident in parliament. When Pierre Mendès-France formed his government of all the talents in 1954, he turned to Mitterrand for help in selecting the members of the Cabinet. Mendès-France described in glowing terms Mitterrand's masterly knowledge of his fellow politicians: 'No one knew better the deputies, their talents and weaknesses, their current performance and past record, their secret ambitions and confidential dealings. He knew everything and everybody and played parliament like an expert.' Writing in 1955, one political correspondent offered his zoological description of Mitterrand: 'He resembles a gazelle with an ecclesiastical allure, a mixture of bishop and leaper. He has eyes which have a surprising caress the first time they alight on you. But there is a steely look behind the velvet pupils. He proceeds in thought and word by nimble leaps. But at the least alert, he's quickly off and is seen no more.' As Mitterrand's political stature grew he increasingly became a target for the French Right.

Their intense dislike for him had been made worse by a scandal which led to their accusing him of giving national defence secrets to the French Communist Party. The 'Leaks' affair as it was called in France was more than an attack on Mitterrand. It had all the hallmarks of a concerted effort to discredit the Mendès-France government and to try and brand its liberal policies as Communist-inspired.

In a sense, Mitterrand brought the 'Leaks' affair upon himself by sacking reactionary Paris police chief, Jean Baylot, only a few weeks after taking over as Minister of the Interior. Baylot was a fanatical anti-Communist. He had organized teams of former Nazi collaborators to infiltrate the Communist Party and produce forged leaflets inciting workers to riot. These he would use as an excuse for disruptive searches of Communist Party premises and he allowed his police free rein in brutal attacks on left-wing demonstrations. It was Baylot who authorized the arrest of the acting General Secretary of the Communist Party, Jacques Duclos, in 1952. Two dead pigeons were found in Duclos' car. It was suggested that Duclos used the pigeons to pass messages to Moscow. Duclos was released after a threat of a general strike but not before the President of the National Federation of Pigeon-fanciers had declared that the pigeons in the car were of an edible variety and destined for Duclos' dinner.

Mitterrand's decision to replace Baylot was described in the *Figaro* newspaper as a success for the Communists. Hard-liners in the police department also disliked the young minister's decision to cut back severely on wire-tapping. In future, Mitterrand announced, if the police or security services wanted to listen in to telephone conversations they would have to get authorization from a judge or it would have to involve major state security cases. A few days before Baylot's dismissal, two police inspectors had called on Christian Fouchet, the Minister for Tunisian and Moroccan Affairs. Fouchet was handed documents containing an account of the most recent meeting of the French Communist Party's political bureau – its top leadership body. A quick reading of the document left Fouchet shaken. Included in the proceedings was a detailed account of what had been said at the last meeting of the National Defence Council which grouped senior ministers, including Mitterrand, and generals, and was responsible for taking major decisions concerning France's military policy. How on earth had the Communist Party obtained this highly classified information? asked Fouchet. The proceedings also recorded the Communist leaders saying that the information came from a government minister, and one of the policemen said he believed it was Mitterrand. The credentials of the two police inspectors who came to tell Fouchet should have served as a warning. One had worked for the security forces during the Vichy regime while the other had been convicted of collaboration with the Nazis. Fouchet none the less took the dossier to Mendès-France who launched an immediate enquiry. Mitterrand was soon to be cleared because the enquiry showed that the Communist Party had obtained minutes of a National Defence Council meeting held in May 1954 a month before Mitterrand took his seat on it and, therefore, whoever the leaker was it was unlikely to be the Minister of the Interior. All this, however, was unknown to Mitterrand because Mendès-France did not tell him about the enquiry nor that he had been accused of leaking vital national defence secrets. Mendès-France later explained his failure to tell his colleague:

> It may be difficult to believe but I really did not think that this affair was connected with the Minister of the Interior. I thought above all it was a military matter connected with the Ministry of Defence. I asked the senior civil servant investigating the matter to speak to no one in the government but that did not mean that I suspected any minister. Like other ministers, Mitterrand was not informed. I know he has always held this against me but in my mind there was no question that he was implicated in any way at all.

The rumours swept Paris; even the editor of *Le Monde* was 'confidentially' informed by a right-wing deputy that Mitterrand was betraying national defence secrets. Mitterrand finally learnt about the suspicions around his name when the investigators were forced to call in experts from one of the Interior Ministry departments, who at once reported to their Minister. Mitterrand was furious with Mendès-France and a gulf in terms of political relations opened between the two men that remained visible for the rest of Mendès-France's active political life. Frantic with worry about his reputation, Mitterrand used the resources of the Ministry of the Interior to widen the enquiry. These efforts were frustrated as key documents mysteriously vanished and important meetings between senior police officials and civil servants somehow managed to escape observation.

The puzzle was solved almost by accident when the police inspector who had originally alerted Christian Fouchet returned with yet another document from the French Communist Party headquarters which contained extracts from the most recent minutes of the National Defence Council. Mitterrand's men stopped and searched the inspector and discovered that he had been given the documents by an informer he had planted in the Communist Party headquarters. In turn, the informer's home was raided and it was discovered that he had been given the classified secrets by two junior civil servants, a committed pacifist and an extreme left winger, who worked in the secretariat of the National Defence Council.

The affair might have ended there save for the coolness between Mitterrand and Mendès-France. But it had revealed a network of people in politics, the police and security services ready to do anything to discredit the Mendès-France government for having concluded the peace treaty with the Vietminh and moving towards independence for Tunisia. They wanted Mitterrand's head as he had shown himself willing to dismantle the parallel police operations aimed principally at the Communist Party. Despite the arrests, the rumours about Mitterrand continued to circulate in Paris. Some right-wing deputies carried documents purporting to show that Mitterrand was a secret Communist, while there was a strong whiff of anti-Semitism in some of the attacks on Mendès-France. In December 1954, there was a debate in the National Assembly. A speech by one right-wing deputy gives a flavour of the poisonous atmosphere of the time. Pointing his finger at Mitterrand he said:

The inner workings of the civil service have been infected

69

with the gangrene of Communist penetration. The top echelons of the police service have been similarly infected by people with peculiar habits who belong to that currently fashionable brotherhood of homosexuals. I acknowledge that you are sufficiently broadminded not to be shocked by amusements of this nature but you should not forget, M Mitterrand, that these sort of people have defaults that make them especially vulnerable for the positions that you have given them or in which you have confirmed them.

Another right-wing deputy, Jean Legendre, went further and implied that Mitterrand was made to resign from the government in 1953 because he, already then, was leaking defence secrets. 'Why Dien Bien Phu? Why was the French army, superior in men and supplies, defeated in Indo-China?' asked Legendre. He told the deputies:

The answer was because it was betrayed in Paris. To publish details of the National Defence Council (in the summer of 1953) was to give away our plans to the enemy. Why was the author of these leaks not tracked down? I do not have the answer but M Mitterrand could tell us. He was a member of the government at the time and took part in the Cabinet meeting on 5 August 1953 when the President, Vincent Auriol, announced, 'Gentlemen, there is a traitor amongst us!' Three weeks later, M Mitterrand left the government.

The National Assembly was stunned and Mendès-France shouted at Legendre, 'What are you insinuating?' A white-faced Mitterrand walked to the speaker's rostrum to meet the challenge. Calmly, he explained the history of the latest case and then turned to the innuendo that he had left the 1953 government because he had betrayed defence secrets. 'There are several members of that government sitting with us. They know I resigned because of disagreements with government policy on Tunisia and Morocco. If any of my former colleagues shares M Legendre's opinion, he should say so. If not, on what basis does M Legendre advance his slander?'

The silence was long. Mitterrand waited patiently at the rostrum, sipping a glass of water as the crowded assembly looked at the faces of those who had been members of the Cabinet from which Mitterrand had resigned. No one rose to confirm Legendre's accusation and Mitterrand had won. His victory in the National Assembly did not, however, put an end to the 'Leaks' affair. The investigation and trial of those arrested continued for another eighteen months and right-wing lawyers used the privilege of the courtroom to continue the attacks and accusations against Mitterrand. There was a desire, almost a pathological longing within the Right to find a 'traitor' whose 'treason' would explain away French defeats at the hands of the Vietminh, and, later, the Algerian National Liberation Front. Mitterrand, the equivocally progressive, smooth-tongued young minister was an obvious target. Most politicians who make one of the top offices of state before the age of forty arouse the envy of their colleagues and the personal dislike, often hatred, of their opponents. In addition, Paris was cluttered with colonial bureaucrats and policemen sacked by Mitterrand for reactionary behaviour and attitudes. Together with army officers bitter at the defeat in Indo-China, they sat over their *pastis* moaning about the France which had been betrayed. They needed a traitor and Mitterrand fitted the bill.

François Mauriac, the Nobel Prize-winning French writer perceptively noted after the National Assembly debate, 'The deep-rooted hate of his opponents marks Mitterrand as one of the leaders of the French Left – and, it will need several – which will sooner or later emerge.'

By the beginning of 1956, the thirty-nine-year-old Mitterrand was already acknowledged as one of the chieftains of the French Left. Together with Mendès-France and the SFIO leader, Mollet, he formed the anti-conservative 'Republican Front', an electoral coalition of parties and groups, lacking any clearly defined programme, beyond a vague offer to be conciliatory in Algeria which won a majority of seats in the 1956 elections. The 'Republican Front' shared 166 seats, compared with 151 for the French Communist Party, and with the remaining 200 seats split between conservatives, independents, a small rump of Gaullists and the newly victorious Poujadists, who were committed to right-wing economic policies that they claimed would protect the small businessman, shopkeeper and farmer and from whom they garnered two and a half million votes. The left-wing majority produced the Mollet government that led France to collude with Britain and Israel over the invasion of Egypt at Suez and which stepped up repression in Algeria. Under pressure from the trade unions, it passed progressive social measures, including legislating a third week's paid holiday for workers and improved social security schemes.

The Mollet government also helped launch the Common Market. From the late 1940s onward Mitterrand strongly supported the idea of European economic integration and closer political unity. He has never seen any contradiction between being, at one and the same time a passionate Frenchman and a passionate European. Nor did he find membership of the EEC any obstacle to the implementation of extensive nationalization and other wide-ranging Socialist measures after he became President.

The Mollet government, like the other left and centre-left coalitions that had on and off managed since 1947 to win approval from the National Assemblies, would have nothing to do with the Communist Party despite the solid block of 151 deputies. Visceral anti-Communism manifested itself in arrests of Communist militants and suspension of Communist publications charged with helping the Algerian liberation movement. Mitterrand's presence in the government implicitly endorsed these decisions, but shortly after leaving the government in May 1957 Mitterrand gave an interview to *Paris-Presse* in which he reflected on the need to broaden the Left's base in France. He was asked if he would like to see a party like the Labour Party and a regrouping of left-wing forces.

> The regrouping of the small parties of the left and centre-left is desirable . . . The Communist Party is on the left if one looks at the five million electors who vote for it. It isn't if one recalls its methods of action, its refusal of free discussion, its authoritarian sectarianism. Without Communist voters there is no left majority, but instead centre-left majorities or rather 'third force' majorities stretching from the Socialist Party to certain liberal conservatives.

The answers were couched in that elliptical style that

Mitterrand was already making his own. But they show a watering down of the simplistic politics of the French non-Communist Left that tried to pretend that neither the Communist Party nor its mass support in the population actually existed. In the crisis leading up to de Gaulle's arrival in power, Mitterrand was briefly to find himself shoulder to shoulder with Communists as he searched for allies amongst the few political forces brave enough to challenge de Gaulle.

It was Algeria that brought de Gaulle to power and finished off the Fourth Republic. By the beginning of 1958, there were 400,000 French soldiers, including conscripts, stationed in Algeria to try and keep the National Liberation Front in check. Twenty-eight per cent of the French budget was being spent on prosecuting the war in Algeria. Hard-line French colonialists controlled the local administration, ever ready to denounce as treason against France any suggestion of negotiations, reform or even compromise that emanated from Paris. Not even the Communist Party was ready to come out with the straight policy of French withdrawal from Algeria which was rapidly becoming the only solution which would satisfy the nationalists. The greater the repression applied by the authorities, the more the Algerian population became radicalized and supported the National Liberation Front. The French army kept searching for that final defeat that always seems to elude a colonial army facing armed liberation forces commanding genuine popular support. Army officers blamed the Paris government for not providing them with sufficient men and supplies or for not allowing a ruthless enough policy against the local population. The increasing international publicity about the behaviour of French troops became an important factor for the government. In February 1958, a French warplane crossed the Tunisian border and bombed what the army claimed was a hide-out for Algerian nationalists. The village may well have been used as such, but on the day of the bombing it was full of Tunisian villagers attending the local market. Seventy-five people were killed in this attack on what was now an independent state and the world was shocked. The Tunisian government succeeded in getting the matter raised at the United Nations Security Council and, rather than turn the issue into a full-blown UN affair, the French government accepted the offer of a 'good offices' mission by the United States and British governments.

All this was too much for the right-wing 'ultras' in Algeria and their supporters in the National Assembly. In April 1958 the government that had accepted the 'good offices' mission was overturned and for thirty-eight days none of the main party leaders could find sufficient support to form a government. It was a vacuum exploited by supporters of General de Gaulle who had been busy in Algeria, within the army and inside the right of French politics urging the return of de Gaulle as the only man who would keep Algeria French and resolve the crisis of policy.

De Gaulle was living in a kind of internal exile at his home in Colombey-les-Deux-Eglises. He had resigned as Prime Minister in 1946, his haughty authoritarian style unable to adjust to, nor having any taste for, the resurgence of party-based activity. He had campaigned for a new constitution based on a strong executive under the leadership of a powerful head of state. The Fourth Republic constitution went completely the other way, delivering all power to the deputies in the National Assembly. In 1947 he founded his own party, the 'Rally of the French People' which had no discernible programme save an unquestioning belief in the need for de Gaulle to govern France. The 'Rally of the French People' took on a hue that seemed to many reminiscent of pre-war mass populism. Huge meetings and excessive glorification of the leader, de Gaulle, were its characteristics. To thwart both its and the Communist Party's electoral chances, the main parties changed the French voting system in 1951 and gerrymandered the general election in favour of themselves. With no prospect of gaining power via the ballot box and angry at the desertion of some of his deputies who accepted government jobs, de Gaulle dissolved the 'Rally' in 1953 and retired to his country home to write his memoirs. If he publicly stayed aloof from political involvement, his supporters did not. They seized on Algeria as the weak point of the Fourth Republic's existence. Gaullist agitators went to Algiers for the not very difficult task of stirring up the French colonialists against Paris and in favour of de Gaulle. For the French army, de Gaulle was almost a god. Once when de Gaulle arrived in Algiers to pay a visit, he greeted the French commander in the jocularly cumbersome manner that passed as his wit: 'Good morning, Massu. Still stupid and a shit, eh?' Massu replied loyally, 'Yes, my General and still a Gaullist.'

On 8 May 1958, the National Assembly breathed a sigh of relief when Pierre Pflimlin, the leader of the Christian Democrat Popular Republican Movement, emerged as a potential Prime Minister able, just, to form a government and secure a majority. He was thought to be a liberal who would continue the policy of allowing other countries like the United States and Britain to offer their 'good offices' to help resolve Algerian problems. This policy was denounced by the French Resident Minister in Algiers as a 'diplomatic Dien Bien Phu'. During the day of 13 May, there were demonstrations in Algiers against Pflimlin and the National Assembly. Egged on by Gaullist supporters, the demonstrators occupied the government buildings while French soldiers, supposedly there to maintain order, looked on impassively at this usurpation of central authority. Instead, the French army in Algeria joined in the rebellion and, along with Gaullist and 'ultras', set up what they called a 'Committee of Public Safety', an echo of the similarly named body created in 1793 to safeguard the French revolution. As news of these developments was given hour by hour to the anxious deputies in the National Assembly in Paris, it was clear that Algeria, still in everyone's eyes an integral part of France, was in open rebellion.

The putsch of 13 May, as it became known, threw the deputies and much of France into confusion. On 14 May, speaking in the Assembly, Mitterrand attacked the putschists saying it must be made clear that 'the government of the Republic, in short the Republic itself, remains in control'. But it was too late.

The military situation worsened with the resignation of the head of the French army and more units in Algeria declaring support for the 'Committee of Public Safety'. De Gaulle refused to condemn the army revolt; instead, he announced he was ready to 'assume the powers of the Republic'. On 24 May, paratroopers from Algeria flew to Corsica and proceeded to form a 'Committee of Public Safety' for the island which was more unquestionably French soil than even Algeria. It seemed merely a matter of time before the military takeover spread to Southern France. The atmosphere in Paris was unrelievedly tense. People looked anxiously to the sky above Paris half expecting the arrival of paratroopers. The threat of civil war or a military dictatorship was in the air. An appeal by the Communist Party to the SFIO, to combine forces to resist the military threat was rejected out of hand by the Socialist leader, Guy Mollet, who still contemptuously described French Communists as 'Bolsheviks'.

Instead Mollet turned to de Gaulle, travelling, as had rightwing leaders, to Colombey-les-Deux-Eglises to implore the General to take power to avert civil war. A more dramatic intervention came from the French President, René Coty, who said he would resign unless the deputies agreed to make de Gaulle Prime Minister. (It was Coty's obeisance in front of de Gaulle that moved a British journalist, sent to Paris to cover the crisis, to write the scornful line: 'All the perfumes of Arabia cannot sweeten the name of Coty.' The journalist was Michael Foot and he was expelled from France because of his critical reporting in the *Tribune* and the *Daily Herald*. Foot was not allowed to re-enter France until 1961.) De Gaulle agreed, but on condition that the party leaders guaranteed his investiture with exceptional powers which would include putting a new constitution to a referendum. It would mean the end of the Fourth Republic.

As the continuing military threat pushed Fourth Republic politicians further into de Gaulle's grip, Mitterrand and Mendès-France, who had found common cause in their opposition to de Gaulle, were taking part in a demonstration alongside leaders of the French Communist Party. As many as 200,000 Parisians took part in the demonstration on 28 May, but it was lacking in vigour and was as hostile to the memory of the Fourth Republic as it was opposed to the idea of de Gaulle arriving in power on the shoulders of French paratroopers. The hope of popular resistance to the putschists on 13 May faded, if it had ever really existed. No one appeared to have an alternative to de Gaulle. After the Paris demonstration, de Gaulle arrived in the capital to confer with all the main party leaders, including Mitterrand but excluding the Communists.

Mitterrand was the only party leader to criticize de Gaulle. He told him he would withhold support while de Gaulle refused to denounce the 'Committees of Public Safety' and the military insurrection. De Gaulle told the party chiefs that he would defend the Republic. Before the meeting, Mitterrand walked up and down the left bank of the Seine turning over in his mind what his attitude should be. That de Gaulle was going to get his majority in the National Assembly there was little doubt. That the Fourth Republic had run out of life was also clear. That de Gaulle had, to his credit, restored the Republic and democratic institutions in 1945 was an historical fact. Yet set against all that was the manner by which de Gaulle was moving to power and the clear indications of the authoritarian way in which de Gaulle intended to use that power. In a book published eleven years later, Mitterrand described his feelings as he ruminated under the clear blue Paris sky:

> Behind de Gaulle I saw the closed battalions of those who wanted vengeance on the poor. In Jarnac, Nevers, in Paris, in the prison camp, I had already met them. To a certain extent I was one of them. Because we came from the same stock, pronounced the same words with the same accent, because we had been given the rudiments of the same culture and wore the same clothes, they treated me as an accomplice or an associate. I knew I had no longer anything to say to them and could not bear to hear them speak any longer.

It was more than a quarrel between members of the same class. If Mitterrand followed the majority of Fourth Republic politicians and fell in behind de Gaulle in order to save France from civil war, it would not be an illogical act. But it would mean acting according to the same safety and career-first political criteria as had governed most politicians' attitudes during the years between 1947 and 1958. 'The only way to be at peace with myself,' wrote Mitterrand, 'was to refuse de Gaulle's takeover.'

On 1 June 1958, the day de Gaulle's investiture as Prime Minister was debated and voted upon in the National Assembly, Mitterrand came out in open, public defiance against the General. His colleagues sat around him and begged him to keep quiet but Mitterrand was angry with the number of former ministers, even prime ministers, who had accepted office under de Gaulle. He did not bother defending the Fourth Republic.

'We will not fight for the rites, the customs or the faults of this system which has been so often denounced. In any case, some of those who surround General de Gaulle in his government are qualified to undo this system which they created, they managed and now have lost.' Against a background of shouts and interruptions from right-wing deputies, Mitterrand pressed on: 'When General de Gaulle, after his struggle abroad and in the resistance, arrived in front of the provisional Assembly in September 1944, he had with him two companions called honour and the nation. His companions today, which doubtless he has not chosen but which have arrived with him call themselves insurrection and sedition.' Mitterrand knew that this was to be the last big debate in the National Assembly before it was prorogued until after the referendum on the new constitution. His peroration was worthy of de Gaulle himself:

> Since General de Gaulle invites us to keep quiet or allow ourselves to be silenced, it is now the time to tell the nation that those who fight for freedom and the sovereignty of the people, even if their hearts are full of concern and anxiety, will not fall into despair. There is much to do and France continues to exist. At the end of the day, with faith and with will, freedom will emerge victorious in a nation reconciled with itself. That hope is enough; it stays with me and encourages me now as I vote against the investiture of General de Gaulle.

Proudly, Mitterrand cast his 'No' vote along with the Communist deputies, Mendès-France and a breakaway group of SFIO deputies who were not ready to fall in behind their leader, Mollet. It was an act of political courage for a man who up to that moment had been considered to be mostly obsessed with his career. At the age of forty-one, perhaps Mitterand thought he could wait a few years until the sixty-eight-year-old de Gaulle vanished and the traditional political forces re-emerged. De Gaulle was to stay in power for eleven years and Mitterand was to wait until six months after his sixty-fourth birthday before he once again held office.

In the summer of 1958, Mitterrand, together with Mendès-France and the breakaway left-wing of the SFIO tried to regroup the non-Communist Left. Loosely gathered around a platform of opposition to de Gaulle's proposed new constitution, the Union of Democratic Forces was launched in July 1958. The new body also attracted the support of the young Socialist intellectuals active in the Catholic trade union confederation, CFTC, though they were at best half-hearted, at worst downright suspicious, of such Fourth Republic veterans as Mitterrand and Mendès-France.

It was too early a try for left unity. Firstly, Mollet and other mainstream SFIO leaders, like Gaston Deferre, had entered de Gaulle's government: the SFIO was to campaign in the November election under the slogan 'De Gaulle and Mollet saved the Republic!' Secondly, the Union of Democratic Forces excluded the Communists and at the same time its component parts, Mitterrand's Democratic and Socialist Union of the Resistance (even some deputies in Mitterrand's party had crossed over to support de Gaulle), Mendès-France's Radical Party followers, the left-wingers from SFIO and the Catholic trade unionists all had their own party allegiances and as many political differences with each other as they had with de Gaulle.

The September 1958 referendum which proposed the abolition of the Fourth Republic, confirmed the failure of the opposition to de Gaulle. Mitterrand campaigned vigorously in his Nièvre constituency for a 'No' vote and was rewarded with a 78% vote in favour of de Gaulle. Worse followed. In November, a new National Assembly was elected, and despite the Communist candidate standing down in his favour, Mitterrand was heavily defeated by a Gaullist. Everywhere the Left was humiliated. The 160 SFIO deputies were reduced to forty. The French Communist Party won only ten seats and saw its vote slump to a pre-war level. Three-quarters of the National Assembly owed allegiance to de Gaulle who, having taken over as a figure above politics and claiming to recognize no force save national unity, now found he had a solid block of conservative, often downright reactionary deputies who strictly identified the national with their own interests. Mitterrand, Mendès-France and other anti-Gaullist leaders lost their seats. The Fourth Republic was well and truly sunk. At the end of 1958 it appeared to have taken French Socialism down with it.

7
Into Opposition

Behind de Gaulle, in his shadow, the
conspirators are busy preparing for tomorrow.
With de Gaulle they are daily taking over the
levers of power. After de Gaulle,
they will stay there.

Mitterrand had lost his seat but had found a cause, that of
anti-Gaullism. The French Left was engulfed by the wave of
Gaullism that swept France in 1958. Not only had the referendum and the National Assembly election overwhelmingly
endorsed de Gaulle but an enlarged electoral college of 80,000
national and local politicians as well as other notables had
elected him President.

Previously the President had been chosen by parliament and
had no effective power. De Gaulle's Fifth Republic changed all
that and made the President an executive head of state. The
success of the referendum as a means of appealing over the heads
of parties and political leaders direct to the people, combined
with a ruthless exclusivity in using the state television and radio,
strengthened de Gaulle's populist authoritarianism though it
also allowed him to make radical changes in Algerian policy,
which would have been unlikely to win their way through the

National Assembly. The conduct of foreign policy was left entirely in de Gaulle's hands. Here too he veered away from the Atlanticism of the Fourth Republic, ploughing ahead with the development of French nuclear weapons despite an Anglo-American ban on sharing any nuclear bomb secrets with France; he also held out the hand of friendship to Russia, and to Washington's disgust, started moves to recognize China. In Europe, he refused Britain's application to join the Common Market and started to disengage the French military forces from NATO.

Once his position in France was secure, he began distancing himself from the Algerian hard-liners and tried to open up negotiations with the National Liberation Front. A second putsch against this policy collapsed in 1961 and this time de Gaulle had the generals involved arrested and put on trial. The popular disgust mingled with sheer weariness with the Algerian war allowed him to move to a final settlement which gave Algeria its independence in 1962.

A devaluation of the franc combined with an increase in economic liberalism allowed the French economy to push ahead with businessmen and managers happier to operate in the climate of political stability created under de Gaulle. In fact French production had grown by an annual average of 7.5% under the Fourth Republic and the economy developed no faster under de Gaulle. (It was still impressive: by 1963 France's Gross Domestic Output was already greater than the United Kingdom's.) The investment in the 1950s had gone into the industrial infrastructure, whereas by 1960 it was more consumption-oriented. The new apartments, cars, television sets, the high-speed trains and burgeoning autoroutes had been conceived and to a large extent paid for under the Fourth Republic but came to fruition in the Fifth. The increased material prosperity was thus credited to de Gaulle.

After the Gaullist victory in November 1958, Mollet and the other SFIO ministers did not stay in the government long. They resigned in January 1959 in protest over the government's deflationary economic policies, though to have stayed much longer in what was clearly a right-wing administration would have compromised forever Mollet's fading reputation as a

Socialist. Mollet had effectively wrested the party leadership of the SFIO after the war from the ageing Léon Blum. He had attacked Blum as a revisionist, a kind of French forerunner of Hugh Gaitskell, anxious to move French Socialism to the centre, to shed the SFIO's Marxist vocabulary and, worst of all, according to Mollet to transform the SFIO into something like the British Labour Party.

Rank and file delegates at the 1946 SFIO Congress were swept by Mollet's militant denunciation of Blum's reformism and elected him General Secretary. Mollet's leftism, however, was not broad enough to encompass the French Communist Party and after the 1947 split he said French Communism 'does not come from the Left but from the East'. His pitiless waging of the Algerian war and adventurism in Suez did not reinforce his Socialist credentials, while his invitation to de Gaulle to take over in 1958 completed the transformation of a man who had appeared to many as a Marxist militant in 1946.

Nevertheless, right into the 1960s (he did not quit the party leadership until 1969) the blunt-spoken Mollet, with his direct northern manner held sway over his party. His most effective critics within the party resigned or were removed and those on the French Left who might have reinvigorated it stayed active within the Socialist trade unions or in other protest and pressure groups; anything rather than join the sclerotic SFIO. His power base rested in the municipalities, especially in the North, his own personal fiefdom, and the Rhone estuary, which was very much the estate of Gaston Deferre.

Still, Mollet could charm most audiences. He never played the national figure or elder statesman but remained, oratorically speaking, the rank and file delegate. In 1957, at the height of the Algerian war repression, he addressed university students in Paris, who by any standards could be expected to be an aggressively hostile audience. He left his Prime Ministerial mantle at the door and offered himself as an honest Socialist surrounded by hostile forces in the National Assembly and outside it but trying to do what was right and best in extremely difficult circumstances. He left his audience feeling almost sorry for him as he drove back to his office to turn a blind eye to a fresh wave of torture in Algeria.

Mollet's entry into de Gaulle's first government had angered the left wing of the SFIO, which broke away to form the Autonomous Socialist Party, later to change its name to the Unified Socialist party in 1960. Pierre Mendès-France joined this party now that the bulk of his Radical Party colleagues had either made their peace with de Gaulle or been swept away by the Gaullist electoral victories. In 1959 Mitterrand applied to join the Autonomous Socialist Party but the party leadership were against his admission. In particular Alain Savary, one of the founders of the Autonomous Socialist Party, who had resigned from the Mollet government in 1956 in protest over its North African policy, was adamantly against Mitterrand becoming a member. Mitterrand was to get his revenge, if that is the right word, in 1971 when he displaced Savary as First Secretary of the Socialist Party. Had Mitterrand entered the Autonomous Socialist Party in 1959, his career would have been lost in the imaginative but always uncompromisingly oppositionist policies and tactics that the party developed in the 1960s. Mitterrand dropped his application but was angry at the rejection.

Although he had lost his seat in the Nièvre, Mitterrand was determined to keep contact with the region. French deputies, like United States Congressmen, are expected to keep in close touch with their constituencies. Deputies will spend every weekend in their constituency and often their family home will be there. They also take an active part in local and regional politics – most leading French politicians are mayors of a town in their constituency, while some current senior ministers, including the Prime Minister Pierre Mauroy and the Minister of the Interior, Gaston Deferre, were for many years mayor of the cities of Lille and Marseilles respectively. Even senior national figures were expected to look after parish pump interests and a deputy who wanted votes for the National Assembly would have to fight for funds to build local swimming-pools or to get a new roof for the primary school.

A few months after his November 1958 defeat Mitterrand set about reconquering his electoral base. In March 1959 he was elected mayor of Château-Chinon in the Nièvre, a post he held until his election as President. He later became President of the Association of Mayors in the Nièvre, President of the area's general council and even managed to secure a special post on the Gaullist-dominated Regional Economic Development Commission. Mitterrand was determined never to lose his local base again.

This assiduous cultivation of the towns and villages in his constituency paid off in April 1959 when he was elected a member of the Senate. The Senate, France's upper house, is elected on a different basis from the universal suffrage of the National Assembly. For the Senate, an electoral college is formed in each French department consisting of delegates sent from the villages and towns. This electoral college elects a certain number of senators according to the population of the department. Mitterrand won a seat easily, as did other defeated left leaders like Mendès-France and Deferre. Although virtually powerless to block government legislation or action, the Senate in the early 1960s became the focus of opposition to government policies and journalists tended to report the debates and speeches in the Senate which were politically more interesting and intellectually superior to those of the Gaullist-packed National Assembly. It looked as if Mitterrand might be on the road to some kind of comeback. But in the middle of an autumn night in 1959, there was a burst of machine-gun fire in the centre of Paris. To the delight of his enemies, what became known as the 'Observatory' affair nearly finished him altogether.

The 'Observatory' affair began quietly enough when a former extreme right-wing deputy, Robert Pesquet, approached Mitterrand and said he had to see him urgently. Mitterrand knew Pesquet's political antecedents but did not know that he had a police record and was an associate of one of the Paris policemen who had tried to implicate Mitterrand in the 'Leaks' affair in 1954. Pesquet told Mitterrand that there was a plot to kill him. According to Pesquet, right-wing extremists in Algiers had a hit-list of those who were favourable to a negotiated settlement in Algeria and Mitterrand was top of the list. Pesquet asked Mitterrand about his routes to and from home and advised him to vary them. He explained that, much as he was opposed to Mitterrand politically, he could not support a murder attempt on a man who had made an impressive showing when in the National Assembly. In the days that followed Mitterrand began receiving letters and telephone calls threatening his life. A week later, Mitterrand once again met Pesquet who told him the assassination attempt was imminent. That night, Mitterrand slept at a friend's house. The next day, there was another long meeting during which Pesquet warned Mitterrand to be careful about his children and begged him not to reveal his informant's name under any circumstances because, if Pesquet's name was mentioned, then his life would be in danger. This Mitterrand promised to do. To add to his alarm a Paris evening newspaper carried a report that ten armed men had crossed the Spanish border and were heading to Paris as an assassination squad.

After dinner with a friend late on the night of 15 October 1959, Mitterrand got into his Peugeot 403 car to drive home. After a few minutes he had the sensation of being followed and saw in his rear mirror a small dark car with two men inside. He drove this way and that but the car stayed doggedly behind him. By now thoroughly frightened, Mitterrand raced through the Latin Quarter until he got to the Observatory gardens just behind the Luxembourg Palace. He stopped his car, scrambled over the wall and threw himself head down into a geranium bed. Seconds later, there was a squeal of brakes and the rattle of a sub-machine-gun. Seven bullets slammed into Mitterrand's car. When the police arrived Mitterrand described what had happened but, keeping his promise of silence to Pesquet, did not mention what had passed between them. The attack was a sensation in France. Messages of support and sympathy flowed in. An examining magistrate opened a case into the murder attempt. Mitterrand met Pesquet four days after the attack and thanked him for the tip-off.

Three days later, the scandal broke. Pesquet called a press conference in which he announced that the assassination attempt was a fake, a plot contrived by Mitterrand and carried out by Pesquet who waited until Mitterrand had safely taken cover before giving the order to open fire. The motive, according to Pesquet, was that Mitterrand wanted to discredit the Algerian hard-liners and give the government an excuse to search their homes and disrupt their activities. To back up his case Pesquet produced two letters which were posted before the incident and set out in some detail where the attack would take place and what

Mitterrand's conduct would be. The only discrepancy was over timing, with Pesquet's letters putting the attack thirty minutes before it actually took place. The interval, Pesquet told reporters, was because they had to wait until first a passing taxi and then a courting couple moved away so as to ensure no witnesses for the attack. The press in France and abroad was overwhelmed. The London *Daily Herald* headlined its page lead story: MP FAKED HIS DEATH PLOT with the subheadline 'A story which could come from a thriller shakes France. Was the Mitterrand murder bid a fake? The background is that rumbling volcano Algeria.'

Once again, Mitterrand was enveloped in clouds of suspicion. The most damaging charge laid against him by his enemies and even by some friends was that he had not mentioned Pesquet's name nor the warnings he had brought to anyone either before or after the night of 15 October. Worse, he had not told the examining magistrate about this vital piece of evidence, his excuse being his promise of silence to his informer. As the press dug their teeth into the scandal, organizing unsuccessful searches for the taxi and courting couple that had delayed the attack, the two men, Mitterrand and Pesquet, stuck firmly by their own versions of the story. The government, headed by an old opponent of Mitterrand, Michel Debré, decided to increase the humiliation by seeking to lift Mitterrand's parliamentary immunity. François Mauriac noted in *L'Express*: 'In this ignoble business, killing is nothing, smearing is everything.'

The Senate had to debate the lifting of immunity and Mitterrand defended himself vigorously. He pointed out that Mendès-France had received a similar death warning two years ago. More importantly, Pesquet had gone to another politician, Maurice Bourges, a month previously and had warned him his life was in danger. Bourges shrugged off the threat saying, 'If they want to kill you they don't tell you in advance' but, unlike Mitterrand, he had had the sense to go to the authorities and tell them of Pesquet's approach.

Although the government had this highly relevant piece of evidence as to Pesquet's character, the examining magistrate had not been informed. 'Was the government not equally guilty of keeping evidence from the magistrate?' asked a sarcastic

Mitterrand. He also told the senators of an incident in 1957 when he was a Minister of Justice. A deputy arrived to protest his innocence in the plot to kill the French commander in Algeria. The deputy begged Mitterrand for time to establish his innocence and not to lift his parliamentary immunity. Mitterrand agreed to keep a lid on the affair. Who was the man he had thus protected? Mitterrand asked the Senate. Why none other than the current Prime Minister, Michel Debré. Debré retorted that Mitterrand was a liar and in due course the Senate lifted Mitterrand's immunity. The case against both Mitterrand and the separate case against Pesquet came to nothing. But they were never closed and the dossiers remained open for years afterwards. Three theories were advanced at the time. Firstly, he had genuinely believed Pesquet's story of a death threat. The whole thing was an elaborate plot to discredit Mitterrand but without any intention of killing him. Secondly, that Mitterrand had faked the attack with Pesquet in order to damage the Algerian hardliners. Thirdly, that Pesquet convinced Mitterrand that he was under orders to kill him and that if he failed then Pesquet himself would be murdered. In order to protect Pesquet, Mitterrand had gone through with the sham attempt. Mitterrand has always stuck by the first version. If he had wanted to fake a murder attempt in order to discredit the 'ultras' he surely would have found a better conspirator than the dubious Pesquet. The third possibility seems unlikely as Mitterrand would hardly have exposed himself to the subsequent obloquy when a simple call to the police would have secured Pesquet's protection. Under almost all conceivable circumstances, Mitterrand would have emerged from the plot with his reputation damaged. To have initiated it therefore seems contrary to his reputation as a canny politician. In 1965 and again in 1975, Pesquet claimed that the murder attempt was a plot organized by extreme right-wing deputies to discredit Mitterrand. Pesquet even named Debré as one of the instigators. Even those admissions have to be treated with reserve as Pesquet's reliability as any kind of witness is open to question. What really happened we shall never know, though Mitterrand's explanation is the most satisfying. He had given his word to Pesquet and he would stand by that word despite embarrassing and politically damaging consequences. Yet his behaviour, and especially his keeping secret what Pesquet had told him both before and after the attack, shows a vulnerability, a lack of the surefootedness that is generally considered his chief political attribute.

Whatever the motives of those involved in the affair, it succeeded in making Mitterrand an object of derision. For years afterwards Gaullist deputies would shout 'Pesquet, Pesquet' in an effort to embarrass Mitterrand. The 'Observatory' affair haunted him all during the 1960s and only ebbed from the political consciousness as a new generation took over the Socialist Party, for whom 1959 was a long way back in history. Badly wounded by the 'Observatory' affair, Mitterrand took refuge in travel, writing and spending more time with his young children – he is said to have been an excellent father. He began practising as a lawyer and though he had no previous experience he quickly built up a successful practice – having a former Justice Minister as an advocate was an attractive proposition in some quarters. In January 1961, he set off on a three-week tour of China where he had a long meeting with Mao Tse-tung and annoyed his hosts by comparing French military behaviour in Algeria with the Chinese invasion and occupation of Tibet. On his return he wrote a short book *China Under Challenge*. Like nearly all Western visitors to China in the period Mitterrand was fascinated by how the Chinese Communists had reorganized society and seemingly had banished famine and food shortages. 'The Chinese Communist Party inherited a weak, corrupt, scattered empire. From that they have created a nation.' But he was critical of the 'massive propaganda campaigns which give no one a moment's rest', and the need for continual praise of 'the correct line of the party' added up in Mitterrand's eyes to 'an intolerable mental pressure'. Following his trip, Mitterrand began calling for France to establish diplomatic relations with China.

Back in France, Mitterrand campaigned vigorously against de Gaulle's proposal to change the constitution and have the President of France elected by direct universal suffrage. This had been de Gaulle's ambition since 1946 and was seen by him as the mechanism to consolidate the authority of the presidency by connecting it directly with each citizen. Mitterrand though differently. 'I do not believe that in France any more than in any other Latin country we can both grant a man considerable powers and seriously guarantee our public institutions and freedoms. I see a fatal risk of a slide towards authoritarianism,' he wrote in *L'Express*.

His vision was not shared by his countrymen, who in November 1962 agreed by a two-thirds majority to have a President of France elected by all voters. That referendum like the others that had preceded it on Algeria pushed the Left in France into further disarray. Their dislike of de Gaulle led both Communists and Socialists to call for a 'No' vote in the referendum on Algerian self-determination in 1961. In fact, de Gaulle had stolen a suit of progressive clothes and was moving towards a disengagement from Algeria. Already the black African states to which he had offered the choice of staying linked to France or casting off for full independence had chosen the latter with a speed that had melted Mitterrand's beloved 'French Union' like a snowball in the Sahara. The Left called for a 'No' vote but the French people overwhelmingly endorsed de Gaulle's proposal. When the time came for the final 1962 Algerian referendum, the Left had realized their mistake and grudgingly supported de Gaulle's settlement. The Left claimed credit for pushing de Gaulle towards disengagement from Algeria but Left opposition was at best unco-ordinated and often, as when the French Communist Party refused to take part in a national demonstration in favour of Algerian independence in October 1960, hopelessly sectarian.

Some modest advances had been made. As part of the 1958 constitutional reform, de Gaulle abolished the proportional representation electoral system which had so richly contributed to Fourth Republic instability and brought back a first past the post system split over two ballots. This system, which still obtains in France, allows any number of candidates to run in the first ballot. If one candidate gets more than 50% of the votes on the first ballot he or she is elected. If no such majority is achieved there is pressure on the less well placed left or right candidates to drop out and unite behind the candidate who did best in the first round. In presidential elections only the top two from the first ballot can proceed to the second. Voters can express a generalized preference in the first ballot but they have to make a choice – usually between Left and Right – in the second. In National Assembly or municipal constituencies where a left-wing victory was possible Socialists vie with Communists to come ahead of each other in the first round of voting. Whoever does best in the first ballot can then, in theory, expect to have all the left-wing votes transferred for the second ballot. This system of mutual support between Socialists and Communists is now well instituted under the name of 'republican discipline' but in the aftermath of 1957 and the long, mutual, hate-filled exchanges of words between Socialists and Communists ever since 1947, it seemed almost to be another piece of Gaullist trickery to embarrass the divided Left. True to their anti-Communist inclinations, most SFIO candidates preferred to come to an agreement with Radical or Christian Democrat anti-Gaullist candidates rather than embrace or acknowledge the need for Communist support. It took some time before the voting imperative of a ballot spread over two rounds sunk in.

In the 1959 municipal elections, Mollet had reluctantly agreed to some limited support for Communist candidates who were best placed for the second round. In the 1962 National Assembly elections, he had said that in a few seats where, as he churlishly put it, there was 'a choice between an unconditional follower of de Gaulle and an unconditional follower of Khrushchev' it would be all right for Socialists to vote for the latter in order to obtain a victory for the Left. With such a lukewarm endorsement from their leader, it was not surprising that Socialist voters did not always display 'republican discipline'. In Paris, nearly two thirds of the Socialist voters would not transfer their votes to the better placed Communist candidate in the second round and in the provinces, two out of five Socialist voters stayed at home rather than vote Communist. Mollet, on the other hand, was luckier. His precarious seat was saved thanks to a full transfer of Communist votes in the final run-off. The Communists' order of the day was: 'No worker's vote to fail comrade Guy Mollet.' Historians of post-war France have usually treated the result of the 1962 National Assembly elections as a major breakthrough for the Gaullist party. For the first time, a single party had obtained an absolute majority in the National Assembly. Unlike the freak election of 1958 which revolved around the need to keep de Gaulle in power, the 1962 election was after the Algerian settlement which had removed the dominant electoral problem of the past six years. It was much more a test of the government record. The Gaullist majority, unwelcome as it was to the Left, had none the less increased the stability in French politics. The Left regained some strength after the 1958 humiliation. With the Socialist and Communist standing down in his favour, Mitterrand was returned as a deputy for the Nièvre and there were now sixty-six Socialist deputies, thirty-nine Radicals and forty-one Communists.

More interesting was the narrow margin between the total number of votes for the majority and the total number of votes for the opposition. Leaving to one side the 10% of votes cast for the Popular Republican Movement whose deputies could shift from support to opposition depending on the issue, the Gaullist majority and its allies obtained 46.7% of the votes, while the Socialists, Communists and Radicals obtained 44.2% of the votes cast. In short, the gap between a Right and a Left majority was really rather small despite the overwhelming domination of the state by the Gaullist machine. It only needed a few extra percentage points for the Left to overtake the Right. But finding those extra votes in either Presidential or Assembly elections was to take another two decades.

If the official parties of the opposition were still barely on speaking terms, there was a modest resurgence of left-wing ideas and political debate which was not party-linked. The students' union had shaken off its right-wing image and had tried to build contacts with Algerian students. In agriculture, young farmers were beginning to take over the National Federation of Farmers' Union and demanding a more rapid modernization of farming structures. Inside the main non-Communist trade union con-federation, CFTC, there were strong currents urging that it drop the word 'Christian' from its title and thus deconfessionalize itself. All three main trade union confederations were able to sink their differences during a miners' strike in 1963. De Gaulle had reacted to the strike by conscripting the miners but both the workers and the communities reacted with a vigorous, united front that won considerable public sympathy. In the National

91

Assembly, Mitterrand championed the trade unionists' cause. Unlike 1947 and 1948, there was no blacklegging and de Gaulle discovered that even with the army behind him there is no way you can dig coal with bayonets. It was a major defeat inflicted by the working class on de Gaulle and helped tarnish his seemingly invulnerable image.

Much of the animation for this new energy on the Left came from young Catholics in the trade unions and the Unified Socialist Party. The Catholic tradition has been strong on the French Left ever since Pope Leo XIII's *Rerum Novarum* encyclical of 1891 acknowledged working-class rights and urged the creation of unions and parties that would lead working people towards social progress but away from 'godless Marxism'.

The hierarchy of the Catholic Church in France remained, for the most part, a key component of the authoritarian establishment but there were many Catholics whose religious commitment led them to a political championing of the underprivileged sections of French society: in its ultimate form, this kind of politicized left Catholicism manifested itself in the shape of worker-priests. The reforming winds that were blowing from Pope John XXIII's Vatican Council also encouraged those who wanted their faith to have greater social purpose than Sunday mass and contributing to Peter's Pence. This resurgence of Catholic activity sat uneasily with the traditional French radical and Socialist values which for over a hundred years were sternly anti-clerical. One of the great post-war political issues in France was the state support for church schools against which SFIO stood adamantly opposed. The Catholic activists did not therefore look to SFIO as the automatic resting place for the non-Communist Left.

Another important development on the Left since 1960 had been the creation of the 'republican clubs', curious bodies without any real Anglo-Saxon equivalent. A cross between debating societies and political organizations they linked together like-minded people who work on political analyses and campaigns. (Perhaps the closest British equivalent would be the Fabian Society.) One of the most important was the Jacobins' Club, presided over by Charles Hernu, formerly one of Mendès-France's associates who had moved closer to Mitterrand. The clubs were important because within them took place the development of new political ideas that were to be refined and capture the imagination of many who looked askance at the traditional parties. Five themes can be picked out from the policy ideas that were being produced and discussed by the clubs.

Firstly, the idea of participation: democracy must involve the fullest participation, industrial authoritarianism must be subject to democratic control, the state must have an organic link with the citizen and not simply impose orders from above. Secondly, the need for political parties to live and act jointly with the extra-parliamentary forces such as trade unions, teachers' and students' associations, and other social groups not connected to parties. Thirdly, there should be a devolution of power from Paris with a return to life based on the region, or even to the commune. Fourthly, a preference for planning rather than the continued spread of the economic liberalism favoured by de Gaulle's new Prime Minister, Georges Pompidou. Fifthly, an acceptance, indeed a welcome for the presidential system.

These themes were to be picked up, developed and re-shaped by the Left over the following twenty years but, in essence, they were among the main planks in Mitterrand's election programme in 1981.

The clubs were farsighted enough to realize that the Fifth Republic constitution and its strong presidency were gains for France, gains which need not permanently disfavour the Left. In 1965, Mitterrand, a popular contributor to the clubs' debates and discussions, was to discover that far from being a device to keep the Left forever in its place as an opposition, the Fifth Republic Presidency was to begin the process of reforging unity on the Left and would help take Mitterrand to its leadership.

8
Presidential Candidate – 1965

I am not the representative of a party. I am the candidate of all the Left.

In September 1963, one thousand leading left-wing figures sat down to dinner with Mitterrand in his Nièvre constituency. His stylish and penetrating speeches in the National Assembly underlined his growing importance as the most effective critic of the Gaullist regime. Although he was given few opportunities of appearing on the tightly controlled television or radio, he wrote regularly in the wide-selling *L'Express* and contributed to other newspapers like *Le Monde*. He was much in demand as a speaker at meetings and seminars organized by the republican clubs. In December 1963, he told a colloquium organized by the SFIO leadership:

> None of us has been spared the sectarian quarrels within the Socialist ideology. But when it comes to making a choice, whether it be of friends, enemies, issues, or for the kind of future we want for our country, I believe with all my heart that the Socialist choice is the only answer to the Gaullist experience. That is my basic belief and I do not expect to have to take an exam in Socialism every six months.

The last remark was a rejoinder to those in SFIO who queried Mitterrand's left-wing credentials. In fact, Mitterrand was, if anything, outflanking the SFIO's incorrigible anti-Communism. In September 1963 he wrote:

> My attitude towards the Communists is simple: everything that helps the struggle against a regime that tends towards the dictatorship of an individual and the establishment of a single party is good. Four to five million voters, ordinary people and workers, vote Communist. To neglect their support and their votes would be unpardonable or extremely stupid. I am always against those who want to lock up the Communists in a sort of political ghetto and who want to treat them as second-class citizens.

Mitterrand's clear stand on involving the Communists in any left-wing campaign was significant because already by late 1963 the question of who would be the candidate to oppose de Gaulle in the presidential elections due to be held in 1965 had become pressing. Two possible left-wing candidates had ruled themselves out. Pierre Mendès France had maintained his stand, not simply against de Gaulle but against the idea of a president replacing parliament as the source of legislative and executive power. He had also failed to regain a National Assembly seat in the 1962 elections. His new minority Unified Socialist Party was also against any left candidate standing against de Gaulle. 'Gaullism without de Gaulle is more dangerous than Gaullism with de Gaulle,' was the party's slogan. The other left-wing leader Guy Mollet was also staunchly opposed to the presidential system. He suggested the Left should put up no official candidate but nominate a Nobel peace prize-winner like Albert Schweitzer to turn the presidency once more into a powerless figurehead position. Le Monde's political editor also noted that for Mollet control of the SFIO was more important than sitting in the Elysée or the Matignon: 'Mollet holds tight to his post as General Secretary. Neither the presidency nor the prime ministership interests him, not because of modesty or pusillanimity, but because he would have to give up his place as General Secretary. It is in his party headquarters that he is really himself.'

The Communist Party was reluctant to run a candidate against de Gaulle. Everyone agreed that de Gaulle would win but of all the possible left candidates a Communist would probably be the most decisively beaten. In addition, de Gaulle's anti-American, pro-Soviet foreign policy initiatives were beginning to blunt the edges of all-out Communist Party opposition. Maurice Thorez' death in 1964, also meant a temporary loss of stability in the Communist leadership. It was all very well to produce good reasons for not running against de Gaulle but there was going to be a presidential election and there would have to be an opponent. De Gaulle would be seventy-five years old when he stood and everyone was muttering about the period after de Gaulle. Whoever challenged him in 1965 would stand a good chance of being the most favoured candidate when de Gaulle finally left the stage. Late in 1963, after a publicity campaign launched by *L'Express,* Gaston Deferre, the Socialist mayor of Marseilles put his name forward. Deferre was a successful lawyer who had been in the SFIO since 1933. He had led a Socialist-oriented resistance group in the war and had won control of Marseilles in 1945. He was a determined anti-Communist, and although, like Mitterrand, he had made a reputation as a progressive on colonial questions while briefly a minister in the Fourth Republic, he had endorsed Mollet's welcome of de Gaulle in 1958. Deferre was a superb local-machine politician and had built up the SFIO in Marseilles and the surrounding industrialized Rhone estuary into the biggest section of the party. While Mitterrand concentrated on ministerial politics in the 1950s, Deferre was making his name as an energetic and competent mayor of Marseilles, ridding the city of much of its criminal underworld and efficiently integrating French refugees from Algeria after 1962.

His campaign organization was called 'Horizon '80'. Mitterrand supported Deferre's candidature and served on the 'Horizon '80' committee. The SFIO also adopted the Mayor of Marseilles as candidate early in 1964, although Deferre made it clear that he believed in and would continue the Fifth Republic's presidential system. His programme was not dissimilar to the British Labour Party programme that narrowly won the 1964 election in the United Kingdom – economic planning, decentralization of power to the regions, educational expansion, more involvement for trade unions. Deferre, unlike the Harold Wilson of 1964, was strongly pro-European and against the French nuclear bomb. Mitterrand put forward the 'Horizon '80' line on nationalization when he spoke in an Assembly debate late in 1964:

> Nationalization is not good in itself. Our banks and insurance companies provide us with a good example of nationalizations that have gone wrong. The nationalization of Renault after the Nazi occupation shows how difficult it is to take over enterprises that have to continue existing in a competitive climate. But each time private interests come together to exercise an effective monopoly over an important sector of the national economy, each time an individual or a group has sufficient financial power to dominate the state, then I consider it necessary for the state to free itself of such domination.

While Mitterrand quietly supported Deferre's candidature he continued to strengthen his own base. In June 1964, Charles Hernu brought together fifty-four of the republican clubs and formed the Convention of Republican Institutions with Mitterrand as its President. Mitterrand's Democratic and Socialist Union of the Resistance merged with the convention. The original convention had ruled France from 1792 to 1795, consolidating the gains of the revolution, and the choice of title was a deliberate echo of the republican traditions that Mitterrand accused de Gaulle of betraying.

The Mitterrand-Hernu Convention of Republican Institutions was always more of a paper organization than a potential political party with real roots and organization. But during the seven years of its existence it made up for the ephemerality of its position in French politics by the liveliness of its ideas and the flair with which they were promoted. While the SFIO seemed locked in a backward-facing trajectory, the Convention gave the impression of being the force on the non-Communist Left which looked to the future.

Mitterrand further confirmed his return to a commanding position in the French Left with the publication of the *Permanent Coup d'Etat*. It is a remarkable polemic, sustained by an almost

Swiftian anger through 250 pages of detailed criticism of de Gaulle's regime. Rich in historical comparison, Mitterrand charges de Gaulle with turning France from a republic into an elective monarchy. He compares de Gaulle's arrival in 1958 to the arrival in 1830 of Louis-Philippe, Duke of Orléans. Both men were military commanders who answered the call of the people for a strong man to lead France out of a period of social turbulence. But Louis-Philippe's reign, as every French school-child knew, ushered in a period when the bourgeoisie reigned supreme. Furthermore Louis-Philippe and his ministers had used troops against demonstrating workers and had indulged in ill-fated foreign policy initiatives. His reign crumbled in the revolution of 1848. Was that the outcome that awaited de Gaulle, pondered Mitterrand. As the memories of the putsch of 13 May 1958 that had brought de Gaulle to power were fading away, Mitterrand reconstructed those anxious days in his book with flamboyant journalistic detail. De Gaulle may have legitimized his takeover through referendums and elections but the sources of his arrival in power were the paratroopers of Algeria, not the citizens of France. De Gaulle, Mitterrand wrote, was a harsh, and justly so, critic of the ever-changing ministers in the Fourth Republic. But, Mitterrand pointed out, in the first four years of de Gaulle's rule he appointed and dismissed more ministers than there had been in the Fourth Republic. The coming and going was, in any case, neither here nor there. 'There are ministers in France. There are even whispers that we still have a Prime Minister. But there is no longer a government. It is the President who alone gives or makes decisions.'

Almost as if he were writing a doctoral thesis in constitutional law, Mitterrand carefully goes through the Fifth Republic constitution, picking it apart and showing how de Gaulle had power to do almost anything he liked. He is especially scathing about de Gaulle's interference in judicial procedures and his creation of the special State Security Court (abolished by Mitterrand in 1981) which he wrote: 're-established the royal privilege in the judicial sector'. With wicked delight, he recalled the case of a man who was arrested and fined 1,000 francs for having whistled rudely as de Gaulle's car went by:

This little whistle has shaken the foundations of the state. Honest people now know that a country capable of punishing a whistle with a fine of 1,000 francs is a country defended against anarchy, terrorism, regicide, in short against anti-Gaullism and, above all, against spontaneous, rude, loud anti-Gaullism which dares to manifest itself in the middle of our well-kept streets.

Mitterrand also attacked the great extension of police powers, the creation of new secret police groups to harass de Gaulle's opponents and the new brutality of the police in handling demonstrations – eight people were killed by the police in a 1962 demonstration against Algeria. 'Gaullism,' concluded Mitterrand, 'lives without laws. Going from one *coup d'état* to another, it pretends to be constructing a state while it only succeeds in sanctifying an adventure.'

After six years of de Gaulle's stultifying hold on French politics, the book was hard-hitting, and fresh. Far from the frenetic criticisms of Mitterrand that surrounded de Gaulle's 1958 takeover, the *Permanent Coup d'Etat* was well-argued, sustained in its analytical criticism not just of the individual but an entire regime, and written with considerable elegance. It caught and helped shape the growing public mood, that though de Galle may have been necessary in 1958, his style of government was at odds with republican traditions and that individual and collective liberties had greatly diminished under the Fifth Republic.

While Mitterrand was cultivating the grass roots of the Left by means of his writing and through his position as President of the Convention, Deferre was running into difficulties with his candidature. The problem was the position of the French Communist Party, whose votes Deferre needed but whose involvement or formal support he categorically rejected. Mitterrand told him he ought to work with the Communists but Deferre ignored the suggestion. The municipal elections in May 1965 in Marseilles turned into a pitched battle between Deferre's SFIO and the Communists. The latter nearly succeeded in dislodging Deferre who had to scuttle around making electoral alliances with Christian Democrats and other strange bedfellows of the Right. Reversing the famous popular front slogan, Deferre said he would have 'no enemies on the Right'. It looked as if Deferre was trying to resurrect the 'third force' – a political regrouping based in equal measure on anti-Gaullism and anti-Communism. After the municipal elections Deferre moved further to the Right, entering into negotiations with the rump of the Popular Republican Movement. To tempt them he offered to modify his opposition to state support for church schools. This was too much for the old guard in the SFIO for whom anti-clericalism and in particular a refusal to contemplate public money going into Catholic education remained an inviolable party shibboleth. Furthermore the Popular Republicans refused to have the word 'Socialist' in the title of any group formed to support Deferre's candidature. Deferre's campaign was collapsing around him and at the end of June 1965, he withdrew from the race. A few months before he decided to launch himself forward as a candidate Deferre had been quite modest about his abilities: 'I can claim to be a good mayor and I think I was a decent minister – but the President of the Republic, that's in a different class.' But Deferre's eighteen-month candidature had at least demonstrated one crucial political fact. His search for allies in the Centre had proved fruitless. From now on, an effective candidate against de Gaulle would have to be based in the Left.

Deferre's withdrawal with only four months to go placed the Left in a quandary. Neither Mollet nor Mendès-France were runners while the Communists under their new leader, Waldeck-Rochet, continued their policy of not putting forward a Communist candidate. Aside from the Marseilles fight, the Communists had successfully entered into mutual voting pacts with the SFIO in a number of municipalities: to promote a Communist candidate for the presidency could ruin these tentative moves in the direction of popular frontism. Communist political strategy was moving away from complete emphasis on class struggle towards the idea of an autonomous French Socialism. To achieve this a broad front extending well beyond the fifth of the population that habitually voted Communist would be needed. Such a broad front could only afford one candidate for the presidency. The Communist decision to opt out of the 1965 presidential contest was of historic importance as it allowed Mitterrand to put himself forward as the representative of all the forces of the Left, not simply the non-Communist Left.

From the moment of Deferre's withdrawal Mitterrand's three closest political associates, Charles Hernu, secretary of the Convention, George Dayan, a university friend of Mitterrand who had worked with him in government and followed him into the political wilderness and Claude Estier, a left-wing journalist, began to put out feelers to the leaders and personalities on the Left to see what kind of support a Mitterrand candidature would receive. Mendès-France promised his endorsement and for the Communists Waldeck-Rochet, who had first met Mitterrand in London in 1943, was surprisingly warm: 'Some of our leaders see Mitterrand, as a Fourth Republic politician, longing for the "third force". But let's not forget that since 1958 he has always been found alongside us fighting de Gaulle's personal power.' Guy Mollet indifferently promised SFIO support, at least for the first round. Mollet privately believed that Mitterrand would be beaten into third place in the first round and that the final candidate against de Gaulle would be a centrist.

Of the left-wing parties only the Unified Socialist Party was against his running, though it came round to supporting his candidature during the campaign. Mitterrand hurried through these consultations in order to announce his candidature publicly on 9 September 1965. It was a casual enough beginning to a campaign that would change his life. In the press conference announcing his candidature, he was vague about what his actual political programme would be. He was opposed to 'arbitrary personal power, chauvinism and social conservatism' and he was for 'the respect of laws and freedoms'; he was strongly pro-European and called for economic expansion based on democratic planning. Mitterrand was offering no hostages to fortune: he willingly accepted the support of the left parties but he was not entering into any political negotiation with them on a joint programme.

The press reaction to Mitterrand's announcement was scornfully dismissive. Jean-Jacques Servan Schreiber, editor of *L'Express*, said that Mitterrand risked obtaining the lowest number of votes for the Left since the Second Empire. An exception in the midst of the hostile reaction was François Mauriac, whose political perspective was Gaullist but, as on previous occasions he had a kind and prescient word for Mitterrand:

> From his point of view, François Mitterrand is not wrong to put forward his candidature. Not that he has a chance of winning, he is not so naïve as to believe that. But, given the feebleness of the old parties and the political vacuum which is bad for all of us, the arrival of an intelligent, courageous and talented individual can count. It can give him an important position tomorrow or the day after tomorrow but on one condition: that he does not descend into the gutter.

Mitterrand had no intention of doing that. In 1969, he wrote that ever since 1958 'I knew I would be a candidate against de Gaulle'. Hindsight can thus make firm what was, at best, a flickering, uncertain ambition. Until Deferre's bid collapsed, there is no indication in Mitterrand's writings or speeches that he saw himself challenging de Gaulle, nor did any commentators mention his name as a possible presidential candidate. He had no party, and his name was still besmirched by the 'Observatory' affair. Alain Savary, one of his left-wing critics, acidly noted that a Mitterrand campaign 'would fatally provoke a series of personal attacks'. To run was to re-establish himself not just in the public's mind but in his own mind as well. Mitterrand took a brave step in putting himself forward; after all, the initial opinion polls only gave him 11%, a figure which if confirmed in the election would be a crushing humiliation. But his gamble paid off. As France was to find out, a presidential election polarizes the country. Whoever represented one of the two poles would gain enormously in stature.

The first move in the campaign was to form the Federation of the Democratic and Socialist Left which grouped the SFIO, the Radical Party and the Convention. The Federation was to continue its life after the December presidential elections and all through his campaign Mitterrand stressed the need to look forward to the elections for the National Assembly due to be held in 1967. Mitterrand himself avoided too close a contact with the parties and worked with a small team of old friends, enlarged for the campaign by a few people seconded from the SFIO and the Radical Party. One of those who came from SFIO was Pierre Mauroy, who was already being talked of as a possible successor to Mollet. Mitterrand told *L'Express:* 'I believe in the dynamism behind my candidature, the dynamism behind the United Left. And I will use all my weight to ensure that the legislative elections in 1967 will be fought in a completely new way with a new style of campaign.' Mitterrand projected himself as the youthful foward-looking alternative to the ageing de Gaulle dwelling in the past. 'A young President for a modern France,' proclaimed Mitterrand's yellow election posters. To boost the dynamic image he travelled around the country in a helicopter and secured the endorsement of personalities ranging from Jean-Paul Sartre to Brigitte Bardot. He kept his distance from the Communists: a few days after announcing his candidature he went to Brussels and made a passionately pro-European speech to the European Movement. On this issue he was totally at odds with the French Communist Party and his decision to make the Brussels speech was publicly to mark his distance from them. He also avoided meetings in town halls where a Communist was mayor. Mitterrand would only allow himself to be introduced by Socialist or Radical mayors. Support flowed in from trade unions, and other groups and institutions opposed to de Gaulle.

There were two other serious candidates in the race. Jean Lecanuet had been put forward by his party, the Popular Republican Movement. He was aiming to attract the votes in the Centre, still questing for the elusive 'third force'. Lecanuet offered himself as a candidate in the 'Kennedy' style, an evocation potentially alarming to the average French voter who prefers his leader to present a certain gravitas. Although Mitterrand's publicity underlined his youth, the plain fact was that he was nearly fifty. His good looks had become a little faded with a receding hair line and the beginnings of a quite definite paunch. His jowly dark features were always broken by a smile but one reporter noted that even if his eyes were laughing his mouth stayed tightly puckered. Another reporter was struck by the similarity on television of Mitterrand to an American politician, one Richard Nixon. A fourth candidate, Jean-Louis

Tixier-Vignancour had been busy promoting himself for several months. Tixier-Vignancour was a brilliant, extreme right-wing lawyer who had defended OAS terrorists. He had also been Mitterrand's chief tormentor in the law cases that followed the 1954 'Leaks' affair and his running against de Gaulle was a gesture of hate against the man who had taken France out of Algeria.

De Gaulle himself stayed well above the electoral fray, the solitary giant in the Elysée barely noticing the insects outside. It was not until 4 November, one month before the first round of polling was due to take place that he announced he would allow his name to go forward. De Gaulle played his favourite theme, re-elect me or face disaster. He told the press conference called to announce his candidature that unless there was a massive vote for him, 'France would suffer disorder such as it has never seen before and this time without a possible redress'. Philip Williams, one of Britain's leading historians of post-war France, summed up de Gaulle's campaign launch: 'His brief announcement of his candidature showed all the old hallmarks: before de Gaulle – nothing; under de Gaulle – perfection; if not de Gaulle – catastrophe.' De Gaulle's election slogan was simply: 'Me or chaos'. Having announced he was a candidate de Gaulle retired to the Elysée and disdained campaigning. He even refused to use the two hours of television time each candidate was allotted. An announcement from the Elysée said: 'The broadcasting time allocated to de Gaulle will be filled by a variety programme' though de Gaulle did make one fifteen-minute broadcast on 29 November.

Mitterrand had refined his electoral programme with the publication of twenty-eight propositions which he wrote out himself without reference to any of the parties backing him. They made anodyne reading. Better government, constitutional modifications, reform of television and radio, repealing of anti-strike laws, more workplace rights for unions, support for the nuclear non-proliferation treaty, European political integration, increased aid for the third world, the list meandered on worthily but it seemed almost designed to damp down arguments rather than engage strongly committed support. On one controversial issue of the day, Mitterrand broke new ground when he called for

104

the repeal of a 1920 law making the sale or advertising of contraceptive devices a crime. Instead Mitterrand advocated family planning and wanted the birth-control pill made available to French women. In what was still formally a Catholic country, it was a courageous stand to make. It cost Mitterrand votes; in the first round only 8% of France's practising Catholic population voted for Mitterrand compared with 88% for de Gaulle and Lecanuet. Nevertheless, his call for the introduction of contraceptive measures caught de Gaulle by surprise and he had to promise to set up a government commission on the subject.

If Mitterrand had studiously avoided having a common electoral programme agreed between the left parties, his opponents, particularly de Gaulle's ministers who were doing the grass-roots campaigning that the General believed was below his dignity, painted Mitterrand as an advocate of a new Popular Front. Mitterrand treated the charge as a compliment; 'When they insult me by saying I am the candidate of the Popular Front, that gives me pleasure because there has been no government for a hundred years that did so much for the people of France.'

Mitterrand campaigned with vigour, shaking hands, kissing babies and scattering promises to farmers, doctors, war veterans and shopkeepers. His crowds got bigger and by the end of the campaign he was addressing 20–30,000 people. He was not at his best on television but as France had been deprived of any criticism or opposition to de Gaulle on the government-controlled television and radio, the French people were fascinated and delighted with the attacks on the General. He was caustic about those around de Gaulle: 'The only difference I can see between Pompidou (de Gaulle's Prime Minister) and Giscard d'Estaing (de Gaulle's young Finance Minister) is the name of their banks.' Again the crowds loved it. The London *Guardian's* correspondent captured Mitterrand's appeal when he spoke to car-workers outside the Peugeot factory at Sochaux:

> Bare-headed in the drizzle, he spoke for half an hour perched on the back of a lorry. In his light overcoat and muffler, his stocky figure and short profile looked astonishingly Napoleonic. One half-waited for him to slip his hand under his coat in the imperial style. Hundreds of men in

overalls cut short their lunch break to give him an enthusiastic reception. They were tied mechanically to slogans such as 'a United Left', 'an Alliance of Republicans', but it was easy to sense their initial curiosity in Mitterrand the man change to admiration and a warmth for 'a mere candidate' who was carrying the workers' banner against enormous odds.

In the television address he made on the eve of the first round of the 1965 presidential election Mitterrand summed up his campaign. He denied that he stood for a return to rule by parties.

The present regime is that of a single man and when the time comes for him to go he will designate an unknown successor who will appoint his friends, a faction that will be worse than a party, an anonymous collection of interests and intrigues. I am not the representative of a party. I am not the representative of a coalition of parties. I am the candidate of all the Left, the warm-hearted Left, the fraternal Left which before me and after me has been and will be the expression of our people's worth. Let me give you what are perhaps old words but for me, for all of us, men and women of the Left, women and men of progress, they have kept all their value. These words are Justice, Progress, Freedom, Peace. . . . I ask you to choose for independence and against arbitrary justice, for the freedom of the media and against the abuse of propaganda, for trade-union freedom and against the return of privilege, for freedom at the communal level – handed down to us from the Middle Ages and against the encroachment of the state . . . To believe in justice and to believe in happiness, that is the message of the Left.

This gushing eloquence is treacle-like when translated into English. In French, it is solemn, moving and showed that the Left's candidate had just as much right to appeal to his country's historical traditions as de Gaulle. The quicksilver orator who delighted in irony and sarcasm in the National Assembly and at public meetings could become slow and stately when appealing to all of France. But his language was too rich for the intimacy of television. It was to be several more years before Mitterrand mastered the medium.

The results of the first round of the presidential election held on 5 December 1965 were not at all to de Gaulle's liking. After his personal triumphs in the referendums of 1958 (78% vote) and 1962 (66% vote), he had failed to persuade even one out of two citizens to vote for him. He received 44.6% against 31.7% for Mitterrand and 15.6% for Lecanuet. It was almost as if Mitterrand had won. In a way, he had if his objective was limited to re-establishing the Left's presence in France. After seven years during which de Gaulle had towered over everyone and the Left had been reduced to sullen disunity, here was new hope and a new man.

The second round of the presidential campaign lasted two weeks and was developed at intense speed. Having coasted through the first round on the assumption of a walk-over, the Gaullist machine began taking Mitterrand very seriously indeed. There was a massive propaganda barrage reckoned to have cost 20 million French francs (about £1.5 million at 1965 exchange rates) on posters and newspapers delivered to homes. Mitterrand's campaign costs amounted to a more modest 2 million francs (£150,000). De Gaulle climbed down from Olympus and appeared on television chatting knowledgeably about everyday problems affecting ordinary people. The 'Charles the Great' was hidden from view to be replaced by a more welcoming 'Uncle Charles' and French viewers enjoyed the transition.

But if, in a bid to capture votes, de Gaulle appeared less godlike that only served to remind people of his age and mortality. Mitterrand played on this theme. It was necessary to look beyond the election to a time after de Gaulle. As the sole opposition to de Gaulle, Mitterrand began picking up support from everywhere. Lecanuet, disappointed at his failure to get a new centre party off the ground told his followers either to vote for Mitterrand or to abstain. Tixier-Vignancour strongly endorsed Mitterrand, his arch-enemy of only a few years ago: anything other than de Gaulle. Jean Monnet, who had devised the planning system which led to France's post-war economic take-off came out in favour of Mitterrand. Again it was more anti-de Gaulle than pro-Mitterrand. Monnet, known as the 'Father of Europe' was distressed at de Gaulle's ruthless pursuit of national interests at the expense of the European ideal. Most of the 900,000 French who had been repatriated from Algeria also switched their votes to Mitterrand – de Gaulle was still the man who had sold out Algeria. Despite gathering in all these votes Mitterrand refused blandishments to move to the centre. He ignored appeals from *L'Express* and the defeated Popular Republican candidate Lecanuet. 'Let's have no illusions,' he told a friend, 'I have no chance of beating de Gaulle but rather than give pledges to the centrists I prefer to remain an intransigent man of the Left.'

In his final television appeal, Mitterrand returned to the theme that had motivated him continuously since 1958.

> General de Gaulle behaves like a citizen above law, above even the supreme law of the constitution. He is the master of our foreign policy and he alone chooses our alliances; he is the master of our military policy and he alone chooses what arms we will have. He is master of our judicial system and chooses the judges and looks after them and punishes those who criticize him; he chooses who can be kept in prison and who can be released. He is the master of economic and social choices and how the budget is divided, giving priority to the atomic bomb over national education. . . . Who thus claims that without him France would be nothing? No, General de Gaulle is making a mistake. France does not belong to him. France identifies herself with no one other than her own people.

On 19 December, Mitterrand received 44.8% of the votes against de Gaulle's 55.2%. If the votes from the overseas territories are excluded and there were many suspicions about the validity of the immense Gaullist majorities that always appeared in these far-off islands, Mitterrand's score goes up to 46%. He had persuaded an extra 3 million voters to support him. A few days before the election, the London *Observer* had profiled Mitterand under the headline: THE UNKNOWN MAN AGAINST DE GAULLE. The sub-editor had got it wrong. The campaign through October, November and December had turned

Mitterrand into a recognized national personality. His exposure on television made him a media star. If the headline in the *Observer* was wide of the mark, the anonymous journalist who profiled Mitterrand summed up what all France was thinking when he wrote: 'When all is said and done, however, he remains a mystery. He behaves as if he is not yet sure about himself.' The campaign had not really revealed what kind of man Mitterrand was. His political ideology remained unclear. That he was *against* de Gaulle was obvious. But what, apart from a humanistic commitment to liberty, to the democratic traditions of republican France, a medley of woolly social democratic *cum* centrist policies, did he stand *for*? Despite the haziness of his political positions no one could deny the immense energy he had put into making the campaign the most successful united Left effort for thirty years. Single-handedly he had given the Left a new sense of its strength. His decision to run, which appeared so casually taken, almost capricious at the time, had been completely justified. The Left, under Mitterrand's banner, had delivered an immense snub to de Gaulle and had re-appeared as a political force in France.

9
From Triumph to Disaster

The daily life of a formal opposition
taught me a lot.

The 1965 presidential election constituted only the first two
rounds of a three-round fight. For the Left and Mitterrand, the
elections to the National Assembly in some fifteen months' time
would show whether the Left could unite and continue its solid
electoral progress. The obvious vehicle was the Federation of the
Democratic and Socialist Left which had hurriedly thrown
together the SFIO, the Radical Party and the Convention of
Republican Institutions as a campaign vehicle for Mitterrand's
presidential bid. Mitterrand wanted to take the loosely knit
Federation further and merge the three wings into a cohesive
party. A new party could be an equal partner for the Communist
Party which still, on the basis of votes cast in the 1962 and 1965
national and municipal elections was the best supported left-
wing party in France. Already in January 1966, the Communist-
dominated CGT trade union had signed an agreement with its
rival, the CFDT, setting out certain common objectives and
campaigns. The two major French trade union organizations
held to their separate ideological perspectives, but – they felt – in
the fight against de Gaulle's deflationary economic policy, and

continued repression of trade union rights it was better to march together than march apart.

The question of what kind of relationship the Federation should have with the Communist Party remained a difficult subject. Guy Mollet had been swung around to the idea of a common electoral pact with the Communists based on mutual second-round voting support, but he remained hostile to any notion of a common electoral programme or the idea of sharing power with Communists in the event of a victory and a Left majority in the Assembly elections. Gaston Deferre still dreamt of making alliances with Lecanuet's Popular Republicans and other centrist groups. There was some vote-gathering logic in this. Although Mitterrand's 45% vote in the presidential election had shaken de Gaulle, nearly one third of Mitterrand's second-round votes came from those who were hostile to de Gaulle but by no means left-wing. A more accurate reflection of the natural left-wing vote, combining the Federation and the Communist voters, was the 32% Mitterrand received in the first round. Nearly half the industrial working-class vote had gone to de Gaulle. Lecanuet's 16% was up for grabs and, argued Deferre and some members of the Radical Party, it was better to go hunting for those centre votes than to lock the Federation too tightly with the Communists.

The arguments went back and forth all during the summer of 1966. Mitterrand's reputation for equivocation was increased as he made a series of speeches which seemed to bend both ways at once. Sometimes he acknowledged the logic of trying to attract centre votes, on other occasions he went to the other extreme, musing over the possibility of a common programme with the Communists. As the re-alignment debate continued, Mitterrand introduced a peculiarly British institution into French politics – the Shadow Cabinet. It was the first time in France that opposition leaders were asked to take shadow portfolios and to set themselves up as a kind of government-in-waiting. The idea caught the public imagination in France and abroad, though Mitterrand's choice of Fourth Republic veterans to take the major posts – Mollet had Foreign Affairs and Defence, and Deferre was shadow Social and Administrative Minister – led to derision in the right-wing press which dubbed the effort: 'a phantom government full of ghosts of the past'. The Shadow Cabinet system in the time-honoured British manner could never be completely grafted on to France's more fissiparous political structure but it was a constructive innovation that gave expression to the idea of the opposition as a coherent entity ready to take over. Mitterrand explained that the idea of putting old-timers in top posts was deliberate – they were the only colleagues he had with direct ministerial experience. But he added several younger politicians in order that they could gain experience from working with the old hands and to get a feel of departmental affairs. He wrote, of this time:

> The daily life of a formal opposition taught me a lot. There were crises and contradictions. One could see that the opposition had not yet rid itself of some of its old practices and it would need to suffer some rude shocks before being able to take on its full responsibilities. But little by little a team spirit developed and we realized that we had a very effective body for political discussion and action.

While Mitterrand was trying to give the Federation a more heavyweight image, the French Communist Party was also snapping at his heels demanding the conclusion of an electoral pact. In a rare television interview, the Communist leader Waldeck-Rochet read out the text of a letter he had sent Mitterrand asking for a commitment to second-round support in the forthcoming National Assembly elections. The issue could not be put off much longer with the elections due to be held in March 1967. Finally Mitterrand came off the fence in October in a long interview published in *Paris-Match*. There would be no link-up with the Centre: its leader, Lecanuet, Mitterrand declared had already defined himself as a man of the Right. Mitterrand went further and said that between Communists and the Federation there would be more points of agreement than disagreement. For the Radical Party, such abrupt rejection of the Centre was almost too much. This time Mitterrand turned the pressure on the Radicals – either they agreed to a joint left-wing electoral pact with the Communists or they could quit the Federation. The Radicals grumbled but stayed put.

On 20 December 1966 the pact with the Communists was

signed; the first time since 1945 that the signatures of the Socialists and the Communists had appeared on the same piece of paper and more than thirty years since the formation of the electoral pact that led to the Popular Front. The pact condemned the regime of 'personal power', i.e. de Gaulle, promised mutual second-round support in all constituencies for the best placed first-round left-wing candidate and talked of continuing co-operation and discussion between the two sides once the election was over.

The Communists got less than they wanted – a jointly agreed programme; but at least now they were much more part of a united Left than in 1962 and 1965 when the electoral agreements with SFIO had not covered all of France, nor were such stringent disciplinary rules attached to them. Commenting on the pact, Mitterrand said: 'We have embarked on a very profound study so that the whole of the Left can join in the battle. Effectiveness is the outcome of a good understanding of the Left which must reject all stupid sectarianism. Thus it will obtain a majority, or, failing that, will be the powerful axis of a minority.'

Although in the National Assembly elections held in March 1967 Mitterrand developed themes similar to the presidential election – the arbitrary power of the regime, the bias of television and radio, the increasing power of big monopolies – the contest was quite different from the Mitterrand–de Gaulle presidential duel. For a start, the President stayed out of the fight while the Gaullists, ably directed by the Prime Minister, Georges Pompidou, projected themselves not as men of de Gaulle but as men (and in a few constituencies, women) of the Fifth Republic. They claimed that it was the stability of the nine-year-old regime that was at stake. Since 1962, at least, there had been peace in France and no external military involvement. On the other hand, unemployment was rising and there was a great housing short-age. The economic and social policies of the government became, for perhaps the first time in twenty years, the most important issue in a French election. The Unified Socialist Party, which although not a signatory to the Federation-Communist electoral pact, campaigned along with the left-wing parties and managed to produce the most effective economic critique of the government from their chief spokesman, Pierre Mendès-France, who was finally to win his way back to the National Assembly. Once again television played an important part and Mitterrand was the main speaker for the Left. In addition his face stared out from thousands of posters endorsing local Federation candidates. He had carefully placed several of his own young supporters in winnable seats; as ever he kept half an eye cocked on improving his political base in the future.

In addition to the standard attacks on the regime's authoritarianism, Mitterrand, on the Left's behalf, promised equal pay for women, earlier retirements, better social security for peasants, more schools, homes and jobs. There was disagreement between the Communists and Mitterrand on NATO and the Common Market: they were against, he was for. But all the Left joined in denouncing de Gaulle's proposals for a nuclear strike force. It almost worked. In the first round, the Communists, the Federation and Unified Socialist Party obtained 43.5% of the votes. Now the electoral pact came into operation and the best-placed left-wing candidate went forward as the united Left candidate for the second round. The discipline was tough. Three SFIO candidates, who put themselves forward for the second round despite coming below a Communist in the first round, were expelled. The united Left showed it meant business. In the 1936 Popular Front elections, by comparison, there had been thirty-two breaches of republican discipline.

The inter-party discipline may have been tight but that did not guarantee a matched response from the voters. Whereas Communist voters usually loyally switched all their votes to a Federation candidate, there were several seats where not all the Federation first-round votes were given to the Communist second-round candidate. In some seats, the reluctance of the Federation voters to support a Communist handed to the Right what should have been a Left victory. These minor problems aside, the Left did well out of the election: the Communist Party gained thirty-two seats and the Federation twenty-eight. The Left now had 193 seats compared with the Gaullists' 244; the balance was held by the rump of the Popular Republican Movement and other centrists who had been squeezed by the continuing bi-polarization in French politics.

The electoral pact strategy had paid off. Left-wing voters, for the most part, were not frightened at the thought of having to vote Communist though the bigger increase in seats achieved by the Communist Party strengthened the fears of some SFIO stalwarts that continuing togetherness between the Communist and non-Communist Left would be much more to the benefit of the former. For most however the mood was happy at another important advance for the Left which was finally able to display real unity. Mitterrand, who had patiently put the whole package together, was duly given the credit for his achievement and was re-elected President of the Federation. He was the acknowledged leader of the opposition. Yet within two years all this crumbled and Mitterrand and the Left had plunged into electoral disaster. The Federation of the Left was dissolved. Once again, as in 1958, he was to be back in the political wilderness. How did this come about?

The answer lay in the lack of policy and ideological clarity within the Left. The success of the electoral pact and the advances of the Left's position in 1965 and 1967 had disguised the underlying differences within the Federation, and between the Federation and the rest of the Left, especially the Communist Party. Under the pressure of electoral annihilation the parties had sunk their differences to form an anti-Gaullist front. But following their electoral successes their separate conceptions of what a post-Gaullist left-of-centre France would look like began to draw them apart. The Common Market was one acute point of difference. The Communist Party was hostile; Mitterrand and the rest of the Left were strong Europeans and enthusiastically supported the British Labour government's application to join the Six. There was disagreement over the Middle East six-day war in June 1967. France under de Gaulle had leant towards the Arab side while Mitterrand was pro-Israeli. The Communist Party lined up behind Moscow and criticized Israel. De Gaulle's decision to take France out of NATO's military command structure was welcomed by the Communists. For Mitterrand, it was a hollow gesture as France would remain part of the Atlantic Alliance and maintain its nuclear bomb, of which Mitterrand, at the time, said: 'There is no more terrible danger to the survival of the human species. What France wants for herself, Israel and Egypt, India and Pakistan will want for themselves and Germany

115

in its turn, and all the states of the earth. We must not hesitate to proclaim it: the proliferation of nuclear arms leads to the extension of conflicts.'

On domestic policies, there was more convergence between the Communists and the Federation. The government took special powers to rule by decree half way through 1967 and rushed through several measures to increase social security contributions which effectively cut the real wages of workers. Unemployment was sneaking upwards and, by the beginning of 1968 when it reached half a million it was double what it had been in 1965. For the Communist Party, the defence of workers' needs was safe and sure ground. In a list of social objectives put forward by the Communists in 1967, the defence of wages, pensions, jobs and social security was seen as the top priority rather than securing improvements or gains in those areas. As the champion of proletarian rights, the Communist Party was unchallengeable. As a promoter of a constructive, positive and imaginative policy that would engage people beyond the numerically shrinking industrial working class, the Communist Party left much to be desired. Their best hope was to construct some common policy agreements with the Federation. Mitterrand was cagey, telling one interviewer in December 1967: 'The "Common Programme" is a phrase used by the Communist Party and represents its aim. The Federation of the Left considers it absolutely vital to maintain a "contract of the majority" and therefore a common platform but one should note with precision the points of disagreement that cannot be settled simply by waving a magic wand.'

It was a balancing act that could not go on forever. The internal problems did not damage his public reputation and mid-way through 1967 he overhauled de Gaulle in the opinion polls. One poll claimed that he would easily beat Pompidou in a presidential election following de Gaulle's departure. He managed to court constituencies that were widely separated. On one hand he now accepted the Fifth Republic constitution with the office of all-powerful President against which he had railed in 1958. This satisfied those who feared that Mitterrand and the Left stood for a return to the parliamentary chaos of the Fourth Republic. On the other hand, he pleased the young, Left and far-Left with criticisms of American policy in Vietnam and Latin America. In 1967, he paid tribute to Che Guevara whose fight, declared Mitterrand, 'is that of free men'. To endorse both the Fifth Republic constitution and Che Guevara is neither contradictory nor insincere but it does suggest a desire to win support based on political capability of some elasticity.

In February 1968, an agreement was reached with the Communist Party. It laid down common policy objectives as well as reconfirming the mutual electoral pact. According to preference and the importance different parties wanted to attach to the agreement, it was described as a 'Common Programme' (by the Communists), an 'enlarged agreement' (by the right-wing members of the Federation) or a 'common platform' (by Mitterrand). In addition to laying down areas where the Federation and the Communists agreed on policy the text was quite candid on disagreements. Both sides called for modest constitutional reforms such as reducing the presidential term to five years, introducing a supreme court and abolishing the worst aspects of de Gaulle's personal rule. On a wide range of social questions – education, mass media, housing, public health, social security and taxation – there was complete agreement. On foreign policy and external alliances, there was the by now traditional divergence. There was also a sharp difference between the two partners' stand on nationalization. The Federation accepted the nationalization of merchant banks plus the aerospace and armaments industries. The Communists wanted to go much further and put forward a list that included all banks, insurance companies plus the following industries: electronic, automobile, petroleum, nuclear, chemical and steel.

Mitterrand described the agreement as 'the most frank confrontation between political partners ever put in front of public opinion'. One small phrase in the agreement, however, provoked a storm: the two partners agreed to hold further discussions on 'the measures to be taken to stall attempts of all kinds to prevent a government of the Left from carrying out its programme'. Pompidou seized on these words and said that, after the election of a Left government, democratic opposition would be done away with. It was, claimed Pompidou, 'the thin end of dictatorship'. The public criticisms embarrassed

Mitterrand and his efforts to defend the 'little phrase' sounded unconvincing.

The agreement with the Communist Party was another important step in Mitterrand's campaign to build a united Left. Apart from predictable right-wing attacks, it had been well received by the majority of activists in both the Federation and the Communist Party. There was increasing joint trade union activity and the prospects for genuine left unity looked good. The fear that in any re-grouping of the Left the Communists would dominate their rivals was offset by the emergence of Mitterrand as the leader, either as President or Prime Minister, in any future left-wing government. Whatever else people thought of him he was clearly no Communist and would maintain democratic Socialist principles within any Left union. Shortly after the agreement was signed, the political editor of *Le Monde* published a short biographical essay on Mitterrand which tried to sum up the complex character of the leader of the opposition as it appeared in 1968:

> One does not believe in his sincerity as much as his agility. Everything seems calculated and nothing left to chance. His resignations, his warnings, his bitter attacks appear profitable rather than prophetic. He can be friendly, angry or evasive but one does not believe in his smile, his temper or even that his 'No' is final. But with him the façade is false. Behind the suspicions he provokes and at the bottom of the extremely violent and hurtful attacks directed against him – he is more insulted than any other leader – one fact stands out: François Mitterrand, unlike most politicians, is worth more than he appears.

While Mitterrand was surviving double-edged praise like that and keeping busy strengthening the opposition's cohesion, policy and organization, the political geology of France, unperceived by professional politicians, was shuddering on the point of an earthquake.

The famous 1968 May 'events' in France have entered popular mythology as almost exclusively a student revolt when the young of France came close to toppling the government. The students were the detonator of what happened in those extraordinary weeks, but the government only came under real pressure when the French working class decisively entered the lists. Mitterrand's two sons were at university in Paris in 1968 and kept him informed on the feelings and turbulence to be found in the faculties. But Mitterrand only moved to try to exploit the situation once the anti-government pressure had shifted from the Latin Quarter and the Sorbonne and out into the factories and workplaces of France. The excitement of being a student in the late 1960s is something that people in many different countries now well into their thirties remember with awe. It seemed as if each nation, no matter what its ideology, was infected. The catalyst in the West was the Vietnam war and the nightly horror on television of America's industrial military machine trying to napalm a small South-East Asian country off the map of the world. In East Europe, a generation that had grown up since the war were more and more restless under the restrictive one-party control of political, social, economic and cultural relations. In Warsaw and Washington, in Prague and Berlin, in Rome and London, students took to the streets to protest in the spring of 1968. In the United States, President Johnson decided not to run again because of the public protests against his Vietnam policy while in Czechoslovakia, Dubcek took confidence from the tide of university-based support for his reform policies. Direct action seemed to pay off and shift policies and politicians towards change. In Paris, the students had more local problems to complain about. The student population had expanded well beyond the capacity of the university structures. There were 100,000 students in Paris alone, double the entire student population of France twenty years previously. The main students' union, which had earned government displeasure because of its stand against the Algerian war, had lost its ability to act as a single voice for students. Trotskyist and Maoist groups and grouplets had sprung up and their targets were what Daniel Cohn-Bendit called the 'crapulent Stalinists' in the leadership of the French Communist Party as much as the conservatives in power. The centralized Education Ministry which administered the university system with bureaucratic rigidity did not help to defuse the various rows that broke out over faculty organization, the provision of facilities and the form and content of courses. (Though, in passing, it should be pointed out that the university authorities in Britain and the United States were hardly any better at judging or handling student grievances in the same period, even though American and British universities are not under the control of state administration. It was the difference of age and the poverty of imagination of the university administrators of the epoch that rendered them helpless in face of student pressure: whether the administrators were elected academics or ministerial civil servants was by the way.) As the university administrators in France ignored student demands, the students developed new forms of protest, such as faculty occupations or the interruptions of classes with demands that they be turned into seminars on third world liberation.

In turn, the response of the Ministry was to close down the faculty and to discipline the student leaders. This tactic and response had been mainly restricted to the overspill buildings in Paris University at Nanterre in the western suburbs. But early in May, the students, led by Daniel Cohn-Bendit, decided to occupy the administrative centre of the Sorbonne in the heart of the Latin Quarter. They did so in protest against a university attempt to discipline Cohn-Bendit. As thousands of students milled into the eighteenth-century courtyard, the authorities reacted by calling in the police who evicted the students with a savage brutality. Six hundred students were arrested and several dozen taken to hospital. The rhythm of protest, demonstration, police repression, and official indifference mounted. A march of 20,000 students along the Champs-Elysées – the first time that students had crossed the Seine and 'invaded' the Right Bank – and an attempt to snuff out the flame around the tomb of the unknown soldier underneath the Arc de Triomphe lifted the protests on to the front pages. Most newspapers condemned the students: one of the harshest criticisms came from Georges Marchais, number two in the Communist Party. Writing in *L'Humanité*, he attacked 'the false revolutionaries and sons of the bourgeoisie who are serving the interests of Gaullist power and the great capitalist monopolies', while Cohn-Bendit was nothing more than a 'German anarchist'.

That the French Communist Party, along with the parties in the Federation, were so completely out of touch with the students was to become much clearer as the days went by. Only the far-left Unified Socialist Party and the CFDT which were groping towards an idea of workers' control (the French word is *autogestion* which literally translated means self-management but the concept extends well beyond the English sense of the phrase) as the answer to French industrial and social problems, actively supported the students and their claims. In general, the students were left to their own devices and the first week of May turned into a running battle with the police. This culminated in the building of more than fifty barricades late on 11 May 1968 to try to turn the Latin Quarter into a student-held fortress. In the middle of the night the riot-police stormed the barricades with a force that seemed equivalent to a military assault. School-children from nearby high schools had excitedly joined the university students behind the barricades and a horrified France listened on the radio to the sound of street fighting, the dull crump of exploding tear gas bombs, the coughing of those unable to breathe and the shouts and screams of police and students. For those taking part it was a moment of political exaltation. One militant pariticipant recalls: 'It was joy in the quasi-Nietzschean sense of the word, people were happy to die for it, you see, and I remember for me it was the most beautiful night of my life.' For the parents of the masked seventeen-year-olds tearing up paving stones to hurl at the police, there was rather more fear for their offspring's safety and for the disruption which would be caused to the preparations for the all-important *baccalauréat* examination.

In the middle of the night of the barricades, as weary students were crumbling before the police assault, a group of them are said to have telephoned Georges Séguy, the general secretary of the Communist-dominated CGT and pleaded with him to mobilize workers. 'Three o'clock in the morning is no time to rouse the proletariat,' is said to have been Séguy's reply and he put down the receiver. But the trade unions were already moving. The spring months had seen a wave of strikes breaking out in many different sectors ranging from the traditional metal industry to banks; even clerical workers at the Paris Stock Exchange went on strike. The riot-police, who were lashing into students in the Latin Quarter, had often been used against workers to break up picket lines or evict occupying strikers. They were no more gentle with adult strikers than they were with student demonstrators.

The CFDT issued a statement explicitly linking the students' and workers' struggles:

> When young people demand, with methods which are sometimes anarchistic, shocking and plain stupid in the eyes of adults, a new style of relationship between master and pupil, the participation by the students in the organization and life and choice of courses in their faculties, they join the fundamental struggle which workers are engaged in and which questions the power of capitalism in the workplace, the economy and the nation, and they join the fight for a real democracy which provides for meaningful participation at all levels of society.

The unions decided to organize demonstrations on 13 May to protest against the brutality of the police repression and to demand the reopening of the universities. But the date was also the tenth anniversary of the putsch that had brought de Gaulle to power and the object was to rally all those who wanted to see an end to the Gaullist regime. The demonstration was massively supported but inverted the traditional order with Cohn-Bendit hogging the publicity limelight, having insinuated himself at its head, while the trade union leaders, and well behind them in the rear political leaders like Mitterrand, Mollet and Mendès-France walked glumly, ignored by most of the young people. Mitterrand tried to shift the centre of protest to the National Assembly with a powerful attack on the government's handling of the student crisis, but the scene was in any case moving away from the Left Bank of Paris and into workplaces.

Inspired by the student protest and with a long list of unsatisfied demands and unremedied grievances behind them, workers in many areas, including the important Renault and Peugeot automobile plants, went on strike and occupied their factories. It was a spontaneous movement from below over which the central confederations had little control. The strikes wave went beyond industry, and railways and postal services stopped running. By 22 May, 10 million workers were on strike and petrol supplies were cut off. For the CFDT the movement was 'to construct a democratic society' while the CGT emphasized traditional economic demands of more pay and the future safeguarding of workers' purchasing power. The general strike and the continuing occupation by the students of the Latin Quarter seemed to add up to something approaching a revolutionary situation. The government had no answers and precious little authority. 'Power,' the slogan ran, 'is in the streets.'

For the politicians of the Left, it was a golden opportunity – but how to transform it to their advantage? The Communist Party shrunk from a revolutionary bid. The army was still there and in the event of any insurrection it would be workers' blood that would be shed and workers' organizations destroyed. The students would survive. Mitterrand wanted to exploit the situation and so did Mendès-France who was now back in the National Assembly and whose attachment during the 1960s to the Unified Socialist Party had given him a more pure, leftist image amongst the young. On the evening of 21 May, the two men met in Mitterrand's apartment close to the Latin Quarter. Someone suggested that they go and stroll amongst the students to demonstrate support. Mendès-France counselled restraint and told Mitterrand: 'Don't do it. Remember you are a statesman. A future President of France should not be seen down there.' Two days later Mitterrand was furious to read reports of Mendès-France spending an evening with the students occupying the Sorbonne and even joining in an all-night debate with them. The sixty-one-year-old Mendès-France had, in effect, double-crossed him. As the crisis worsened and if the Left were to be able to exploit it it was clear that Mitterrand would have to act by himself.

On 24 May, de Gaulle returned from a state visit to Romania and broadcast to the nation. It was an unconvincing performance, weak, and lacking in authority. He offered a referendum around the vague idea of increased participation. If the result was a 'No' vote, he would resign. The broadcast did nothing to staunch the growing stike wave. On 25 May, Mitterrand addressed 8,000 people in his constituency and told them: 'We have in front of us a tottering power on its knees which has capitulated in front of the growing force of an angry people. The

Republic lies in front of us.' It was a reasonable analysis based on publicly available knowledge but behind the scenes the state was regathering its forces. As soon as the strikes had grown in strength the Prime Minister, Pompidou, had called the unions and the employers' federation to begin negotiating on the union demands. With nearly every workplace occupied or on strike the employers were beaten and along with Pompidou they made major concessions. There was to be an increase in the minimum wage of 35%, all wages would go up by 10%, there would be a two-hour reduction in the working week and new laws promoting workplace rights for unions would be introduced. It was a major package of economic gains, more than the unions had won at any single moment since a similar general strike produced similar concessions from the employers in 1936. While Pompidou was busy finding a solution to the strikes, de Gaulle had flown to Germany for secret meetings with French army generals. In exchange for releasing senior brother officers still in prison as a result of attempted coups dating from the Algerian war, the French generals promised de Gaulle full military backing should he need it. This time, unlike 1958, the French army would stand by the government.

On the surface, however, it looked to everyone as if there was simply a growing power vacuum. Mitterrand met with other leaders of the Federation and on 28 May they decided to try and fill the emptiness. Mitterrand called a press conference and announced: 'Since 3 May, the state no longer exists and what is holding it together cannot even maintain the appearance of power.' The referendum was irrelevant and both de Gaulle and Pompidou should go. In their place Mitterrand called for a ten-member caretaker government to take over and for fresh presidential and National Assembly elections. For the office of Prime Minister, Mitterrand suggested Mendès-France and said that he himself would run for President. The effect of his pronouncement was the opposite of what Mitterrand intended. He read out his statement to the cameras and microphones in an ornate Paris hotel and the tired, poorly shaved Mitterrand made a poor impression on the evening television news bulletins as a by now nervous and disoriented population watched him make what seemed to border on an unconstitutional bid for power. (He claimed later that French television had broadcast a doctored version of his statement.) In Paris, the feverish politicians of the Left were failing to pick up the waves of fear and anger from the peasantry, the shopkeepers, the concierges, the scores of thousands of small businessmen for whom May was a non-stop nightmare. The left-wing party leaders discussed Mitterrand's announcement seriously. He went to see the Communist Party who were angry at not having been consulted prior to the announcement. They were insulted when Mitterrand said that at best he could only give them one seat in any government he led, and became furious when Mendès-France said that the caretaker government would have to include the new forces in the factories and the universities, forces that from a Socialist perspective were hostile to Communism and which were threatening to ruin the Communist Party's influence in the working class and the intelligentsia. With their trade-union confederation, the CGT, making clear progress in the wage negotiations, the Communist Party drew back from what many people were now saying was the mirror image of 1958 – an attempt to take power on the basis of a breakdown of order and fear of anarchy: a takeover that would be later legitimized through elections

Mitterrand's call was killed stone dead on 30 May when a revitalized de Gaulle broadcast to the nation in the middle of the afternoon. He announced a postponement of the referendum and the dissolution of the National Assembly to be followed by elections in June.

An immense sigh of relief went through the bourgeoisie at the return of a strong, confident, dominant de Gaulle. Early that evening a million Parisians poured into the Champs-Elysées to express support. All those who had looked upon the students' and workers' revolts with a mixture of terror and loathing felt relieved. If May 1968 saw the awakening of a young, class-conscious, quasi-revolutionary movement, it also saw the resurgence of the French bourgeoisie that discovered it still had strength and numbers. The wave of change that had swept France in May was replaced by a wave of reaction that swept the country in June. The trade unions ordered their people back to work, reluctantly in the case of the CFDT, more eagerly in the case of the CGT which argued, almost certainly correctly, that to have spasmodic strikes and occupations continuing during an election campaign would only play into Gaullist hands. The students denounced participation in the elections as a betrayal of the hopes of May. The Gaullist candidates concentrated their fire upon Mitterrand, ridiculing his attempted takeover and associating the Left with the riots, strikes and disorder that were so fresh in the memory. Mitterrand tried to rally support. He wrote:

> The government is trying to exploit the fear of civil war, a fear for which it is primarily responsible. The government which has so often scorned the peasants, the shopkeepers and craftsmen and which has never helped them in any serious manner – is it because they are the only groups never to have revolted? – is now trying to rally them to their side. But the government is forgetting that we are talking about serious citizens who know how to think carefully and how to make an honest judgement of a government's record.

It was a waste of time.

The government campaign was virulently anti-Communist and they managed to transfer all the hate and blame for the chaos of May on to Communist shoulders. Mitterrand stuck faithfully by the 'common platform' and electoral pact and side by side the Federation and the Communist Party went down to massive electoral defeat. The Federation lost sixty-one seats and were reduced to fifty-seven seats in the new Assembly and the Communists went down to thirty-three seats having lost thirty-nine. In the National Assembly Mitterrand was shunned and former colleagues did not want to sit beside him. In July, Gaston Deferre told him that he should resign his leadership of the Federation of the Left. Again, and still only fifty-one years old, his political life was in ruins.

10
Birth of the Socialist Party

*Anyone who cannot accept a rupture with
capitalist society cannot be a member of the
Socialist Party.*

Like the 'Observatory' affair in 1959, Mitterrand's television
appearances during the May 1968 crisis in which he announced
his readiness to take over the reins of government was to linger as
a bad memory in the public's mind for several years afterwards.
At key moments Mitterrand's judgement seemed to stumble and
he was mercilessly punished for his mistakes. The May events
amongst both students and workers caught the established politicians and trade-union leaders by surprise. The government's
initial reaction was to ignore the manifestation of student dis-
content then to repress it. The Left failed to understand that the
students' upsurge would spread to the working class and by the
time Mitterrand and others tried to take advantage of the power
vacuum it was too late; the workers had secured major economic
gains and the public fear was turning towards thoughts of
revenge. France may have been in an insurrectionary situation
for a brief moment in 1968 but an overthrow of the state was
never taken seriously as an option. Young Unified Socialist Party
militants gathered in a Paris cellar stocked with small arms and

grenades for one crucial night late in May but their purpose was rather to defend Paris against a feared paratrooper takeover following de Gaulle's visit to French army units in Germany. The irony therefore was that this, the most radical section of the mainstream French Left, wished to defend the republic rather than take it over. For a short while, power was in the streets but no one knew how to use it and most shrank from the consequences of acting unconstitutionally. Although the advocates of various forms of direct action would remain influential on the Left in the years ahead it would have to be the long march through the institutions and the accession to power through the mechanisms of electoral democracy that, from now on, would be seen by more and more as the strategy to change French society.

If that was one lesson from the May events, there were others equally important. General de Gaulle had claimed that only he stood between France and chaos. During the May crisis they found they had both de Gaulle and chaos. A few months later they would vote him out of office. But it was more than de Gaulle's stature that had suffered. The whole Gaullist regime, based on personal control, an authoritarian exercise of power and the exclusion of formalized political opposition could not cope with the kind of pressures that exploded in May 1968. In its place the French bourgeoisie would move to instal a more modernized open, capitalist democracy in which an opposition would have a more important public role as an escape valve for complaints and protests that otherwise might build up again into explosive density.

Many of the young activists who had built the barricades in Paris or occupied the factories in May 1968 would stay loyal to the Marxist revolutionary groups that emerged at that time. Trotskyist and Maoist groups had a strong hold on those who had participated in the May events and those who wished they had and now wanted to make up for it. Trotskyist candidates standing in the 1974 presidential election received half a million votes, which indicates the level of support that existed. The vigour and presence of the ultra-Left in workplaces, educational establishments and in the streets was a factor that Socialist and Communist leaders had to take into account. Many of the 1968 generation, while retaining their political libertarianism, arrived at the conclusion that only a political party with mass electoral support could be an effective vehicle for achieving what they yearned for in those glorious days of May. One immediate beneficiary was the Unified Socialist Party which saw its membership nearly double between April and July 1968. The search for a new vision of Socialism based on younger new ideas and younger activists had already begun in the SFIO before 1968. In 1966, a group of young SFIO members had signed an appeal in which they described themselves as a new generation for whom Gaullism was already antiquated and the Fourth Republic an academic memory. Their object was to 'bring about the adhesion of new layers of French society to Socialism'. They criticized Mitterrand for being too obsessed with negotiating organizational unification and suggested that instead the Left should 'formulate in clear terms what it means to do if it gains power, what model of society it wants to lead us to and by what means it intends to achieve its ends'.

This call for clearly stated objectives had met with little response: as we have seen both the Federation and Communist Party concentrated more on manoeuvring for electoral gains. As the dust settled after the May events and the June elections, the problem of developing policies for the Left remained a pressing need. The Gaullist, or perhaps now one should say the Pompidou victory, in the National Assembly elections had not resolved the economic problems, nor would the continuing demands of students and other disadvantaged groups for reforms go away. Constitutional opposition to the government would remain as needed as ever.

Like most political groups who take a hammering at the polls, the French Left turned in upon itself and began a process of recrimination in the months following the June defeat. In August 1968 the Soviet tanks rolled into Prague and the French Communist Party was once again tarred with the brush of Soviet repression. Waldeck-Rochet had flown to Moscow and begged Brezhnev on behalf of all the West European Communist Parties not to suppress the Dubcek experiment in reform Communism, but as in 1947, 1956 and in Poland in 1981, the domestic consequences in France or Italy of Communist intervention in East Europe counted for little in Moscow. The French Communist

Party Political Bureau was split over what reaction to adopt towards the arrival of Russian tanks in Prague – there was still a hard core of Stalinists in the Communist leadership, and in the end the French Communist Party decided that it 'disapproved' of the Soviet invasion. The word 'condemn' or 'denounce' could not be forced from its lips. The choice of verb was by the way as the French Right, Centre, Left and far-Left swept into attack against Communist behaviour, East and West. Although few made the explicit connection, the fact that Mitterrand was the chief advocate of a United Left based on collaboration with the Communists and had established his Socialist credentials as the architect of the Federation-Communist 'common platform' meant that the tide of anti-Communism washed in part over his defeated and dejected figure. For Mitterrand the answer was to speed up the process of forming an homogeneous Socialist Party out of the three sections of the Federation of the Left. He made this call at the Congress of the Convention of Republican Institutions in October 1968 where he told delegates: 'The Federation of the Left has suffered a defeat. They suffer much more from their incapacity to heal the wound they received than from the blow itself.' But the Convention Congress was more interested in a post mortem on the June defeat and Mitterrand had to sit through some bitter attacks on his behaviour in May. The next month Mitterrand resigned as leader of the Federation of the Left and sat back working on a new book while Gaston Deferre and other SFIO leaders tried to get what they called a Social Democratic Party off the ground.

One SFIO veteran, Gaston Deferre, was still haunted by the search for the elusive centrist formation. Deferre's chance to put his conception to the test came in April 1969, when de Gaulle was defeated in a referendum on reforming regional organization and the Senate. As usual de Gaulle had threatened to resign if the referendum went against his wishes. This time it did, as his reforms angered people right across the political spectrum. After the May events and with a competent and efficient Pompidou waiting to take over, de Gaulle was no longer indispensable. De Gaulle quietly stepped down and the different groups began casting round for candidates. Pompidou was the obvious Gaullist choice. The Communists suggested Mitterrand and another united left-wing campaign as in 1965. The SFIO rejected this. There would be no link-up with the Communists. Mollet was thought to favour Alain Poher, the popular if politically colourless President of the Senate who became acting President of the Republic on de Gaulle's resignation. Deferre, whose Rhone Estuary section of the SFIO continued to be the most important element in the party, pushed himself forward and was chosen as the SFIO candidate against the wishes of Mollet, who took the occasion to retire. To the Communist Party, Deferre was unacceptable as the standard-bearer of the Left, and they decided to run as candidate one of their veteran leaders, Jacques Duclos. The far Left ran two candidates, the Trotskyist Alain Krivine while the Unified Socialist Party put forward their General Secretary, Michel Rocard.

The thirty-nine-year-old Rocard was a brilliant economist and civil servant who had served in the prestigious Finance Inspectorate. His Socialism dated from student campaigning against the Algerian war. He had been a mainstay along with Alain Savary in the Unified Socialist Party from its inception in 1960. After Savary rejoined the SFIO, Rocard took over as General Secretary. He worked closely with the advocates of workers' self-management in the CFDT and supported the new political issues like ecology and women's rights. But his left radicalism was always tempered by his direct personal knowledge of the inner workings of the state machine; passionate for well worked out, economically feasible reforms, Rocard had become increasingly irritated by the utopian revolutionaries who flocked to his party during the May events. Standing for President, especially with its television exposure, would give him a national standing and meant he could distance himself from the more extreme elements in his own party.

The presidential election also saw the last significant appearance of Pierre Mendès-France on the political stage. Mendès-France agreed to run with Deferre as the future Prime Minister under a Deferre presidency. The most popular of France's left-wing politicians who had spurned Communist support when invested as Prime Minister in 1954 was now embarking on his last attempt to seek electoral success without Communist Party involvement. Deferre and Mendès-France did not expect to beat

Pompidou but they hoped to gain more votes than the Communist Duclos and open the way to a viable non-Communist grouping of the Left and its Centre allies. Mitterrand played no part in the campaign save to warn Michel Rocard against being manipulated by television. It must have been with grim satisfaction that he heard the results of the first round. They were disastrous for Deferre and Mendès-France. Deferre received only 5.01% of the votes while Duclos received 21.52%, thus demonstrating the bedrock Communist vote, one-fifth of the electorate, which could not be dislodged from the Communist Party.

Pompidou won the run-off with Poher but not as comfortably as he would have liked. Pompidou campaigned as the faithful inheritor of de Gaulle's tradition, though hard-line Gaullists blamed Pompidou for the General's failure in the referendum – during it Pompidou had announced he would be available as a candidate to succeed de Gaulle and many voters accordingly plucked up courage to ditch the old man. But Pompidou had little of the appeal of de Gaulle's historic universality and failed to pick up de Gaulle's working-class vote. (42% of French industrial workers voted for de Gaulle in 1965: Pompidou could only win 29% of the industrial workers' votes in 1969.) Pompidou had welcomed the support of Giscard d'Estaing and his Independent Republican Party even though Giscard's internationalist, business-oriented political philosophy was at odds with the Gaullist tradition of national grandeur and a centralized state. Pompidou was a banker and had to secure himself through various political concessions with a wide range of right-wing political forces. De Gaulle could afford to disdain such politicking but with his disappearance the homogeneous Gaullist bloc quickly unglued itself. Although the Right were to hold power throughout the 1970s one would see a curious inversion, with the Right becoming more divided and internally antagonistic while the Left came together, at least until 1978, to present a reasonably cohesive front.

While the Left contemplated the disaster of the 1969 presidential election, Mitterrand brought out a book, *My Part of the Truth*, which marked a significant development in his political position. In it he openly embraced Marxist concepts, though he admitted that he had never made a detailed study of Marx; instead he had picked up elements of materialist analysis from reading extracts of Marx or from the books and articles by the new school of French political scientists who were rediscovering Marx. His 'intellectual excitement' about Marxism came, he wrote, from observation of everyday life. 'That the exploitation of man by man is linked to social relationships determined by the mode of production is now evident to me,' he wrote. But he stressed that a simple materialistic explanation is not sufficient. A constant theme in the book is the demand for justice, which he considers to be the most important by-product of a Socialist society. His Socialism, he wrote, did not come from his family, nor from having been exploited as a wage-labourer in a factory, nor, even, from his wartime experiences. It developed in him little by little. Each time there was a great division in France, the bourgeoisie rallied behind the forces that would guarantee their privileges. The ruling class would hop from Pétain to de Gaulle or from de Gaulle to Pompidou and each time the mass of the population was denied the possibility of justice. In the meantime, he argued, France had become bewitched by the false belief that what was wrong was the particular political system used to govern the country. This was a mistake. The choice was not between a Fourth and a Fifth Republic: the choice was between capitalism and Socialism.

> For twenty-five years I have been looking at our society and I believed that under the pressure of competing interests there had been some progress. Now I have to admit that it amounts to nothing. The ruling, dominant class rules and dominates more than ever. Look beyond the dry statistics. A quarter of French families do not earn enough to pay for a municipally subsidized home. A fifth of the homes in Paris do not have running water. There is the sadness of the old and unemployment of the young. Look at the cultural segregation and the subservient position of women. All this has brought me to meet, to understand and finally to accept the idea of Socialism.

Another section of Mitterrand's book is devoted to an attack on East European Communism and the Soviet intervention in

Czechoslovakia but Mitterrand continued to insist that the future of the French Left lay in working with the French Communist Party. He explained why he believed the French Communist Party still kept its hold over 5 million voters.

In the last few months in my constituency of the Nièvre, fourteen shop stewards have been dismissed for trying to set up union branches at work. Attempts to protect these people are brushed aside by employers whose belief in their divine right to rule has not changed in a hundred years despite what Paris sociologists believe. Low wages, factory closures, unemployment, strikes, slums, evictions, high rents, the exodus from the countryside to the overcrowded cities, an unfair tax system, the growing misery of exploited peasant farmers, the anger and weariness of young people confront an indifferent state in no hurry to put into effect its promised reforms or to create new relationships at work. Can one imagine the weight of worry that hangs over our people? One cannot be, at one and the same time, on the side of exploiters and the exploited. At the political level the Communist Party declares its willingness to fight and shows a solidarity in struggle which the other left-wing parties do not display: in fact, sometimes they work hand in hand with the powers that be. Communism is weak in Great Britain, Sweden, Denmark, Belgium and Holland. The proletariat in those countries votes for the Social Democrats or the Labour Party while the French pro-letariat votes Communist. That is no accident. Workers will support those who support them.

The book is far from strident class politics. In the first section he describes his youth and is positively elegiac about the French countryside in which he grew up. Mitterrand the man with roots in the soil of provincial France was now making his first studied self-revelations and it would be an image he would increasingly cultivate. His love and knowledge of rural France is genuine but the rural, pastoral, often melancholic, Mitterrand softened the contours of the abrasive Socialist Mitterrand. He makes appropriate noises about pollution and ecology but argues, 'a belief in Socialism cannot be separated from advanced industrial development. A Socialist government must be as capable as a capitalist government in achieving growth and expansion.' He also began the process of changing his position on France's nuclear weapons, advancing two arguments for his turnaround. Firstly de Gaulle's nuclear policy had been endorsed at successive elections and therefore was clearly the democratic choice of the French people. Secondly, the Soviet invasion of Czechoslovakia showed that the superpowers still behaved as if the Yalta agreement permitted them to do what they liked in their own sphere of influence. The foreign and defence policy of France was independent and separate from that of Washington and Moscow. To maintain that independence, France would, regrettably, have to keep the strongest weapon available.

The book appeared at just the right time. The mistake that Mitterrand had made in May 1968 seemed trivial compared with the humiliation of Deferre and the Left in 1969. Mitterrand's consistent argument that only an alliance with the Communists made sense was now the only alternative for the Left. Shortly after the presidential defeat, a SFIO Congress was held and the SFIO officially changed its name to the Socialist Party. The new Socialist Party proclaimed that 'the Union of the Left would from now on be the principal basis of a Socialist strategy.' A new First Secretary, Alain Savary, was elected in place of Guy Mollet. Savary was an efficient, precise economist who had resigned from the Mollet government in 1956 in protest at Mollet's Algerian policy. He had helped set up the Unified Socialist Party but had moved back to the SFIO as a protégé of Mollet. Discreet, unflamboyant and an indifferent speaker in front of either large crowds or small groups, Savary was a good organizer who swiftly got hold of the party and started getting rid of regional chiefs who had been in place since the war and, in some cases, longer. By 1971 he had replaced more than half the Federal Secretaries with much younger people.

As Savary was setting about reorganizing the Socialist Party, Mitterrand and the Convention of Republican Institutions were keeping their distance. Mitterrand called the new party 'the ex-SFIO' and said it was a 'hundred years old before it was born'. The period between 1969 and 1971 was one of manoeuvre as Mitterrand bided his time until the political moment was right to seek a fusion with the new Socialist Party. He spent the period busily captivating the grass roots of the Left, aiming his speeches and articles at both those who had entered political activity after or as a result of the May events and those whose attitudes had been completely shaken up by May 1968 and the Left's defeat in the 1969 presidential election.

Mitterrand is not a conventional political work addict in the sense that he always seems to have time for a good lunch or dinner, keeps up with the latest novels and will find the odd couple of hours to see a new Hollywood thriller. But he had a tirelessness in tramping around the country preaching his beliefs and putting himself in contact with his supporters and those he hoped to convert to the Mitterrand cause. Now after the summer break in 1969 he worked his way round France talking to small meetings, opening summer fairs, conducting weekend seminars, always preaching the need for a Union of the Left.

On the surface, there was no division between his position on left unity and that of Savary. The latter accepted the principle but wanted a lengthy ideological debate with the Communist Party and sought to get the French Communists to put down on paper assurances about political democracy and liberty and to promise publicly that they would voluntarily surrender power if a left government were to lose an election. Even after six weeks of discussion in 1970 between representatives of the Socialist and Communist parties on a possible common programme, Savary took a look at the proposed text, announced it was 'too Marxist', re-wrote it, and put it in a pigeon-hole. The difficulties with the Communist Party were exacerbated by a power battle for the leadership after Waldeck-Rochet had fallen incurably ill, his breakdown caused by the festering divisions inside his Party over the Communist handling of the May events and the invasion of Czechoslovakia. The winner was Georges Marchais, the Communist Party's organization chief, whose main aim was to take the Communist Party out of its political ghetto. Marchais could display a Stalinist ruthlessness inside the Party while outside he put on a façade of Eurocommunist pluralism. Or, he could just as easily invert the roles and become a political bully in public and a conciliator within the Party depending on his estimation (often mistaken) of the balance and direction of political forces inside the Party, and in French politics as a whole. The aftermath of 1968 had led, in 1970, to the expulsion of Roger Garaudy, a leading Communist intellectual and member of the Political Bureau. Garaudy had tried to get the Communist Party to embrace some of the currents unleashed in the May events and to condemn the Soviet suppression of Dubcek's attempt at reform Communism. To secure his succession to Waldeck-Rochet, Marchais could not afford to lose the support of the Stalinist, workerist wing of the Party leadership and Garaudy was sacrificed to appease the hard-liners. This may have made life more difficult for those in the Socialist Party advocating the fullest partnership with the Communists but Marchais would always put the interests of the Party and his position within it (like most political leaders, he tended to think the two were identical) before the need to worry about upsetting Socialist sensibilities.

If such Communist behaviour strengthened Savary's preference for a cautious approach to negotiating an agreement with the Communist Party, it did not stop Mitterrand from calling for a 'contract of government' between the Socialist Party and the Communists. Despite the unease at Communist illiberalism, the rank and file of the Left wanted unity at almost any price. The municipal elections were due to be held in March 1971 and to defeat the Right, Socialists and Communists would have once again to promise mutual second-round voting support. In 1973 there would be the legislative elections and the message of 1965, 1967, 1968 and 1969 was obvious. United, the Left did well; divided they stood no chance. Whatever flickering hopes that right-wing SFIO old-timers like Gaston Deferre had for a non-Communist re-alignment disappeared when the Radical Party, the third partner in the old Federation of the Left, broke apart in 1970. The Radical Party's new chairman, the brilliant polemical journalist Jean-Jacques Servan-Schreiber (or JJSS as he was known in France) had issued a manifesto calling for massive public investment in the framework of a deregulated market economy. But the ideological principle underpinning the Servan-Schreiber manifesto (modestly entitled *Between Heaven and Earth*) was outright opposition to nationalization in any form. Servan-Schreiber had been elected a deputy for Nancy after a highly publicized campaign and already had major successes in the media behind him with the launch and development of *L'Express* and the publication in 1967 of his best-selling *The American Challenge* which argued that French and European industry and markets were now being taken over by American companies and which called for a fight-back against this trans-Atlantic financial colonization.

Like others swept along with some genuinely good ideas and the enthusiastic support of the mass media, Servan-Schreiber believed he could bring about radical re-alignment in French politics. He took his wing of the Radical Party and merged it with the Democratic Centre of Jean Lecanuet, who last appeared when he came third after de Gaulle and Mitterrand in the 1965 presidential election. Then Lecanuet was the candidate of the centrist Christian Democratic Popular Republic Movement. He and Servan-Schreiber co-existed for a while miserably watching their longed-for Centre shrink in face of a growing Left and a growing Right. Both made their peace in due course with the Right, Lecanuet becoming a minister in Giscard's government after 1974. JJSS, true to his headline-grabbing style, remained a Giscard minister for a fortnight, leaving after he had made some critical remarks about France's nuclear programme. The half of the Radical Party that stayed true to the Left re-named itself the Radical Movement of the Left and would stay as a minor independent party, taking up regional and environmental issues with some flair but generally situating itself under the mantle of the Socialist Party. The Radical Party split served to confirm the trend towards a more solidified Left in French politics.

In 1970, Mitterrand published a short book called *The Socialism of the Possible* which brought together the arguments he had been advancing since de Gaulle's disappearance.

We must define a Socialism that is possible. Socialism is the science of or the scientific approach towards existing economic, and social facts in a given place, at a given time. If Socialism proposes methods inappropriate to the level of evolution of a country it claims to reform and lead, or a Socialism that is contrary to a country's civilization and customs, then a Socialism like that will be utopian and counter-productive.

A key mechanism for introducing Socialism was increased public domination of the growing number of industrial, commercial and financial monopolies. But public ownership under modern Socialism should be qualitatively different from the immediate post-war nationalizations: 'The nationalizations such as were carried out in 1945 did not fundamentally change the worker's status. The worker only exchanged one boss for another. That is why in changing the nature of state ownership it is necessary to go further in the direction of co-determination and self-management.'

Having attempted to lay down some kind of theoretical basis for what he believed French Socialism in the 1970s should be, Mitterrand proceeded to take over the vehicle for turning the theory into practice, the Socialist Party. Although the SFIO had re-named itself the Socialist Party and had a new First Secretary, the lively Convention of Republican Institutions remained separate and outside the party. Inside the Socialist Party the powerful regional federations around Marseilles and Lille continued to operate as independent fiefdoms. Officially in retirement, Guy Mollet nevertheless exercised a considerable influence over his successor, Alain Savary, and each evening one of Savary's assistants went to see Mollet to report on the day's events. Neither Gaston Deferre who headed the Rhone Estuary Federation based in Marseilles nor Pierre Mauroy who was joint chief of the Northern Federation based in Lille had much love for Savary and behind him, Mollet. For Deferre, Mollet was one of those who had scuppered his presidential bid in 1964 and had tried to stop him running in 1969. Mauroy, a solid, capable right-winger, had long been considered Mollet's successor as First Secretary and had been surprised and hurt when Mollet handed the post to Savary. Mauroy had been impressed by Mitterrand's leadership of the Federation of the Left between 1965 and 1968. Mitterrand developed his contacts with the two men partly to sound them out on their attitude towards a fusion of the Socialist Party with the Convention and partly to see if they would back him as a candidate to replace Savary. The response was positive on both counts. The fact that Mitterrand, who by now was seen as a leading French Socialist, had never been a member of the SFIO was inestimably to his advantage. He had never played a part in the internal fights of SFIO and although he had few passionate supporters inside the party, he, unlike Savary, had few dedicated enemies. As so often in political life, the lack of enemies was to weigh heavier than the presence of friends.

In the summer of 1971, the Socialist Party and the Convention agreed to hold a unity Congress at Epinay just outside Paris. The merger had already been worked out; everyone knew the real fight would be the election for the post of First Secretary in the new enlarged Socialist Party. Mitterrand had the votes of the Convention plus votes from Deferre and Mauroy which together added up to nearly half the delegates. To find the extra votes that would clinch his takeover, he turned to the left-wing CERES* group. CERES had been founded a few years previously by young intellectuals anxious to move the SFIO to the left. It had come into its own after 1968 under the able direction of Jean-Pierre Chevènement, author of a pamphlet, *Social-Mediocrity*, which attacked the dominant reformist currents in the SFIO. The young, more class-conscious activists who joined up as Socialists after 1968 gravitated towards CERES. The party leadership regarded CERES with distaste and in 1971 Savary ordered a commission of enquiry into CERES. Chevènement therefore went to the Epinay Congress uncertain as to what the future of CERES would be if Savary were to continue as party leader.

It was this unusual alliance of two right-wingers, Deferre and Mauroy, with the left-wing Chevènement, that was to help Mitterrand to victory at Epinay. The issue was always in the balance, however, throughout the three days of the Congress. The first test came with a row over voting procedure. Savary wanted a simple proportional representation system which would have ensured a majority for his position. Chevènement successfully argued for the right of the main tendencies in the party to be represented in the party's collective leadership. Savary's defeat indicated the shift of mood away from the old leadership amongst 1,000 delegates. Mollet sat glumly on the platform watching his beloved party cast away its old SFIO coverings and don strange new clothes. The decision to protect

*CERES – Centre d'Etudes, de Recherches et d'Education Socialistes (The Centre for Research, Studies and Socialist Education)

140

the right of each main tendency to have seats in the party leadership committee was attacked at the time as a return to a sort of Fourth Republic politics inside the Socialist Party – everyone being guaranteed a little portion of power. In fact, the system of automatic representation for tendencies helped strengthen the Socialist Party in the 1970s. No single group within the party felt totally shut out, even if it was unable to be represented at the highest level. As in all broad-based political parties, there would be policy divisions, dominant factions, changing alliances, majorities and minorities but there was an acceptance, if sometimes grudging, of the right of tendencies to exist and be represented within the party leadership.

The key vote on who would take over as party leader depended on the amount of support for the two main motions put forward by the Mitterrand and Savary camps. Mitterrand's speech in support of his motion was a masterpiece of seduction and Socialist fervour. He told the delegates that they were pioneers who, after sixty-five years of searching for Socialism, could now construct a Socialist France. There were kind words for those who believed in Marxism and for those who preferred the Church as a source of inspiration. 'We are here to conquer power but only after we have won over the minds of our fellow citizens.' The Socialist Party had to win over those who currently supported Communist, ultra-left or liberal positions. 'What shall we go for? Reform or revolution? For me, the daily struggle for a complete reform of existing structures is of a revolutionary nature. This presupposes a rupture and I have to say that anyone who does not accept a rupture with the established order, with capitalist society, cannot be a member of the Socialist Party.'

Mitterrand put himself forward as a committed believer in the Union of the Left with the Communists. The time had come to stop the endless search for clarification of ideological differences and get on with drawing up a Common Programme. 'What we have to overturn is the power of the monopolies, by which I mean the power of capital which corrupts people, buys people, destroys people, kills people, ruins people and which can rot the conscience of mankind.' The answer, Mitterrand told delegates, was to 'base ourselves on a class front'.

It was his most explicitly left-wing pronouncement so far. But it was more than quasi-Marxist rhetoric. The essence of Mitterrand's speech was the offer of both the pursuit of power and the means – Left Unity – to achieve it. The final vote was narrow and Mitterrand scraped through with a majority of 51%. Only a few days before the unity Congress at Epinay Mitterrand had received his card as a member of the Socialist Party. Three days after it finished he moved into the Paris headquarters of the Socialist Party as its First Secretary. The party and the man had come together.

11
The Common Programme and the Union of the Left

Nationalization does not equal Socialism:
but it is the key to changing the power
structure in France.

Once installed at the Socialist Party headquarters in Paris, Mitterrand proceeded to shake up the party organization. He brought with him close collaborators from the Convention and gave Jean-Pierre Chevènement the task of developing a Socialist Party programme. He continued the process already started by Savary of replacing old regional stalwarts with younger men. New sections were launched for students and youth. Mitterrand's first public statement after becoming First Secretary confirmed his keynote Epinay speech. The Socialist Party would keep left. "The Socialist Party will be present in all the areas where people are struggling against capitalist exploitation.'

At first Mitterrand wanted to install Pierre Mauroy as the organizational and administrative head of the party, the idea being to leave Mitterrand free of the day-to-day running of the party and able to concentrate on thinking, writing and political activity. Mitterrand saw himself as the party leader in rather the fashion of the leader of the British Labour Party, with someone else handling party administration. Mauroy refused the offer. He

143

did not want to leave his power base around Lille and with the shrewdness of someone who had served as a SFIO *apparatchik* since his time as head of its youth section in the 1950s, Mauroy knew that it would be important for Mitterrand to keep a firm grip on party administration.

Mitterrand had arrived as head of the party without his own constituency inside it. The distribution of power and the internal influence within a political party lies in the amount of control one has over apparently minor questions – the appointment of an official, the allocation of cash to a particular project, who gets put on a working party or committee – and Mitterrand, though he never came to enjoy fully day-to-day administration, learnt to use his position as party chief to nourish the roots of his own implantation in the Socialist Party. He had, after all, earned a reputation as skilled political manipulator during the Fourth Republic.

The arrival of Mitterrand and his commitment to left-wing policies quickly proved successful in terms of membership. The Socialist Party had 56,000 members at the Epinay Congress. Six months later, the figure stood at 80,300. Shortly after taking over as party leader, Mitterrand went to Chile to meet Salvador Allende who was presiding over the first Latin American government elected democratically through the ballot box on a Marxist programme. Mitterrand returned to France saying that life in Chile was 'perfectly free' and he praised Allende's nationalization measures which, he said, had been carried out within the framework of Chile's constitution.

At the beginning of 1972, the Socialist Party presented a draft programme for discussion at all levels of the party. On each of the main issues; nationalization, workers' control, defence, Europe, constitutional reform, there was a majority and minority opinion put forward from the Socialist Party's working groups which had been in action since Epinay. It was a fresh way of encouraging political debate, though the majority line indicated the leadership's thinking and provided the necessary guidance for party activists who wanted or needed direction from the top. The programme was adopted at a special congress in March 1972 but everyone was waiting for the start of negotiations with the Communist Party on drawing up a Common Programme. The

Communists had published their own programme in October 1971, which stressed an acceptance of a multi-party system and of the alternation of governments. There remained the well-known differences between the two parties and the French population waited to see how these would be composed. But before serious discussions between the two parties could begin, President Pompidou announced a referendum on the question of allowing Britain to join the Common Market. On the face of it, Pompidou's referendum proposal was rather strange. None of the other member countries saw any need to ask their people whether or not Britain should join. It was rather a decision for the British people and their government and the member states of the EEC. Secondly, every opinion poll in France showed strong support for the Common Market and Pompidou knew that he would get a 'Yes' vote in any EEC referendum. The real reason for Pompidou's suddenly announced referendum was to try and split the strongly pro-EEC Socialist Party from the equally strongly anti-EEC Communist Party. Both Mitterrand and Marchais saw the trap, which by the standards of Pompidou's normally more subtle political abilities was crude and obvious, and the two Left leaders neatly sidestepped it. The Communist Party called for a 'No' vote. The Socialist Party condemned the referendum as irrelevant and while welcoming British entry, called for a massive abstention. The abstainers won. Nearly half the electorate did not bother to vote or spoiled their ballot papers and although Pompidou got his endorsement the whole referendum exercise was considered a waste of time and a demonstration of the lack of grip and judgement inside the Elysée. The campaign was hardly a Left victory but it did show that Socialists and Communists could live together despite a major policy difference on which neither was ready to make concessions.

As soon as the referendum campaign was over, the Socialist and Communist Parties got back to discussing the formulation of a Common Programme. Both parties wanted to have a signed and sealed pact as soon as possible. The 1973 legislative elections were approaching and both Mitterrand and Marchais knew that to go into the elections without a formal commitment to unity would be disastrous. Each leader was still relatively new in his post (Marchais was only acting General Secretary of the Communist Party while Waldeck-Rochet was dying) and a successful conclusion of a Common Programme would be a signal achievement that each could claim to have brought about for his party. For the Communists, a Common Programme agreed with the Socialists would provide their official passport out of the political ghetto to which they had been consigned since 1947. To sign such an accord with the Socialists would be to prove to France and to the rest of Europe that the French Communist Party was acknowledged as a fit partner for government. In workplaces and community organizations, Communist militants were under continuing pressure from ultra-left militants and groups spawned after 1968. Apart from ideological attacks, the main thrust of the ultra-Left's criticism of the Communist Party was that it was locked in its Stalinist past and had neither the political imagination nor the democratic flexibility to bring about a Socialist transformation in France. The Communist Party, which since the 1930s monopolized the classic hard Left of the French political spectrum, was irritated almost beyond endurance by the success and flair of these ultra-left attacks. It was a new and uncomfortable experience for the Communist Party to be attacked from the left. The success of the left-wing criticism of the Communist Party was rooted in the political vacuum on the Left that had developed since 1968. The 1968 and 1969 elections had soured many young people's belief in the parliamentary road to Socialism. One slogan of the time had been: 'No to de Gaulle, No to Mitterrand. Power to the people.' Agreeing a Common Programme with the newly revived Socialist Party would wrest back the initiative to the mainstream parties who would be seen as launching a new dynamic against Pompidou's right-wing state.

The Socialist Party also had reasons other than securing Mitterrand's position and the imperative of a pre-election pact for wanting to conclude a Common Programme with the Communists as soon as possible. Because it could only be through the Communist Party that the Socialists would gain access to the French working class. None of the Socialist deputies was a worker and there were no working-class representatives in the party's national leadership. The Socialist Party had less than 200 workplace sections compared with the thousands of Communist

146

workplace cells. The Communist Party still formally considered itself a 'revolutionary' party and at that time still retained a reference to 'establishing the dictatorship of the proletariat' in its constitution. Despite the increasingly left-wing, at times almost Marxist tone of Socialist Party pronouncements, its social base was largely middle-class, and although Socialist candidates would pick up transferred votes from the working class in the second round of elections, the plain fact was that for the vast majority of the industrial working class their first choice of a political party to support was the Communist Party. Hardly any of the CERES group nor the post-May 1968 activists who were pushing the Socialist Party to the left came from the working class, and there was an obvious and embarrassing gap between the Socialist Party's proletarian rhetoric and its social composition. Signing a Common Programme with the Communists would organically link the Socialists with the French working class and begin the process of identifying the Socialist Party as a defender of working-class rights.

After only six weeks of negotiations between Socialist and Communist representatives, a draft ninety-page programme was drawn up. On many key questions – staying as members of the EEC and the Atlantic Alliance, the Communists had accepted the Socialist position. The big differences that remained – nationalization, France's nuclear strike force and workers' control – could only be solved by a face-to-face meeting between the two party leaders. On the night of 27/28 1972 June, Mitterrand and Marchais together with eight colleagues each from their respective party leaderships sat down to try and compose their differences. The Communists arrived with a long list of firms to be nationalized to be met by a sarcastic Gaston Deferre who told them they were no longer living in the 1930s and that what France needed now was workers' control and not more state takeovers. As the night wore on, the two sides came to an agreement on nationalizing nine major industrial corporations which dominated the arms, chemical, electronics, computer, pharmaceutical, and textile industries in France. It did not go as far as the Communist Party wished but it still remained the largest package of nationalizations ever proposed by a European opposition for more than twenty years. The main firms of the industries listed in the 1972

Common Programme were to be those taken over when the Socialists came to power in 1981. A compromise was patched together on nationalizing the steel industry. It was agreed that the state would buy a majority of the equity without taking it into full public ownership.

The second big difference was over defence policy and the retention of the French nuclear strike force. Officially both parties were opposed to nuclear weapons, though the Socialist Party wanted the problem of unilateral French nuclear disarmament to be handled in the context of multilateral negotiations. The Communists insisted that all French nuclear weapon stocks be immediately destroyed. Mitterrand rejected this, telling Marchais: 'I will not go down in history as the person responsible for leaving France unarmed in a world which is not.' The Common Programme itself promised a halt to any further development of the French nuclear strike force and the conversion of the nuclear arms industry to peaceful use. In five years, the Communists were to change their position dramatically and enthusiastically embrace the French nuclear deterrent, a switch of policy that would have great implications for the Left.

On two other issues, the Socialist Party refused to make any concessions to the Communists. The latter had wanted the automatic dissolution of the National Assembly following a decision by one of the partners to leave the government and join with the opposition parties in winning a censure motion against the government. For Mitterrand this was simply a trap which would permit the Communists to pick and choose when to bring down a Left Union government. Mitterrand rejected the Communist proposal; the constitution would not be changed in the direction wished by the Communists and the President would retain the right to nominate another Prime Minister who could try to form a new government should there be a successful passage of a censure motion.

Again, it was an important victory for Mitterrand. Despite the fact that the Communist Party was still polling more votes than the Socialists (or the old Federation of the Left), he had manoeuvred the Communists into accepting the role of junior partner in the new union. Every media commentator and many old SFIO stalwarts in the Socialist Party were waiting to portray the Socialists as prisoners of the Communists. They wanted to be able to say the Common Programme was an example of the Communist tail wagging the Socialist dog. On the question of workers' control, the Socialist Party was ready to be more adventurous than the Communists and lean farther towards the new left-wing currents inside the trade unions. The Common Programme stated that the Socialist Party advocated workers' self-management while the Communist Party restricted itself to wanting to see the development of a 'democratic management' of workplaces. The terminology was opaque but the message was clear. The Socialists wanted to give more power to the workers, the Communists wanted to place factory managers under increased state control.

Finally at five in the morning, the two parties put their signatures to the Common Programme. For the first time since the 1920 Congress of Tours when rank and file militants had left the SFIO to form the French Communist Party, there was an agreed set of left-wing policies that united the main opposition forces. It was a serious, well worked out programme that was rooted in French problems and needs. It reflected the desire for change: even an inveterate opponent of both the Socialist and Communist Parties, the Trotskyist leader, Alain Krivine, said that the Common Programme proved 'there are new stirrings in the working class; however one looks at it, the Common Programme is the result of the working class's fighting spirit'.

Despite the welcome by the Left for the Common Programme and the feeling inside both parties that a momentous step had been taken, neither Mitterrand nor Marchais had any illusions that the ideological differences and political ambitions that separated their respective parties had been ironed out. Two days after the signing of the Common Programme, Marchais addressed a secret session of the Communist Party's Central Committee. His remarks were not revealed until 1975: they would have caused a sensation had they been published at the time. 'We have never lost sight of our partner's real nature,' Marchais told his Central Committee.

The Socialist Party represents, as an organization, the reformist social-democratic trend, as all its past history in

France shows. Its permanent aspects have not been obliterated by the Epinay Congress. . . We are not interested in ideological synthesis. . . We do not look for that; we would not welcome it in the present state of the Socialist Party. . . Now that the Common Programme has been agreed, our Party will loyally respect its terms . . . but it will be necessary to watch very closely and always to safeguard our Party's true position, its independence of thought, of action, and to work for greater organizational influence.

While Marchais was making these private observations to his party leadership, Mitterrand was going on the record in just as blunt a way about his intention to reduce Communist Party influence in France. The day after putting his signature on the Common Programme, Mitterrand flew to Vienna for a meeting of the Socialist International Executive Committee on which he sat along with other European Socialist leaders like Willy Brandt, Harold Wilson, Bruno Kreisky and Olof Palme. Mitterrand tried to set their minds at ease about this formal link-up with the French Communist Party: after all, most of the other Socialist leaders had established reputations as committed anti-Communists and entering into a formal electoral and policy alliance with their Communist Parties was unthinkable. Mitterrand told them: 'Our basic objective is to rebuild a great Socialist Party on the terrain occupied by the Communist Party itself and thus to show that of five million Communist voters, three million can be brought to vote Socialist.' It was a candid enough statement, honest to the point of being reckless. The Communist newspaper, *L'Humanité*, published Mitterrand's remarks and added that they showed that the Socialist Party leadership 'had refused to abandon class collaboration'. In a sense both leaders were reassuring their supporters that the Common Programme did not mean a merging of ideological values. Both were reasonably honest in what they wanted to get out of it – the Communists looked for political respectability, even acceptability in what remained a capitalist bourgeois democracy; the Socialist Party wanted to be taken as a party fit to be considered an authentic representative of the working class.

This curiously ambivalent relationship continued throughout

the five-year life of the Common Programme and in the period afterwards, during which Mitterrand insisted that he would stand by the policy provisions contained in it despite pressure from the right wing of the Socialist Party to renege on the Common Programme. Both Socialists and Communists sniped at each other and made statements designed to underline the separate identity of the two partners who had signed the Common Programme. An easy way for Mitterrand to assert the gap between his party and the Communists was to bring up questions about the Soviet Union's domestic or foreign policy. Two months after signing the Common Programme, Mitterrand wrote to the Soviet ambassador in Paris criticizing the treatment of Soviet Jews in Russia. A few days beforehand, he had announced that the Socialist Party would sponsor an international conference on Czechoslovakia. Mitterrand launched both initiatives at a time when all French politicians were quietly finishing their summer holidays and there was no political news about. He thus ensured maximum coverage for both initiatives which would clearly embarrass the Soviet and Czechoslovakian governments and their supporters, of whom there were many, in the French Communist Party. The Soviet ambassador's angry reply to Mitterrand – he accused him of trying 'to stir up artificially created issues' – and Moscow's decision to cancel a trip that Mitterrand was due to make to Russia showed how much they resented his continued public criticism of East European and Russian illiberality. The French public received the message in a different way. They knew that what Mitterrand was doing was sending out signals that the Common Programme did not mean the Socialist Party was in any way willing to accept moves towards a one-party state.

At the same time as marking his distance with the Communists, Mitterrand was enthusiastically campaigning for the Common Programme. Several joint meetings were held with Georges Marchais and with the leaders of the two main trade-union confederations. Leaving the problem of East Europe to one side, activists from the Socialist and Communist Parties found they shared the same analysis of the failures of contemporary French capitalism and could energetically work together in grass-roots campaigns against the government. It was a period of enthusi-

151

asm. Both parties substantially increased their membership and there was a new drive such as the French Left had not witnessed since the immediate post-war period. Mitterrand warned against placing all hopes in the Common Programme. Addressing a giant meeting in support of the Common Programme in Paris in December 1972, he told the crowd: 'Despite the Common Programme, despite our common will, we will not change our lives unless each one of us as individuals is willing to take responsibility for what we do and is willing to share responsibility for others.' In interviews with journalists, Mitterrand stressed that he was ready to govern with the Communists. He argued that the visits of President Nixon to Moscow and Peking, the de-Stalinization of the Soviet Communist Party following its twentieth Congress, the arrival of peaceful co-existence between the West and the East, Willy Brandt's *Ostpolitik* and the enthusiasm for détente, had ushered in a new era in which the French Communist Party had the right to the fullest participation in the country's political life. International détente should extend to détente inside France. He always refused to be drawn on which ministries would be given to Communists in the event of a victory for the Union of the Left in the forthcoming elections. But the two parties were linked together in the Common Programme which presupposed a joint action both before and after the election.

A contract is a contract. It contains reciprocal guarantees. Those the Socialist Party had demanded concern all French people: party plurality, democratic freedoms, and allowing government to alternate between parties. The Communist Party, which is often unfairly attacked, has the right to count on the good faith of Socialists. We have not signed an agreement between two parties waiting to be duped and we have no intention of duping our partners. That being said, the Communists remain Communists, and the Socialists remain Socialists, as we are constantly repeating. Neither they nor we changed our philosophy in signing the Common Programme. We are linked by the Programme in what it says, not in what it does not say. Happily, it says a good deal of things.

Mitterrand developed his defence of the Common Programme in a new book published early in 1973. *The Rose in the Fist* (the title comes from the French Socialist Party's symbol of a fist clenching a red rose, later adopted as the symbol of the Socialist International) was designed as Mitterrand's personal manifesto for the National Assembly elections and is a forthright political essay written over the four months following the signing of the Common Programme. He explained that it was a programme of government to be phased in over five years. He skimmed over the main provisions of the programme – the raising of the minimum wage, the reduction of the working week, the lowering of the age of retirement, equal pay for women, decentralization of state power and devolution to the regions, the introduction of a Supreme Court and an ombudsman. This would be paid for by a reform of the tax system to increase the ratio between direct and indirect tax by introducing more effective corporation taxation systems, and by bringing in a capital gains tax and a modest wealth tax. According to international comparative studies, the gap between the very rich and the very poor in France was the widest of any in the advanced industrialized countries. Two thirds of state revenue was collected through indirect taxes such as VAT and bore most heavily on the shoulders of the poor. Salaried employees found it difficult to cheat on their taxes while small businessmen and shopkeepers were unable to match the ability of company directors to arrange their affairs so that up to 90% of their income could be declared as tax-free allowances. Worst offenders of all were the big companies which found so many loopholes in the French tax system that only 8% of French tax revenue came from the corporate sector.

As usual, Mitterrand returned to his favourite theme of individual liberty around the world. Again he condemned Czechoslovakia but he took his readers on a journalistically graphic tour of the torture, repression and murders taking place in countries like Argentina, Brazil, Greece, Iran, Uruguay, Uganda and the Central African Republic. We are right in France to condemn the political trials and imprisonments in Prague, he argued, but where was the same moral fervour and sense of outrage about crimes against political and human freedom in countries with which the Pompidou government continued to maintain cordial relations? Nearly one third of the book was devoted to a defence of the nationalization proposals in the Common Programme. In developing his arguments in favour of the wide-ranging nationalizations proposed by the two parties, Mitterrand was influenced by the theoretical work of Jean-Pierre Chevènement. The basic argument was not that nationalization was, in itself, a desirable objective but that the power of certain giant firms or groups of firms to control sectors of the French economy was now so great that only public ownership could ensure that this power was used in the interest of society as a whole.

Where you find ownership, there you find power. The big monopolies, the banks, the giant firms are our new masters. Take away their ownership, which allows a few dozen individuals to benefit at the expense of 50 million French people, and you take away their power. Power to dominate the state by the many pressures and blandishments that they exercise; power to dominate the market where they control the quantity, quality, value and type of goods produced and sold; power to control what we think or how we react to events by their ownership of the mass media and control of advertising. Nationalization does not equal Socialism. But it is the key instrument for changing the power structure which is sought not just by Socialists, but by all free men who want to remove the yoke of a system which is based on and which profits from the exploitation of man by man,

he wrote in *The Rose in the Fist*. By 1985, if the trend towards global cartelization continued on its existing trajectory, the world's major trading and industrial sectors would be under the control of just sixty private firms, three quarters of them American-owned. To offset this mushrooming multinational power, only the power of the state ready to take into public ownership certain dominant firms would be sufficient. In some areas, the argument for nationalization was based on different premises. In the armaments industry the money to support the highly profitable firms involved came from the public purse, in the form of arms contracts. As to export orders for the French arms industry Mitterrand produced several examples to prove that the French government and the private arms firms acted so closely together in the hunt for export orders that to distinguish between private and public interest was impossible. But it was the private firm that retained the profits made possible by state backing. In the pharmaceutical industry, profits for drugs companies were guaranteed through national insurance and social security payments. If the state was putting up the cash that provided such easy profits, surely the state could become the direct owner and retain the profits itself. In both industries there would be the added advantages in directly being able to channel arms and drugs production in the direction of more socially useful ends.

Since writing his justification for an extension of public ownership, Mitterrand's views have not changed. Hitherto, he had not shown a great deal of interest in the economic organization of society, but he was to remain a convinced advocate of greater public ownership even when the mood inside his own party started to shift away from seeing nationalization as a necessary, let alone sufficient objective for a Socialist government. There was (and arguably still is) one great gap in Mitterrand's explanation of why he believed in nationalization. That is, what new forms of management and direction of nationalized firms could be introduced to avoid public ownership simply meaning the exchange of a group of managers who cared little for the consumer or the workforce for a set of bureaucrats who cared just as little or even less. Mitterrand could point to the French electrical power industry or the Renault automobile company which were successful within a capitalist economy, but the workers in both industries were barely conscious that their lives were so very different because they worked for the state rather than for private enterprise. Mitterrand also stressed the Socialists' commitment to workers' self-management, though what this would mean in detailed practice was spelt out neither in his book nor in the Common Programme itself. In any case, workers' self-management was rejected by the Communist Party which regarded the concept as just another form of class collaboration.

Despite this shortcoming in Mitterrand's nationalization proposals, the most remarkable aspect of his lengthy argument in favour of increased public ownership is the force and enthusiasm with which he mounts his case. Elsewhere in the non-Communist European Left, nationalization had been largely dropped as a policy objective of European Socialism. In Britain at this time, Harold Wilson and Denis Healey were engaged in a successful battle to remove a commitment to widespread new public take-overs which radical Labour Party theoreticians wanted to include in the Labour Party programme. Even with those that remained, one had the impression that most of the Labour Party leadership did not believe any longer in public ownership. Voters are not fools. They can sense when there is a gap between what a party puts forward in its programme or manifesto and what party leaders are actually prepared to do on assuming office. Tradition has it that as an election approaches, party leaders start making more moderate speeches or produce reassuring interpretations of controversial aspects of party policy. This was not the case with Mitterrand. *The Rose in the Fist* is a hard, uncompromising Socialist call to arms. No one reading it could accuse Mitterrand of forsaking the Left.

The two parties fought the National Assembly elections in March 1973, with a new vigour arising from their coming together in what was now called the Union of the Left (the third small partner was the Movement of Left Radicals). Opinion polls early in 1973 had put the Socialists ahead of the Communists in the popular vote and had even predicted a majority for the Union of the Left.

Opening the campaign, Mitterrand swept aside bread-and-butter populism and returned to his favourite theme, the search for equality and liberty:

> For us, social justice is directly concerned with economic structures. Frenchmen are gradually becoming conscious of the structural causes of injustice. If the Left has still one more effort to make, it is to give them a clear perception of this. In fact, they are called upon to choose between a system of domination by a few privileged groups and a system of equality which people know the Left alone can promote, on the basis of continued growth. That is the issue. The rest is accessory. Only the Socialist Party is

proposing a synthesis between the struggle for equality and that for liberty.

Under Pompidou the Right quickly gathered their forces. They put together an umbrella organization under which Gaullists, Giscardian Independents and Lecanuet's Centre Democrats would run. Effectively, they were running under the shelter of Pompidou's presidential authority. The Left had to overcome the violent anti-Communist propaganda with which the Right tried to smear the Socialists. There was also the problem that if the Left won, would a right-wing President be willing to appoint a left-wing Prime Minister and work with a left-wing government? The question underlined a major omission in the Fifth Republic constitution. What happened when the President and the government backed by a majority in the National Assembly were at odds politically? In 1973 the issue never came to the test, as the Right held on to its majority. Perhaps a factor influencing voters was a desire to avoid the certainty of confrontation between Pompidou and a National Assembly opposed to him. The fear of a return to the political chaos of pre-1958 politics still lingered.

As it happened, an outright victory for the Left was far from likely given the extremely weak position from which they started. Between them, the Communists and Socialists had fewer than 100 seats after the right-wing landslide in the 1968 elections. The Union of the Left made important gains, winning eighty-five seats and putting into parliament several young Socialist deputies who were under Mitterrand's patronage. For the first time since 1936, the Socialist vote (20.65%) was nearly as big as the Communist vote (21.34%); Mitterrand's strategy of advancing on to Communist electoral terrain appeared to be working. The Right was no longer dominated by the Gaullists. In 1968 the Gaullist share of the total right-wing vote had been two thirds; in 1973 it had declined to 44%. The beneficiaries were non-Gaullists like Giscard and Lecanuet. The Right had won but it was now a divided Right while the large working-class vote on which de Gaulle could count was coming back to the Left. Just before the election Mitterrand refused to be drawn by a journalist who asked him whether it was his ambition to become Prime Minister or President of the Republic. Mitterrand replied: 'I am a candidate to neither office. I do all I can to ensure that the Left and the Socialist Party should win the elections. From there on, it is of little consequence whether it is I or another who assumes the main responsibilities.' This becoming modesty was appropriate for that interview at that time, but Mitterrand would have been lying to himself if he did not privately look forward to leading the Union of the Left into another presidential battle. It was the presidency that contained real political power. In 1965 his presidential campaign had remade his career. He wanted another go.

12
Presidential Candidate – 1974

Apparently I have no right to say that we are
governed by a small minority of the privileged
who look after themselves
first and after others later.

By the middle of 1973, it was clear to all France that their President, Georges Pompidou, was dying. His face grotesquely swollen from heavy injections of cortisone to try and slow down the spread of the bone marrow cancer that was killing him was testimony to the gravity of his illness. Much as the official Elysée spokespersons would deny that there was anything wrong with the President, and much as ministers would leave Cabinet meetings praising Pompidou's continuing strong grip on affairs, the television images and magazine photographs of the shuttling, drugged Pompidou told their own story. Political Paris was awash with speculation about what would happen, who would run, once Pompidou had gone. There was an unpleasant ghoulishness about political commentaries of the period, though the real responsibility lay with the Elysée in refusing to admit the President's illness – one of Mitterrand's first decisions on becoming President in 1981 was to promise to publish a six-monthly bulletin on his state of health. During Pompidou's illness, Mitterrand refused to join in the speculation and even in private stopped all conversation about Pompidou's health. He has a fastidious reserve about other people's private lives and personal problems and looks down on such gossip as improper and undignified. Instead he quietly praised Pompidou's courage in the face of suffering. Pompidou himself, shortly before he died in April 1974, said that Mitterrand had been one of the few politicians to handle himself with dignity during the period when the illness was a major talking point.

Mitterrand behaved as if the presidential elections would not be held until the normal expiry of Pompidou's term in 1976. Straight after the National Assembly election, he reaffirmed his party's commitment to the Common Programme and again rejected the idea of any link-up with the Centre. The National Assembly elections had appeared to confirm the continuing bi-polarization of French politics, with society – and the electorate – split into two great camps, the Left and the Right. The logic of this bi-polarization according to left-wing commentators was that only the Left could bring about change and reform French society. The Right was presented by its political and intellectual opponents as ossified, static and reactionary. But one of the right-wing contenders to Pompidou's inheritance was determined to challenge that image.

Valéry Giscard d'Estaing was a former civil servant who had entered politics and become de Gaulle's Finance Minister while still in his thirties. He had always kept his distance from the Gaullists and his Independent Republican Party had made steady gains since 1967 at the expense of the Gaullists. Now as the most prominent non-Gaullist in Pompidou's government (he held the post of Minister of Finance and Economics), he began bidding for Centre votes and offered himself as the man for reform and movement. In a major speech shortly after the 1973 National Assembly elections, Giscard outlined a political programme that differentiated him from Pompidou and the Gaullist tradition.

The choice Frenchmen made in the election was not between the preservation of a traditional society with its privileges and its transformation. The choice was between two ways of transforming society, and the majority of Frenchmen chose the liberal way. We shall be judged by the extent to which we have proved capable of achieving this transformation. If this transformation is inadequate, Frenchmen will remove us from power, and they will be right. This transformation must produce the greatest possible reconciliation between equality and liberty. Our aim must be to bring closer the living standards of the poorest and those of the richest.

Such sentiments came oddly from one who had himself presided over French financial policy during a period when despite the remarkable economic growth and increasing material prosperity of the country, the gap between rich and poor had remained as wide as ever. An OECD survey published in 1975 showed that France was the most unequal country in terms of wealth distribution of any of the advanced industrialized Western democracies. Even in Franco's Spain, the gap between the rich and the poor was not as marked as in France. The top 10% of the population in France owned 50.2% of the country's wealth while the poorest 50% owned 4.95% of France's wealth. There was less social mobility in France than in other West European countries. Studies carried out in the 1960s showed that 58.5% of middle-class children went to university but only 1% of working-class children. A 1968 survey showed that 85% of managing directors came from upper- or upper-middle class backgrounds while fewer than 3% came from lower-class families. One of the most unusual indicators of the inequality in France came in the OECD survey which revealed that the rich even managed to secure a disproportionate share of social security payments, family allowances and unemployment benefits – the so-called social wage, which in most West European countries operates as a minor redistributive system in favour of the poor. Not so in France where the bottom 20% received 17.7% of such payments. In Britain, by comparison, the bottom 20% received 42.4% of equivalent payments. In France, matters had been arranged so that the poor were actually in the position of redistributing their own social wage in favour of the rich.

Mitterrand tried to pick up these themes as he set about

establishing the claim of the Socialist Party to represent as broad a section of French society as possible. He was quick to realize that the 1973 oil crisis and the massive increase in the price of energy would put an end to the automatic economic growth that had carried France through the 1960s and early 1970s and that the consequent inflation and unemployment would exacerbate class differences in France. In the summer of 1973, the well-known French watch factory LIP was threatened with closure and workers occupied and continued production under workers' control. Mitterrand supported the LIP action as part of his campaign to identify the Socialist Party with the industrial working class. As he tried to give the Party a more workerist image, the actual number of working-class Party members was shrinking. Membership itself was growing and had reached 110,000 in June 1973 but the proportion of Socialist Party members who were workers had gone down from 23% in 1970 to 19% in 1973. There was some compensation in the growing number of young people becoming active in the Party – 90% of the delegates at the 1973 Grenoble Congress were under forty. But it remained a male-dominated party. In 1973, only 13% of the membership were women. To offset this imbalance the Socialists brought in internal positive discrimination with a rule establishing a minimum quota of 10% for women at all levels of party organization. In 1977, this was raised to 15%.

Mitterrand's attempt to widen the scope of the Socialist Party's appeal to include all wage and salary earners, small businessmen, shopkeepers and peasants was helped by the decline of religion as a factor influencing voting patterns. Four out of five babies in France were baptized Catholic but in the 1960s and 1970s there was a continuing decline in religious observance. In 1966, a quarter of France's Catholics declared themselves to be non-practising. By 1974, this figure had increased to half the Catholic population. At the same time the number of priests went down by a fifth in the ten years after 1965 and the age profile of those that remained was rising. This continuing secularization of French society could only benefit the Socialist Party which among older Catholics was still associated with the anti-clerical traditions of the SFIO. And in any case the automatic connection between the Church and the Right was also something that could no longer be taken for granted. In 1972, the French episcopate published *For a Christian Political Practice* which endorsed political plurality and encouraged Catholics to be active in the Socialist and Radical parties though it stopped short of endorsing the Communist Party. The books, articles and films about third-world liberation theology which became a fashionable interest area for left-wing intellectuals in the early 1970s presented the Church in a new role as a champion of the oppressed against racist or authoritarian repression in Africa and Latin America. Works linking the names of Marx and Christ in the title attempted to find a synthesis between Communism and Christianity. The combination of the increasing secularization of the faithful and the embracing of Socialist ideas by some sections of the Church did not produce a mass switch in voting patterns. In the 1973 legislative elections only 17% of practising Catholics voted for Left candidates and in the 1974 presidential election Mitterrand secured the votes of 23% of France's church-going Catholics. On the other hand a 1973 survey showed that 44% of Catholics who were active in lay associations had voted Left. The Catholic activists in the Unified Socialist Party, the CFDT (despite having de-confessionalized itself in 1964, the CFDT tended to appoint as permanent officials those who had been active in the Young Christian Workers' movement) or the Farmers' Association saw no contradiction between their religious and their political beliefs. Since Mitterrand was developing a much stronger line on women's rights, especially in support of birth control and abortion, two extremely contro-versial issues from the Church's point of view, it was a very helpful development to have the Church lose its commanding place in French life.

Shortly after the 1973 legislative elections Mitterrand set out his vision for what kind of Socialist Party he wanted to see develop. The Socialist Party should be a large, broad-based national party aiming to replace capitalist society with a Socialist society. As always Mitterrand becomes elusive and avoids defining exactly what he means by a 'Socialist society'; instead he offered this high-flown ambiguity about the party: 'It cannot be both a big party and be homogeneous. We must learn to bear contradictions. Unanimity is dangerous, and I fear nothing more than conformity. The party must organize its own contradictions.'

Another theme Mitterrand developed in the second half of 1973 was the need for a pan-European policy on the EEC. He called for a stronger, more politicized Europe to compete with the growing influence on multinational companies. Such strong economic power, he argued, must be opposed by an equally strong political power. It would be difficult for a Socialist France to resist the influence of multinationals if it had to act alone. A special Socialist Party Convention was held in December 1973 to debate Europe. The delegates endorsed Mitterrand's call for direct elections to the European parliament. 'Europe must be remade to construct Socialism. Socialists in Europe can work through the present Brussels institutions to bring about changes desired by the Left,' he told the convention. He repeated that a go-it-alone Socialist France would face dangers. 'If France tried a Socialist experiment completely on its own, it could end in repeating the Chilean or Greek experience.'

The overthrow and murder of Chile's President Allende by an American-backed military junta in September 1973 had shocked Mitterrand. Two years previously he had visited Allende in Santiago and was fascinated by the Chilean Socialist's attempts to move Chile towards a collectivist economic organization of society while retaining democratic liberties. If Allende could make his experiment work within the political framework of a relatively stable constitutional democracy then it would be an example for democratic Socialists all over the world. Allende's murder showed how far the CIA, and the American multi-national ITT with the background blessing of Dr Kissinger, would go in order to protect what they saw as their threatened interests in Chile. The question in Mitterrand's mind was: could the same scenario develop in France if a Socialist government determined to implement its Common Programme was elected? In many of his writings after 1973, Mitterrand broods over Allende's death. He clearly saw parallels between his own life and that of Allende. They were born in the same decade into middle-class families. Allende had been a minister at a very junior age and had based his political career on the need to build a coalition of left-wing parties around his Socialist Party and the Communists. Like Mitterrand he had made his name by standing for the office of President and after being defeated had maintained his commitment to left-wing policies. Together with the Communist Party and the more moderate Radicals, Allende had led a coalition, not dissimilar to the French Union of the Left, to victory in the 1970 elections. As with the French Common Programme, the centrepiece of Allende's programme was a series of nationalizations.

In his speech to the Special Party Convention, Mitterrand raised the spectre of a 'plot at a certain level of the army' if the Left got nearer to power. The Gaullist 'animal' had been 'wounded' after the legislative elections and would become dangerous. In November 1973, Mitterrand had published an article in which he claimed that the Ministers of the Interior and the Army were setting up a domestic intelligence network. This referred to an announcement from the two ministers that an inter-ministerial committee had been created to study measures to combat a potential 'internal enemy'. Mitterrand also claimed that certain army officers were ready to stop the alternation of political power in France, though he added no details or names to the broad charge. Those who were ready to accuse him of paranoia were stopped short when the satirical, investigative French weekly, the *Canard Enchaîné*, revealed in January 1974 that both Mitterrand's office and family apartment had been wired for microphone eavesdropping by the French security police.

The alarm felt in left-wing circles about the possibility of military intervention to stop determined left-wing governments which might win a majority at the ballot box from entering into office was not peculiar to France. In Italy, there was a similar right-wing obsession with the growing popularity of the Italian Communist Party and the prospect that it might gain power democratically. The links between the Italian armed forces and the neo-fascist MSI party were well known, indeed the party was led by a retired admiral. Almost every month a new plot was uncovered in Italy showing the inter-connections between the security forces and the anti-Communist politicians. Even in Britain, where there was no question of the Communist Party ever winning a seat in parliament let alone having a place in a Labour government, there was a hysterical anti-Left campaign and the Labour Party's mildly reformist leadership was depicted as a band of extremists poised to turn Britain into a totalitarian state. Private armies were raised by retired colonels and in a remarkable series of interviews published by the *Times*, unnamed British Army officers ruminated on worst-case scenarios in which military intervention might be needed to 'protect' British democracy.

The rise in the level of political violence, both by extremist political groups willing to use terrorist attacks and by the state which stepped up its arsenal of repressive measures to incorporate torture in Northern Ireland and political dismissals of left-wing public employees in West Germany, added to the collective anxiety neurosis of European Socialists in this period. In January 1974, the price of petrol in France went up by 30% and domestic fuel increased by 45%. Economic and political stability seemed to be receding memories. When the *Nouvel Observateur* carried out an opinion poll in March 1974 it found that 43% of those questioned thought that the arrival of the Left in power was a 'threatening' prospect and only 32% thought it 'desirable'. A similar majority (42% against 35%) thought that further nationalizations were not the most suitable way of resolving the economic crises. Nor did those surveyed want to see any Communist Ministers in a Left government, save for the post of Minister of Labour.

All in all, despite the continuing buoyancy of the Socialist Party since the 1973 elections, the political climate was less than favourable to Mitterrand when he set off in April 1974 for his second bid for the Presidency. Pompidou died on 2 April 1974. The news was brought to Mitterrand by the owner of the *Brasserie Lipp*, one of the Latin Quarter's best known restaurants favoured by left-wing intellectuals and the radical editors in the neaby publishing houses. Mitterrand was dining alone, working on a speech due to be delivered the following day in the National Assembly. His reaction then and over the next few days was to stay calm and say nothing. It was more or less a foregone conclusion that Mitterrand would be the candidate of the Left and most interest focused on how the Right would divide.

Mitterrand spent the weekend following Pompidou's death in

his constituency and refused to comment on his plans to the journalists who accompanied him down to the Nièvre. As Mayor of Château-Chinon, he laid a wreath in Pompidou's memory in front of the local memorial and busied himself in discussing plans for how the town would welcome a national bicycle race due to pass through in a few weeks' time. Back in Paris, Mitterrand started to put together his team for the election campaign. He refused to enter into discussions with the Communist Party about his campaign or policies and even refused the private meeting that Georges Marchais asked for. Marchais was insulted when a letter he wrote to Mitterrand was replied to by Pierre Mauroy but Mitterrand wanted to avoid prior obligations and later commitments during or after his campaign. He selected his own team of experts and Jean Pierre Chevènement, who as the Socialist Party's expert on economic policy found himself ruthlessly shunted aside in favour of the less radical Jacques Attali whose reputation as a brilliant economist was only matched by his polymathic abilities as a skier, a pianist, and in writing novels in his spare time. Attali, in turn, recruited his own team of helpers and brought in Michel Rocard for his first taste of high-level mainstream politics. Mitterrand had become concerned at the criticism of the Left's economic programme and the attacks on his own lack of economic experience or expertise. With the help of Attali, he had gone through a crash course in economics and began to master financial statistics, the jargon of macro- and micro-economics and economic policy options. He sent Attali on a secret mission to the West German government to discuss problems that would arise on the international finance markets in the event of a Left victory and especially to seek support by the Bonn government against speculation against the franc. Attali and Rocard put together an economic programme for Mitterrand, which, while it stood by the main economic measures of the Common Programme, including the nationalization proposals, contained a new austerity by making the fight against inflation a top priority.

As the Mitterrand campaign got going, the French Communist Party was obliged to fall in behind it. Marchais told his Party's Central Committee that the Communists would have run a candidate:

If our partners had refused a common candidature based on the Common Programme. This said, and while emphasizing the great significance of the 5 million votes cast for our comrade, Jacques Duclos in 1969, it is evident that conditions are not ripe today for a majority of French people to come out in favour of the election of a Communist to the Presidency of the Republic. Furthermore a double candidature of the Left would have encouraged manoeuvres on the Right with the aim of dissociating the parties united around the Common Programme. It might have led to the absence of a candidate of the popular forces in the second round.

The logic was correct; the 1969 presidential election had demonstrated that more than one major left-wing candidate could simply split the Left's votes to such an extent that the second-round run-off would be between two representatives of the governing majority. But in absenting themselves from what was arguably the most important election in France since 1958, the Communists would, willingly or not, consciously or not, give another enormous boost to Mitterrand's and more importantly, the Socialist Party's claim to be the principal standard-bearer for what Marchais called the 'popular forces' in France.

While Mitterrand consolidated himself as the candidate of the Left (there were two Trotskyist candidates, both of whom ran hard-hitting, entertaining first-round campaigns with clever use of the national television time allocated to all candidates but whose votes would go to Mitterrand in the crucial second round) the Right was badly split. The problem was that with Pompidou's death the Gaullist line came to a dead stop. No one in the Gaullist camp had anything approaching de Gaulle's or even Pompidou's authority. The most impressive of Pompidou's ministers had been Valéry Giscard d'Estaing but he was no Gaullist. In the days after Pompidou's death a flurry of Gaullist candidates declared themselves. The one with the official backing of the Gaullist party machine was Jacques Chaban-Delmas, a former Prime Minister under Pompidou. His successor as Prime Minister, Pierre Messmer, put himself forward as did Edgar Faure, a Fourth Republic Prime Minister who was now President of the National Assembly. Yet another claimant to the Gaullist heritage appeared, Jean Royer, Pompidou's Minister for small traders. Eventually all the Gaullists save for Royer and Chaban-Delmas dropped out but the bickering divisions had badly damaged Chaban-Delmas' campaign at the very beginning and he never really recovered. His flashy good looks, three marriages and the recent highly publicized scandal about how he had avoided paying income-tax while Prime Minister sat uneasily with the memory of de Gaulle who, no matter how great his appetite for power, was thought of as the embodiment of personal virtue.

Another blow to Chaban-Delmas was the lack of support from the young, ambitious Gaullist Minister of the Interior, Jacques Chirac. As Minister of the Interior, Chirac controlled the prefects, the government officers who ran the French provinces. Officially supposed to be politically neutral, the prefects acted as government message-bearers to the political powers in the provinces. Chirac and some other young Gaullist ministers and deputies had said that the Right should unite behind the man best able to defeat the 'Socialo-Communist' candidate as the Right called Mitterrand. No name was mentioned but it was clear they meant Giscard. Chirac ordered the prefects not to help Chaban-Delmas, and, lacking this central guidance, the Gaullist machine in many areas of France could not function as of old. Whether or not there was a formal deal between Giscard and Chirac was never clear but there is a remarkable coincidence between Chirac's desertion of the formal Gaullist camp and his appointment as Giscard's Prime Minister soon after the election was over.

Mitterrand did not dwell on these divisions in the Right in his own campaign. Rather he concentrated on explaining the Common Programme and arguing with much greater force than before for a major extension of women's rights, especially the right to obtain abortions. He had to face rowdy disruptions of his meetings by ultra-leftists though he was spared the humiliation of Jean Royer, one of whose early meetings witnessed some young women opposed to his moralizing about decency and family life slowly stripping off their clothes. Royer's campaign only just survived. The disruption Mitterrand faced was of a more traditional kind but was played up by right-wing press anxious to portray Mitterrand as someone who would bring disorder with him. He attacked these ideas head on with invocations like: 'France's Left is patriotic – in the past it has laid down its life for its country in war and in street battles – in the breasts of our people are the qualities of the heart.' He invoked the early days of Christianity: 'the rejection of violence and compulsion, of man dominating man, the need for the spirit to be free as well as the rejection of profit.' The language seems rich by the more prosaic standards of Anglo-Saxon political rhetoric but Giscard could outdistance Mitterrand in political pomp; when announcing his candidature, Giscard said: 'I want to look deep into the eyes of France, tell her my message, listen to hers.' Mitterrand did not duck the avowedly Socialist aspects of the Common Programme, though he defended himself against charges of wanting to introduce a collectivist society into France.

> Our opponents say that if the Left takes power it will suppress private ownership. They want to frighten the majority of French people who like their possessions, as I like mine. But they mix up the possession of property that we have thanks to the hard work of generations, with the accumulation of capital which allows the big national and multinational firms to make superprofits and to dominate our society. Why do they mix up the two sorts of ownership? Because the candidates of the Right represent capital, the banks, the big capitalist firms. And what have they to say, why they should be concerned living in their privileged world about the millions of French people who live their lives in great difficulty?

Although he had refused any negotiation with Marchais prior to his candidature, once the campaign got under way Mitterrand appeared on television with Marchais and Robert Fabre, leader of the Left Radicals, the third partner in the Union of the Left. It was a sign to grass-roots activists as well as to the country that the Left was united behind Mitterrand.

The results of the first round were extremely promising. Mitterrand secured 11 million votes or 43.24% compared with Giscard's 33% and Chaban-Delmas' 15%. Extreme left candidates had received a further 4% so Mitterrand was tantalizingly close to a majority. Mitterrand also felt that in having Valéry Giscard d'Estaing as his second-round opponent he would be facing someone clearly perceived as a classic representative of the right-wing bourgeoisie. Superficially, it was a reasonable analysis. Giscard came from an upper middle-class family with pretensions to grandeur. His father had changed his name by adding the aristocratic d'Estaing to the family name of Giscard in 1923, three years before young Valéry's birth. Giscard's father was an enthusiastic supporter of the extreme right-wing *Action Française* in the 1920s and 1930s and the family were staunch adherents of the Vichy regime during the war. Giscard himself fought with the Free French in the closing stages of the war. He was a brilliant student who powered his way through university and the highly competitive and highly prestigious National Administration School taking a second postgraduate diploma at the same time. In his twenties he was working in the private office of a Fourth Republic minister, at thirty he was elected deputy and at thirty-six de Gaulle made him Finance Minister. His financial policies were those of a classic exponent of the free market. He tried to reduce the amount of interventionist planning and offered tax incentives to firms to invest in France. He also protected the tax privileges of the owners and managers of big companies and, as we have seen, inequality between the rich and the poor did not diminish during his time as Finance Minister. Unlike de Gaulle, he believed that the French economy had to be fully integrated into an American-led Western economy and he was decidely more Atlanticist in his views than the Gaullists. He spoke excellent English and while Finance Minister arranged for an English lecturer to spend an hour with him one day a week in order to discuss George Bernard Shaw.

Mitterrand was correct in seeing Giscard as a representative of the French bourgeoisie but wrong to think that was how he was seen by many in France. Giscard had surrounded himself with some of France's best image-makers and he carefully followed their advice. He was an excellent television performer and his television appearances, dressed casually in a pullover to explain in a simple manner the economic problems facing France, were popular. Despite leading a protected and luxurious life, Giscard projected himself as the man with the common touch, scoring goals as the centre forward for a local village football team and playing jolly tunes on the accordion at a communal singsong. With his four young children, an attractive wife, and his proficiency at skiing, Giscard came over as an attractive modern politician, with few connections with the discredited Gaullist machine, and his talent and obvious capacity for hard work made him a natural leader. Looking back after his defeat of 1981, it is easy to observe the underlying faults in Giscard but in 1974 he seemed a dynamic, new type of leader, ready for change without the possible risks in electing a President committed to Socialist-Communist policies whose first act would be to dissolve the National Assembly for a fresh round of elections in a France that had become tired of the almost annual trip to the ballot box since the middle 1960s. The forty-eight-year-old Giscard also had considerable personal charm and influential journalists like Olivier Todd and Jean-François Revel and some commentators who had cut their teeth as supporters of the Left were won over to Giscard's vision of the future. In his programme Giscard struck a careful balance between continuity and change. He would try to create an independent and powerful France in which the French people would find justice and security. He promised to extend rights to women, to close down privately run old people's homes and protect the old by means of state provision; he wanted to open the government to those who were now in opposition and liberalize television and radio.

As the campaign developed, Mitterrand portrayed himself as attacking the Right but found his target was disconcertingly centrist, moderate and pledged to reforms, and who was campaigning under the slogan: 'Change without risk'. The enthusiasm for Mitterrand's campaign was evident and he spoke at packed meetings of up to 50,000 in the big provincial centres of France. United around the Common Programme and eager to maximize Mitterrand's vote, Socialist, Communist, Left Radical and other Left activists worked together in organizing meetings, putting up posters and delivering leaflets. Opinion polls put Mitterrand and Giscard neck and neck in the fortnight's hectic campaigning between the two rounds. A decisive event was a two-hour debate on television between the two men. This was watched by 20 million viewers and most commentators reckoned that Giscard came off better. He was more at ease in handling economic questions and was able to trip up Mitterrand on technical aspects of the French economy. He told Mitterrand that he 'did not have a monopoly of compassion' and ridiculed him as a man of the past. Mitterrand tried to pin the blame for the current inflation rate of 15% on Giscard's tenure of the Finance Ministry but, as with other politicians of the period, Giscard simply transferred the blame for inflation on to the Arabs. Appearing successfully on television is as much a matter of practice as technique or talent. Giscard had been using television for five years as his own way of talking to the French people. Mitterrand, although he was no longer totally excluded by the government control of access to the studios, had had less opportunity to practise than Giscard and still felt uneasy in the studio. No matter what the content of their respective messages Giscard's television manner was superior to that of Mitterrand and the public awarded points accordingly.

While Giscard out-pointed Mitterrand in the television debate, those supporting the Giscard campaign were using the French Right's favourite weapon against Mitterrand, the smear. Four days before the second round, Michel Poniatowski, one of Giscard's closest lieutenants said: 'Georges Marchais has donned the clothes of a democrat but he is and always will be the leader of a movement under foreign control . . . Every European country that has a Communist government is currently occupied by Russian troops.' Two days before the election all the mayors in France received an anonymous letter which stated: 'François Mitterrand is too vulnerable . . . He hid away 30 million francs in Switzerland after Pompidou's death and the Communists know this . . . This means he will be completely exposed to the demands of his Communist allies if he wins the Presidency.'

Mitterrand ignored this kind of attack. After thirty years in French politics his skin had become hardened. In the closing days of the campaign he found his touch at the large meetings where he so excels. He is not a demagogue and eschews the arm-waving or hysterical ranting of some powerful platform speakers. Rather he is quiet, persuasively leaning over the rostrum to make a point in an almost intimate way to his audience. He delights in irony and scorn and has the priceless orator's gift of making his listeners laugh with him and against his opponents. He was ready to use angry, aggressive, class-laden language.

> Apparently I have no right to say that we are governed by a small minority of the privileged who look after themselves first and others later. This is regarded as shocking, as the language of a boor, not used in the Finance Minister's distinguished circles. But I am told that the Left is hell, that we spell the end of freedom and property. That we will take away your home, your garden. That we are thirsting for blood. What a cynical caricature by those who are about to dispossess you of the fruits of your labour.

Mitterrand nearly made it. Giscard received 50.81% of the votes and Mitterrand 49.19%. Another 300,000 votes would have put Mitterrand in the Elysée. Again his hopes were dashed. The day after the election he told the senior members of his campaign that he felt ready to take on the responsibilities of office in 1974. The next time he would be well into his sixties. He was sure the Left would win but he would not stand again. For any political leader the immediate aftermath of an electoral defeat is usually an immensely depressing time. For Mitterrand who had not tasted power for nearly two decades, the sense of failure was bleak and the thought of another seven-year wait altogether too depressing. And yet, the Left which had been smashed at the polls in 1968 and 1969, only five years ago, had come within a whisker of winning. The unity and strength of the Left was such as had not been seen in France for nearly half a century. Mitterrand's own position as the repository of half of France's political hope was unchallengeable. The economic and social problems that Giscard had claimed could be resolved would not go away. A powerful and vigorous opposition would be needed. At fifty-seven, Mitterrand still had a role to play. As he told party workers just after the election result: 'Our struggle goes on. Because you represent the world of youth and of work our victory is inevitable.'

13
The Giscard Years

*Our struggle goes on with neither a pause
nor a truce.*

One of Mitterrand's more important political attributes is his sense of when to move quickly, when to slow things down and when to say nothing and stay still. The traditional politician's reaction after losing a vital election so narrowly would be to hide away for a few months, make no speeches, announce no new policy and let the wounds of defeat heal themselves with time.

Mitterrand's defeat in the 1974 presidential elections was not a normal kind of political defeat, however. He had enthused and engaged whole new groups of people and sections in French society with the possibility of a real rupture with the de-Gaulle–Pompidou–Giscard conservative, authoritarian tradition. The generation that had discovered itself in 1968 had now come to accept that some, if not all, of their hopes could be realized through securing power via the ballot box; for many of them the 1974 election was the initiation into active party political work. Mitterrand had secured the support of many intellectuals, film stars, writers and other personalities for whom this, too, was a beginning of political engagement not, as in their candidate's case, one more weary stage in a journey that had been going on for thirty years. According to Jacques Chérèque, the burly leader of the CFDT metalworkers' section: 'Mitterrand in his '74 campaign really made contact with the workers with his humanist conception of Socialism.'

Mitterrand himself wrote in the *Nouvel Observateur* immediately following Giscard's victory:

> I felt myself to be in a moving but simple situation, representing the force of the people against the power of money. It was an historic moment, comparable to the great moments of history. For everybody there was a clear dividing line, visible to all, between those who hold power and those who are dominated by it. When I see those who not so long ago were so divided now come together; when messages flow in from all over France from those for whom the result is not a defeat and are not giving up at the end of this campaign; above all, when I see the young people of France enter our ranks when those in power seem to be keeping it for a long time, I say to myself that our struggle, which goes on with neither a pause nor a truce, is more important than anything else.

With this desire to keep the support for the Socialist Party moving along, Mitterrand announced only one week after the election that he would be calling what became known as the 'Socialist Assizes' to enlarge the party and to develop new political ideas based on *autogestion*. The proposal had been put to him a few days before the second round of the presidential election by Pierre Mauroy and Michel Rocard.

Rocard was still a member of the Unified Socialist Party, though he had left its leadership in 1973 and returned to his job as a senior civil servant. Rocard had developed his thesis in the 1970s, especially after the Arab oil price rise, that getting inflation under control was a major economic priority for Socialists. In a book he published on inflation, he had made only passing reference to the Common Programme. 'I am only returning the compliment,' he said, 'the Common Programme devotes barely a page and a half to inflation which is hardly a serious approach to the subject.' At one level, his political position was to the left of the Common Programme with his commitment to workers' self-management but in terms of its nationalization proposals and commitments to substantial increase in wages and allowances, he believed the Common Programme to be unworkable. At the age of forty-five, Rocard had spent all his political life on the margin of French politics. Although he was well-known nationally ever since his presidential candidature in 1969, he realized that to stay in the Unified Socialist Party would only maintain his isolation from the mainstream of politics and the possibility of power. His proposal to Mitterrand to hold the 'Socialist Assizes' was thus a way of formally breaking with the Unified Socialist Party and by holding out the prospect of bringing with him a sizeable number of its 10,000 members he could also lay claim to a position in the Socialist Party leadership.

That much was obvious to Mitterrand and if Rocard alone had made the proposal, the Socialist leader would probably have ignored it. But Rocard was being strongly backed by Pierre Mauroy whose support was still essential for Mitterrand. Mauroy not only maintained his Socialist fief around Lille but he loyally came to Paris for a day and a half each week to work in the Socialist Party headquarters on administration problems. Much of the strength of the Socialist Party lay in its old SFIO stalwarts in the municipalities. France has 38,000 communes which can range from villages of less than one hundred inhabitants to cities of over a million. It is the local organization that parties have in each commune, big or small, that counts in getting out the vote for the important elections. A well-run Socialist town or an impressive Socialist mayor can make all the difference to the party's impact.

Mauroy was the man who held all this together at the national level of the Socialist Party. He too wanted to capitalize on the excitement engendered by Mitterrand's presidential campaign. Although he had loyally backed the Common Programme, he had all the old SFIO distrust for the Communist Party and enjoyed less than cordial relations with the regional Communist organization in Lille. By having Rocard and his comrades join the Socialist Party, it would widen its political base in a way that would be non-Communist but which could not be said to be going in the direction of the Centre. Mauroy also appreciated the appeal Rocard had for the 1968 generation. As a former head of

the SFIO's youth section in the 1950s, he understood the importance for a political party of engaging the support of people young
enough to be enthusiastic party workers before the arrival of
other interests diverts their energy.

Another enthusiastic supporter of the idea of calling a new
gathering of the non-Communist left forces was Edmond Maire,
the recently elected General Secretary of the CFDT. Maire, at
forty-six, one year older than Rocard, was as strong an advocate
of *autogestion* within the trade union movement as Rocard was in
the political world. For Maire, a stronger more broadly based
Socialist Party might begin to act as a counterweight to the
Communist Party presence in industry. In June 1974, the CFDT
signed a joint agreement with its Communist-dominated rival,
the CGT. Both unions committed themselves to joint campaigns
and to united action at the base. But there was considerable
divergence between the two unions on what kind of wage claims
should be pursued and how industrial action should develop. The
CFDT wanted claims based on an across-the-board rise in which
everyone would get an identical lump-sum increase. This system
favours the lower-paid and reduces wage differentials. The CGT
preferred traditional percentage increases. When it came to
industrial struggle, the CFDT was in favour of allowing
spontaneous grass-roots strikes or occupations to happen with
the union offering support once workers had democratically
decided to engage in struggle. For the CGT this meant a loss of
control by the full-time officials and they were determined to
keep a firm central hand on industrial action before and after it
developed. The CGT and the Communist Party had kept a
suspicious distance from *autogestion* with its overtones of ultra-
left spontaneity bordering on old-style syndicalism. One of the
key elements of *autogestion* was the principle of recallability by
which any workers' or community delegate could be instantly
recalled to account for his or her activities to the electoral body.
This was a proposal much supported by Trotskyist groups, and
anything they proposed was anathema to the Communists. In
fact, the *autogestion* tradition in France predates both Trotsky
and Marx. The leading theorist was Charles Fourier (1772–1837)
who wanted to abolish capitalist competition by dividing France
into self-sufficient communes each of 1,600 inhabitants. These

would share social and financial benefits and elect their own leaders. Fourier developed his theories in six long volumes and his ideas remained influential for the rest of the nineteenth century. Emile Zola's novel, *Work* (1901), is based on a Fourier commune. Louis Blanc (1811–82) in his book *The Organization of Work* (1839) called for factories run on a co-operative basis with workers electing their own managers. It was Blanc who coined the egalitarian slogan: 'To each according to his needs.' Pierre Proudhon (1809–65) left posterity an even more resounding slogan when he announced that: 'All property is theft.' He wanted the land taken from its owners and run by communes who would elect their own leaders. Another important nineteenth-century source for *autogestion* was the Paris Commune in 1871. There the theory of rotation and instant recall of delegates was turned into shortlived practice. The whole trade-union tradition in France has been strongly syndicalist; that is workers taking over their workplaces following a general strike and the economy becoming a linked network of producers' co-operatives under workers' control.

To this ancient lineage the modern advocates of *autogestion* added the examples of Yugoslavia, and those scattered examples around the world where islands of workers' control or co operative production floated in the capitalist and managerial seas. The occupation and continued production at the LIP watch factory was held up as an example and Michel Rocard helped set up a co-operatively run café in his constituency.

There was never a coherent *autogestion* policy as such with an integrated programme ready to be applied. Some called for a factory council elected by the workers, while other models called for the workplace management body to be composed of equal thirds from the workers, the government and the consumers, though no one was ever clear on how the latter would be elected or chosen. *Autogestion* was particularly popular in educational establishments where the idea of junior teachers or untenured lecturers outvoting their seniors and taking control of the school or faculty was irresistible. Nearly one in five of the Socialist Party's membership was a teacher or university lecturer and they were to be amongst the keenest supporters of *autogestion*.

Those in favour of *autogestion* saw it not as an end in itself and they recognized that the state would have to be changed at the same time as *autogestion* was introduced. Planning would be influenced from the base upwards rather than be controlled by the central state bureaucracy. But they argued that nationalization and the arrival of the Left in Paris ministries would not be sufficient unless there was a real handover of power to the workplace and the communities.

The 'Socialist Assizes' which were held in October 1974 were to be more than an acceptance of *autogestion* into the mainstream philosophy of the Socialist Party. It was to welcome into the Socialist family those who had been active on the non-Communist Left but had stayed aloof from formal adherence to the Socialist Party. Rocard brought with him 1,500 members from the Unified Socialist Party and Edmond Maire's decision to become an individual member for the Socialist Party was followed by thousands of CFDT activists, though the confederation as such did not seek organic links with the party. Mitterrand was able to announce other notable recruits for the Socialist Party including Claude Cheysson, France's EEC representative and Léon Blum's son. There were some right-wing recruits too, notably Edgard Pisani, an ex-Gaullist minister. In his speech to the 'Assizes' Rocard said that he considered the Common Programme an historic event but that the oil price crisis of 1973 meant that the economic data on which it was based were now out of date.

> In addition, we believe that when it comes to the problem of devolving authority, the Common Programme is too centralist; or at least the proposed methods of economic management appear to us to be too much based on a hierarchical system rather than from the base upwards. But let me stress that these differences do not stop us from believing in the coming together of all the Socialist forces in the same organization, in which we will continue to fight for an improvement of the Left's policies and capability for action.

Modest and low-key as his speech was, Rocard appeared to many in the Socialist Party and certainly to all the Communists as a cuckoo who had finally found his nest. Outwardly the Union of the Left continued its progress, winning legislative by-elections and municipal elections. Both parties substantially increased membership, but inside the Union there were growing divisions within the Socialist Party itself and between the Socialists and the Communists.

At the 1975 Socialist Party Congress, Mitterrand had ditched the left-wing CERES group whose support had been crucial in winning the party leadership at Epinay in 1971. CERES had been essential then and Mitterrand shared their perspective of close tactical co-operation with the Communist Party, even if he kept some distance from their Marxist analysis of, and collectivist answers to French economic problems. But after 1971, more and more of the young newcomers to the Socialist Party had turned towards CERES as the most exciting and active of the tendencies in the Socialist Party. From being a small group of intellectuals, CERES began developing a real power base inside the party and had managed to take control of the Paris federation of the party. This alarmed Pierre Mauroy who did not want to have CERES threaten his own power base within the party nationally and was not at all convinced that the more extreme style of CERES activists was electorally attractive to the votes in the provincial municipalities.

Mitterrand, too, was annoyed with the criticism of the CERES faction within the party leadership. They had voted against him on the question of Europe in 1973 and he had threatened to resign unless they toed the line. Again when the Arab-Israeli war broke out in 1973, Mitterrand had had to use the threat of resignation in order to get the national leadership to repudiate a statement from the CERES-controlled Paris federation which Mitterrand considered to be too pro-Arab. It was a comment on Mitterrand's dominant position inside the party that, only two years after having joined it, he had become indispensable. Everyone had to back down in front of his resignation threat.

The Socialist Party's internal structure provided for all the main currents in the party to be represented right up to the national leadership. The proportional representation system adopted at Epinay means that delegates are elected to the Congress, the supreme organ of the party, on the basis of the votes received for all-embracing policy motions circulated to the base by the different tendencies in the party. At the Congress, the 130-strong Leadership Committee (*Comité Directeur*) is elected, again on the basis of proportional representation. This meets every two months and elects the Executive Committee (*Bureau Exécutif*) on a similar basis. The Executive Committee meets every week and, from within its ranks, elects the National Secretariat which is in charge of the day-to-day running of the party.

In marked contrast to the British Labour Party, neither the Socialist group of deputies in the National Assembly (the equivalent of the Parliamentary Labour Party) nor the French trade unions have any special privileges inside the party. Membership is on an individual basis (members are meant to pay 1% of their net income as an annual subscription compared with the less than 0.1% of average earnings that the British Labour Party member pays) and trade unionists or deputies have to join and act as individual members if they wish their voice to be heard inside the party. Deputies are actually disadvantaged in as much as they can only fill 20% of the seats on Leadership and Executive Committees.

Although the National Secretariat will be dominated by the majority grouped around Mitterrand, the position of all the main tendencies is protected and they can make their voices heard right up to the highest levels. When in 1975, Mitterrand severed his relationship with CERES and Chevènement, it did not mean they were banished from influence within the party. Mitterrand himself kept a firm hand on the party. He chaired the National Secretariat meetings in a laconic, almost abrupt style. Sometimes he came in late, took over the chairmanship and announced a decision even though he had not participated in the debate. Once, when Michel Rocard was making a report he noticed that Mitterrand was busy correcting an article. Rocard paused and asked if he could have Mitterrand's attention. Mitterrand replied: 'I can do two things at once,' and went on with his article. He placed in the national leadership men like Charles Hernu (now the French Defence Minister) and Georges Fillioud (currently the Minister of Communications), old political cronies whose attachment to Mitterrand went back to Fourth Republic and Convention days.

But he also promoted a new generation, men in their thirties or early forties, like Pierre Joxe (now President of the Socialist group of deputies in the National Assembly) and Lionel Jospin (who succeeded Mitterrand as First Secretary of the Socialist Party in 1981). Both were brilliant intellectuals; Jospin a university teacher, Joxe a civil servant. Joxe proclaimed himself a Marxist and was strongly pro-Common Programme while Jospin was more cautious about the Communist Party and wanted to see a much bigger, stronger Socialist Party that could eventually overtake the Communist Party in votes, membership and implantation in French society.

Mitterrand also encouraged women like Edith Cresson (now France's Agriculture Minister) whom he placed in the National Secretariat in charge of youth and student problems while he made Nicole Questiaux (now the Minister for Social Affairs) the Socialist Party's European representative. He enjoyed talent-spotting and gained pleasure from giving advancement to those he could see in a future Socialist government. That these young Turks owed their position to him also strengthened his position as, on the whole, those he brought on repaid him with an intense loyalty.

Another important new adherent to the Socialist Party was Jacques Delors, a fifty-year-old economist who had worked for the Bank of France where he had been active in his trade union and then as one of the leaders of the team responsible for preparing the French plan. Delors had made his name when he worked for Jacques Chaban-Delmas during the latter's period of office as Prime Minister between 1969–72. He had tried to develop a social policy based on wage indexation and draw the trade unions into a national bargaining process. It was a reformist attempt to develop more modern relationships based on increased state incorporation of the working class after the 1968 explosion. Pompidou put an end to Delors' experiment when he sacked Chaban-Delmas in 1972. After he joined the Socialist Party Delors lived with the tag of having worked for a right-wing government but he defended himself as being a technocrat who wanted to try his ideas out in practice. He was highly respected in banking and business circles and was one of the two French members of the Club of Rome, the highly selective (and self-selective) circle of top European liberal economists and industrialists. Delors was a workaholic who never took holidays, preferring to spend the time chewing over economic problems. In 1975, he argued that the Socialist Party 'has to develop a counter programme. We must show the link between under-employment and inequality, study the relationships between education and work, unravel the tax system and emphasize the need to combat social segregation in housing and health.'

The entry of Rocard and Delors into Mitterrand's team, the removal of the CERES group as an influential segment of the leadership, the emphasis on *autogestion*, and the chatter about new programmes based on developments since the 1972 signing of the Common Programme were all deeply alarming to the Communist Party. Even worse from the Communist point of view was the steady climb in Socialist popularity. A June 1974 opinion poll gave the Socialist Party a six-point lead over the Communists. In six by-elections held in September 1974, the Socialist candidates out-pointed the Communists in five out of the six contests. Mitterrand's ambition of seeing the Socialist Party overtake the Communist Party as the main part of the French Left looked as if it might be more than a long-term dream. He continued to keep his distance from the Communists, refusing a strongly pressed invitation from Georges Marchais to speak at the Twenty-first Communist Party Congress in September 1974. When Marchais asked him why he could not come, Mitterrand replied that on the date of the Congress he would be in Cuba, at the invitation of Fidel Castro.

Marchais had tried to develop a personal friendship with Mitterrand, dropping in at Mitterrand's Paris apartment for a drink and a chat. They never became close. The coldly intellectual, literary Mitterrand had little in common with the bluff, proletarian metalworker Marchais. Their small-talk was reduced to mutual moaning about going bald, a problem from which both suffered. Marchais complained that Mitterrand was patronizing towards him when they were having political discussions. Mitterrand did not demur. He was cleverer than Marchais and didn't mind showing it.

While Marchais tried to maintain reasonably friendly personal relations with Mitterrand, *L'Humanité* launched a series of bitter attacks on the new right-wing economic advisers surrounding

Mitterrand. Following the by-election victories for the Socialists, *L'Humanité*'s editor said that the Socialist leadership had 'an attitude aimed at weakening the Communist Party and it must be said that this attitude links up with the major capitalists who can see a victory for the Left coming along and reckon their top priority is to reduce the strength of the Communist Party.'

Another Communist leader, Paul Laurent, said that Michel Rocard 'talks a lot of rubbish and reactionary rubbish', and even Marchais in February 1975 was stung into declaring that Mitterrand was becoming 'too sure of himself and too domineering'. *L'Humanité* began publishing articles about the right-wing behaviour of SFIO ministers in the Fourth Republic and recalled that Mitterrand had been a minister in governments that had suspended *L'Humanité*'s publication. (The paper did not mention that the Communist Party had applied to the Nazis in 1940 for permission to publish *L'Humanité* at a time when the French Communist Party supported the Hitler-Stalin pact; nor when attacking Mollet's handling of the Algerian war did it mention that Communist deputies in 1957 had voted the granting of special powers to the Mollet government to pursue the Algerian war with even more brutal vigour.)

Another major point of division between the two partners had been the developments in Portugal after the overthrow of the Salazar-Caetano regime in 1974. After an initial enthusiastic welcome by all the European Left for this victory for popular forces, there soon developed differences over how the Portuguese revolution was developing and which forces were worthy of support. The main fight was between the Portuguese Communist Party led by Alvaro Cunhal and the Portuguese Socialist Party led by Mario Soares. Cunhal had led the Portuguese Communist Party from exile in Moscow while Soares had been arrested and imprisoned by Salazar for political activities and had been forced into exile in France where he had become a close friend of Mitterrand. Hovering between the two parties was the Armed Forces Movement, proud, and justly so, of having returned Portugal to democracy but uncertain of what their role in the new state should be and anxious to avoid a return by the right-wing forces that had gone into exile or were hiding, behind welcoming smiles for the arrival of democracy, their real intentions in Portugal itself. There was a great deal of spontaneous working-class, peasant and liberal intelligentsia occupation of factories, land, banks, schools, newspapers and radio stations. Not all of it was entirely spontaneous. The Portuguese Communist Party worked hard at installing its cadres in ministries, newspapers and broadcasting stations. Soares and Cunhal each had ministries in the provisional government set up in 1974 and the Portuguese Communists called for broad-front alliance with the Socialists. This was unacceptable with the Communist Party continuing to infiltrate its people into key positions and its aggressive denunciation of Soares. The Portuguese Socialists insisted on the holding of elections for the Constituent Assembly which took place in April 1975. In these the Socialists heavily out-pointed the Communists. Cunhal was forced to try and build an alliance with pro-Communist officers and to continue to use the Communist-controlled Portuguese trade union confederation, *Intersindical*, as a means of maintaining Communist influence.

The reaction of the French Left depended on political sympathies. Both Soares and Cunhal were heavily funded from outside. Soares could count on the wealthy West German Social Democratic party to pay his campaign bills, while Moscow provided finance for the Portuguese Communists. Mitterrand, both as a personal friend of Soares and a Vice-President of the Socialist International which was co-ordinating international political support for the Portuguese Socialists, spoke out strongly in support of the democratic electoral policy laid down by his fellow Socialists in Portugal.

With equal energy, Marchais and the French Communists backed Cunhal and depicted Soares as the social democratic tool of American and West European capital. A major row blew up when Communist printers who worked for the Portuguese Socialist Party newspaper, *Republica*, locked out the journalists and declared the paper to be under workers' control. The extent to which this action was initiated by the Portuguese Communists was not clear, nor was it apparent how much control they had over their members at *Republica*, but there was no disguising their pleasure at having the rival's daily newspaper shut down. The *Republica* incident was vigorously denounced by the French

Socialists as an attack both on press freedom and on political plurality. *L'Humanité* tried to defend the occupation and denounced a mild suggestion by the pro-Socialist *Nouvel Observateur* that the Portuguese authorities might evict the printers and return the paper to the Portuguese Socialist Party as 'an open invitation to a pogrom'.

Like Czechoslovakia in 1968, the events in Portugal in 1974–75 sharpened the differences between Socialists and Communists in France. In mid-1975, *L'Humanité* published the secret speech Marchais had made after signing the Common Programme in 1972 in which he talked of the Socialist Party's 'real nature'. Marchais' cynical evaluation of his Socialist partner's motives, intentions and what he considered to be the Socialist Party's true nature caused a stir, appearing as it did barely a year after the Union of the Left's achievement based upon Mitterrand's candidature in the 1974 Presidential election. An important role was played both now and over the next six years by Roland Leroy, *L'Humanité*'s editor, who had been passed over for the General Secretaryship in favour of Marchais. Leroy was (and is) firmly in the Stalinist wing of the French Communist Party leadership and he has used *L'Humanité* as a weapon against the liberal elements in the Party.

The extent to which Leroy would have the power to pursue an editorial policy which would deliberately set out to embarrass Marchais is hard to work out. The editor of *L'Humanité* is under the orders of the Party leadership but as Leroy is an important part of that leadership, he has more editorial discretion that would a normal editor.

Mitterrand's response to this wave of anti-Socialist attacks from the Communist Party was one of lofty indifference. He refused to reply to the criticism whether aimed at him personally, at his colleagues or at Socialist policy. It was a sensible reaction. He would be seen as the man committed to Left unity while the polemic came from the Communists.

According to Pierre Bérégovoy, the Socialists' National Secretary in charge of relationships with the Communist Party:

It was not by chance that the polemic coincided with the 'Socialist Assizes'. The 'Assizes' meant a double reinforcement for the Socialist Party. We became more militant with the arrival of the CFDT leaders and more ideological with the adoption of the *autogestion* project. That could only damage the Communist Party which wished to remain dominant in the area of class struggle and which understood that *autogestion* means countering the idea of the bureaucratic state against the dream of a libertarian Socialism.

But it was Paul Laurent, one of Marchais' close associates who told Bérégovoy the real reason for Communist disquiet: 'The moment a Communist voter decides to vote Socialist, that worries us greatly.'

At the same time as this polemic, the Communist Party began the difficult and not altogether convincing process of removing some of its Stalinist encrustations. In November 1975, Marchais criticized the treatment of political prisoners in the Soviet Union. At the Twenty-second Congress in the following year, there was an even more remarkable event, with the relinquishing of a key part of the Party's heritage, the dropping of the reference to 'establishing the dictatorship of the proletariat' from its constitution. It was the Leninist concept of 'the dictatorship of the proletariat' which was one of the original reasons for the split from the SFIO in 1920 and the setting up of the French Communist Party. It was the very idea that made Communism different from Socialism or Social Democracy. The year of 1976 was perhaps the high point of the Eurocommunist wave on which the powerful Italian and Spanish Communist Parties were travelling in the search for a more liberal Communism. They were willing to renounce forever loyalty to the Kremlin, to accept political plurality and enter government on the basis of a 'historic compromise' – an alliance with political parties wedded to the maintenance of capitalism.

The French Communists had always been suspicious of Italian-style Eurocommunism but as they saw the French Socialists make inroads into the working class and the intelligentsia it was felt that some move to change the Party's image and win over those who were flocking to the Socialist banner might be helpful. The symbolic renunciation of the

Communist commitment to the revolutionary overthrow of the state and the setting up of the dictatorship of the proletariat had almost the opposite effect. Firstly, the manner in which such an historic decision was taken was frankly ludicrous. Marchais claimed that a great debate had taken place in Communist cells, federations and at the Congress itself over removing the phrase from the constitution. Yet the vote on the leadership's proposition was 99% in favour. It was the kind of majority even East European Communist governments were ashamed to announce after one of their rigged elections. The Party might be dropping the 'dictatorship of the proletariat', but it was not getting rid of the Political Bureau's control of internal Party decision-making. Secondly, if the Party was no longer a Leninist revolutionary party, why bother to stay in it? What made it different in theoretical terms from the Socialist Party? Did it mean that the Communist Party would become a debating club with no political perspective on how to replace capitalism? These questions were to be argued over endlessly by French Communist intellectuals in the years to come, though those who thought the Congress would open the way to real internal debate were soon to be disappointed.

While Marchais opened up this quasi-theological debate, the Left was making steady electoral progress on the ground. In the 1976 elections for departmental councils the Union of the Left obtained 58% of the votes cast. But the Socialists had received 10% more of the votes than the Communists. In the much more important municipal elections in 1977, it was a similar story. The Union of the Left was extremely successful. The Socialists cut all connections with their old Centre partners, which in some cases dated back to the 1940s and worked closely with the Communists. The Left won control of 155 of the 221 towns and cities with populations of over 30,000. In particular, the Socialists made heavy inroads into the Conservative stronghold of West France, capturing Rennes, Brest, Nantes, Cherbourg, and Angoulême. Like most other countries there are geographical divisions in voting patterns which seem to defy changes in time or demography. The west of France had voted Right since the beginning of the nineteenth century. The 1977 municipal elections saw the Socialists prising loose the conservative grip on the region. Elsewhere, Rheims, the capital of champagne country got a Communist mayor. Nice, an international symbol of corrupt and perpetual right-wing rule came within a whisker of putting the Union of the Left into office. After the major gains in votes recorded in 1973 and 1974 for the Union of the Left, people could now see power changing hands. The Union of the Left really did work. The Left also took power in 140 other towns. Socialist-Communist municipal councils came into action. In dozens of town halls, the Communists were for the first time able to exercise some power. But they owed it to the Socialist Party and to Mitterrand. For the first time the Socialists had polled more votes than the Communists, 28% to 21%. Like the Socialists, the Communists were experiencing a massive growth in membership as the continuing electoral excitement and Left advances attracted more and more people to join the two parties, but the growth in Communist Party members was not being matched by an increase in votes. With the National Assembly elections due to be held in 1978, the Communist Party had to face the possibility of being very much the junior partner in the Mitterrand-led Union of the Left which was now poised to form a government.

14
The Break with the Communist Party

'Yes' to the Common Programme, 'No' to a Communist Programme.

Political parties in democracies win or lose elections, advance or fall back in popularity, according to their handling of domestic issues. Foreign policy usually counts for little. In 1968 the Soviet invasion of Czechoslovakia had profoundly influenced French politicians and commentators. The Communist Party's modest disapproval contrasted with the French Socialists' loudly proclaimed condemnation. As for the Right, in the months following August 1968 they continually used the stick of the Russian suppression of Dubcek's experiment to beat France's own Communists. Yet when the time came to count the votes in the 1969 presidential election, the Communist Duclos received a handsome 21%, well up to the usual Communist vote, while the Socialist Deferre mustered a humiliating 5%. The attitudes the two parties had struck on Czechoslovakia seemed to count for little.

The great battles of Mitterrand's life, from the resistance, through the Fourth Republic, opposition to de Gaulle and the reconstitution of the Socialist Party are to do with the internal

politics of France. Even the problems of African decolonialization and Algeria were perceived and acted upon as questions
belonging on the inside of French politics. Yet Mitterrand has a
passion for foreign travel and for getting to know the people and
leaders of foreign countries. Two of his books are devoted to
China and Africa while in the two volumes of diaries he
published in the 1970s there are constant references to foreign
trips and encounters. His Paris apartment or summer home in
the south west of France were open to those exiled by repressive
regimes; Greece's Mikis Theodorakis, Portugal's Mario Soares,
Czechoslovakia's Jiri Pelikan became friends.

The great division in the geography of France is the latitudinal
line above which the olive tree can no longer grow and where the
warm, emotional, impulsive oil-producing south gives way to the
chillier, hardier, rational dairy-producing north. Mitterrand
grew up in no-man's land between the south and north of France
and as an adult has kept in touch with both halves with one home
in Paris and another only a short drive from the Spanish frontier.
But his face is turned to the south and to the Mediterranean. In
all his books or in speeches or interviews there is very little
comment about northern Europe. The British and Scandinavian
economies and societies receive barely a passing mention while
their politics appear hardly to enter his head. This is surprising,
as both Britain and the Nordic countries have Labour or Social
Democratic parties which since 1945 have held office for longish
periods of time and have attempted with varying degrees of
success to implement policies such as those outlined in the
French Common Programme. Mitterrand once described
Harold Wilson as 'an opportunist, guided by neither moral nor
legal principles', while he lectured Olof Palme, Sweden's Social
Democratic leader, on the lack of nationalization undertaken by
the Swedish party.

By contrast Mitterrand is politically active and intellectually
engaged in the development of Socialist politics in the countries
around the Mediterranean. We have already noted his interest in
Portugal, but the 1970s saw him visiting and revisiting and
commenting upon Spain, Italy, Greece and Israel. Within the
Socialist International, he developed the idea of holding a
regional conference based on member parties in the Mediter-

ranean countries. In the summer of 1981 one of his first presidential acts was to host a meeting of Mediterranean Socialist leaders at his summer home not far from the Pyrenees. Across the Atlantic, the same divergence of interest is marked. Mitterrand has visited the United States on several occasions since his first trip there in 1946 but his fascination is reserved for Mexico, Costa Rica, Cuba or Venezuela, all of which he has visited while real political passions bubble through his writing and speeches on the repressive regimes in Chile, Argentina or Uruguay.

In 1975, Mitterrand made two long trips to meet political leaders in the Soviet Union and the United States. He describes both trips in detail in his book *The Bee and the Architect*. In the Kremlin, Brezhnev greeted him with both arms and took him arm-in-arm to a seat where the Soviet leader poured out his desire for peace. He recounted the 20 million Russians killed in the war and added:

> But even when you count the dead, you don't count the sorrow, the misery, the homes destroyed, the fields abandoned, the work lost, the energy wasted; you don't count the time we have had to spend on remaking our country and its people. Those who say in the West that détente is only a diplomatic trick for us, a passing tactic, are deceiving you. We shall only make war if we are forced to.

Suddenly Brezhnev stopped his outburst and asked Mitterrand if he believed him. Mitterrand paused for a moment and replied: 'Let me think it over. I would very much like to believe you.' In his book which recounts the Brezhnev meeting, Mitterrand describes the continual interruptions from an intercom on the Soviet leader's desk. 'What could they do without me?' asks Brezhnev.

After the meeting with Brezhnev came long discussions with other senior Soviet leaders. Mitterrand gives us polished miniature pen portraits. He describes the Soviet Union's top ideologue, Mikhail Suslov, seventy-seven years old, kneading his arthritic hands and reading out his carefully prepared and interminable statements from large exercise books. Or Boris Ponomarev, the Russian Communist Party's expert on Western

193

Communist Parties, cutting short an economic expert about to begin a long-winded exposition so that everyone could get to lunch in good time.

With Ponomarev, Mitterrand engaged in a dialectical debate about the historical role of Socialism and Communism. At the time of the visit, April 1975, the question of Portugal was high on the agenda. Ponomarev criticized Mitterrand's and the Socialist International's support for Soares and the Portuguese Socialists. Ponomarev compared Soares with the pre-war German Social Democrats who, he argued, had not co-operated with the German Communists in stopping Hitler's rise to power. Mitterrand gently reminded his Russian tutor of the true history of the period and of how, on Stalin's orders, the German Communists between 1928–32 had attacked the Social Democrats as 'social-fascists' and class collaborators. It had been that fratricide on the Left that had helped Hitler's ascension to power. Why had Ponomarev made this bizarre and inaccurate historical allusion, all the more absurd, as in Portugal the Communists were in alliance with the military against the Socialists who were standing on policies similar to those in the French Common Programme? Mitterrand later wrote:

> The incident struck me as a warning that we should nourish few illusions about what Moscow considered to be the outcome of the Union of the Left in France. The moment of truce had not arrived between the two wings of the working-class movement, between Communism and our Socialism. I mentioned this to Gaston Deferre, but the extremely pleasant hospitality that we had received seemed to contradict this impression. The cordial welcome and special attention they bestowed upon us seemed to be more than one would expect on the basis of a party-to-party visit and was closer to the reception one would expect if we had been making a state visit. We interpreted this as a wager on the outcome of the next election. Faced with the choice between developing a solid and friendly understanding of those who would be in power in France tomorrow and their fear of a new model of Socialist society in Europe that would be different, if not directly opposed to the

Communist model, our hosts had decided the former was more important.

Six months later Mitterrand was in Washington being ushered in to the United States' Secretary of State's office by its occupant, Henry Kissinger. The two men had met many years before when Kissinger was a Harvard professor calling on European politicians to research his book, *American Foreign Policy*. Kissinger had talked and talked and talked, so much so that Mitterrand's wife laid an extra place for dinner. Now he was one of the most powerful men in the world. As Mitterrand settled to discuss current issues with Kissinger he found that Washington was as obsessed as Moscow with the question of the possible entry into power of Communist parties in West Europe and the role that Socialist parties would play in the process. Kissinger told Mitterrand that in the Americans' view it was not a question of the internal policies adopted by non-Communist parties of the Left that worried him but the very idea of Communists in government. 'The Atlantic Alliance was brought into being in order to contain Communist expansion. We don't need any Trojan horses.' For Kissinger, Eurocommunism was just a 'tactical variation of a universal strategy'. Mitterrand was not ready to let Kissinger do all the talking and attacked the United States' support for so many dictatorships around the world. He contrasted this with the childhood image he had of America, the land of Jefferson and Lincoln, American straightforwardness and love of freedom, the enthusiastic welcome for American troops in France during the war. 'That image we have of you is worth more than the Vietnam war or the Greek colonels.' Kissinger bristled at the word 'dictatorship' and once again drifted off into an anti-Communist tirade. The discussion, between the two men, as recorded by Mitterrand, had become circular, dialectically pointless and, in any case, the time allotted for the meeting was running out. Mitterrand noted that he wanted to, but did not, put one final question to Kissinger. 'Have you ever wondered? The West will only resist the powerful attraction of a system which it is fighting (i.e. Communism) if it breaks the system on which the West is based (i.e. capitalism).'

Mitterrand was visiting America in December 1975 when

speculation had become intense as to who would be running for President of the United States in the 1976 elections. On the Republican side, the fight for nomination was between Gerald Ford and Ronald Reagan. Of the latter, Mitterrand simply commented on his past abilities as an actor and his attempt to place himself to the right of everyone else in political terms. More interesting is Mitterrand's analysis of possible Democratic candidates. He goes through several including Kennedy, Jackson and Humphrey but does not mention the eventual winner, Jimmy Carter. Carter did not break through to the head of the race until spring 1976, but not to have known at the end of 1975 of his relentless campaigning for the presidential nomination and not to have listed him as a potential candidate suggests that Mitterrand's knowledge of American politics was fairly limited.

It was the United States or rather the power of North American capital, he blamed for the failure of Europe, by which he meant the EEC, to work well or to develop a collective political identity. Mitterrand is what the British Left would dismiss as a 'Euro-fanatic'. This is unfair, as the roots of Mitterrand's Europeanism have little to do with the desires that inspired Edward Heath to push the United Kingdom into the Common Market in 1970–74. For Mitterrand, the construction of Europe and the institutions associated with the Common Market were intimately bound up with solving the German question. For France, far more than for Britain or any other European country, Germany is the biggest problem. Three times in the past century, German armies have smashed their way into France, occupied large chunks of French territory and imposed direct rule on millions of French citizens. Mitterrand recalls his grandparents unable to choke back tears whenever the great Prussian defeat of France at Sedan in 1870, was mentioned. Mitterrand was born during one war with Germany and was marked by a second. The European spirit – what Mitterrand described as the 'mission of Europe' in the immediate post-war years was based on and inspired by the need for the economic and political reconciliation of Germany with France and the rest of Europe. To reconcile the German manufacturing and agricultural economies with those of France coupled with the possibility of some measure of political integration would finally solve the German problem. Mitterrand wanted to see the development of a European political identity accompany economic integration, but it was the latter that took off while the political aspect never left the ground. By the 1970s Mitterrand remained a believer in Europe, as shown by his insistence on the pro-EEC section of the Common Programme. But he had become a somewhat dejected and disappointed member of the faithful. The 1976 European Movement's Congress he described as 'a little troupe wandering from capital to capital with its rituals and habits but no public. They spoke of Europe as if General de Gaulle had not broken it up, as if the United States had not colonized it, as if Germany had not learnt to walk without crutches.'

In particular he felt the EEC had failed to stand up to the challenge of the United States. American-based multinationals now so dominated European and world trade that 'the real capital of Europe is Washington'. The answer to this was to develop a political Europe, with workers participating in its institutions. Only such a Europe would be able to stand up to the power of the multinationals. 'Europe must be Socialist or it will not exist,' he declared.

If Europe was Mitterrand's answer to resolve the great French question of what should be done about Germany, he displayed surprisingly little empathy for the country himself. As with Britain there is barely a mention in his writing and speeches of Germany or the German labour movement. He once complained to Willy Brandt about the German Social Democratic Party's habit of exchanging observers with the Gaullist party in the 1960s. He also crossed with Helmut Schmidt after the West German Chancellor had protested following Mitterrand's public support for those campaigning against the notorious *berufsverbot* law which permitted the dismissal of public employees suspected of having Communist sympathies. Added to that was the irritation of seeing Schmidt and Giscard become such close friends with well publicized encounters between the two leaders every few months. Giscard and Schmidt, it was pointed out, conversed in English. Lacking both that language and German, Mitterrand did not seek to develop his knowledge or understanding of

German political culture. The German Social Democratic Party with its explicit renunciation in 1959 of class-based politics, its hostility to widespread state takeovers, and its vitriolic hatred of Communism within West Germany was far removed from the profile and policies of Mitterrand's Socialist Party in France. A political problem to which, frankly, Mitterrand has never addressed himself, is how to integrate the very different political culture, history and internal makeup of the Socialist, Social Democratic and Labour parties that form the non-Communist Left in Europe. 'Eurosocialism' like 'Eurocommunism' belongs more to the journalist's phrase book than political reality.

In the Spring of 1977 however the idea of 'Eurosocialism' like 'Eurocommunism' remained very much in fashion and seemed to denote a politically coherent innovation in France, Italy and Spain. The dropping of a revolutionary vocabulary, the search for political partnership in and even beyond the Left, a public commitment to political plurality, a refusal to acknowledge the leadership of the Communist Party of the Soviet Union and a denunciation of repressive practices inside Russia appeared to link together the three major West European Communist parties who enjoyed a mass base. In June 1976, in the Italian general elections, the Italian Communist Party had come second by only 3.6% to the ruling Christian Democrats. In Spain the Spanish Communist Party had emerged after Franco's death as a powerful force. While in France the elections of 1976 and 1977 had shown a steady increase for the Union of the Left. It seemed as if there really was a Eurocommunist phenomenon and it was moving from success to success.

A closer examination showed that the differences within Euro-communism were as great, if not greater, than the common elements that were supposed to define it. In Italy, the Italian Communist Party had shaken off its Stalinist coverings twenty years previously. It was socially much broader-based than the French Communist Party with three times the membership while its internal culture and organization was considerably more open and tolerant. If, like the French Communists, the Italian Communist Party had been excluded from power since the end of the war it had none the less become the main focus for opposition to the Italian Right and no other party of the Left approached its place in Italian politics. In Spain, the Spanish Communist Party had a reputation for opposition to Franco earned more by the activities of its militants inside the country than by the squabbling of its exiled leaders. It would have liked to build a Spanish Union of the Left with the Spanish Socialist Party, but the Spanish Socialist leader, Felipe Gonzalez, had been horrified by the behaviour and tactics of the hard-line Communists in neighbouring Portugal and with the backing of the Socialist International and especially under the influence of the West German Social Democratic Party had developed a firm anti-Communist policy. There were also bitter organizational fights between the Communist and Socialist trade unions which did little to foster unity between the political parties. In short, the relationship of the so-called Eurocommunist parties to their members, to other Left parties and to the population in general was very different in each of the three countries in question. In France, the country where the electoral and programmatic alliance between Communists and Socialists had steadily increased in popularity since 1972, it seemed only a matter of time before Communist ministers would be attending their first Cabinet meeting.

In fact, when the National Assembly elections were held in March 1978, the Union of the Left had been ripped apart, the government remained secure in office and the abuse by the French Communist Party heaped on their former partners outdid even the insults of the Right. Giscard and the rest of the French Right, which by 1978 was badly divided itself, could hardly believe their luck in seeing the Union of the Left fall apart. How did it all come about?

In the immediate aftermath of the 1977 municipal elections it looked almost as if the Communist Party would edge closer towards the Socialists. Two major policy-changes were announced, again without consultation with the Party's base. The Party would support direct elections to the European parliament and was now dropping its opposition to nuclear weapons. It now wanted the French bomb aimed in all directions, not just eastwards. The new Communist slogan to add to the one recently adopted of developing 'a Socialism in the colours of France' was that 'neither Washington, nor Rome (i.e.

the EEC Treaty), nor Moscow' would guide France's destiny.

These developments in Communist Party policies and constitution coincided with the Left's steady advance in local elections. If the existing pattern of voting held up it would mean the Communists entering government in alliance with the Socialists in 1978. Although that had been the ambition of the Communists since the early 1960s as the prospect came nearer to fulfilment the Communists had to ask themselves on what terms they would be entering that government. They also had to consider what would happen to their traditional role as the uncompromising champion of France's industrial proletariat.

Would they enter government as an equal partner, with a fair share of the big ministries? In whose interests would they be expected to manage the existing economic crisis? Would they have to act as Thorez had done between 1945 and 1947, and police the working class into accepting austerity? If a government of the Union of the Left clashed with Giscard, the right-wing President, would the subsequent presidential election mean an even more supreme Mitterrand in power? Even if a government of the Left were successful, would it not be Mitterrand and the Socialists who would pick up the credit while the Communists could fade away as being neither sufficient nor necessary for reform and progress in France? What, in any case, were Mitterrand's real intentions – did all this international fraternization mean that he was no different from Helmut Schmidt, Harold Wilson or James Callaghan? What had greater priority – the survival of the Communist Party as an authentic, distinctive grouping in France or the victory at any price of the Union of the Left? Finally, would it mean that the Communist Party would have to give up its position as the leader of the French working class, a role that meant more to it than anything else in the world?

These questions circulated through the French Communist Party's leadership, itself divided on how to analyse the current problems or what the correct line should be. One way to secure an answer to some of these questions was to try to renegotiate the Common Programme and insert into it the kind of guarantees that would give those Communist leaders committed to continuing the alliance with the Socialists the upper hand over those who wanted to return the Communist Party to its isolated position. A fresh look at the five-year-old Programme was a reasonable proposition given the major economic and political changes since 1972 but the way the Communist Party went about trying to change it opens the question of how sincere their wish was to reach agreement, just as Mitterrand's behaviour during the period of discussions over the Common Programme raises the question of how far he was willing to accept a rupture of the Union of the Left provided all, or nearly all, the blame could be pinned on the Communists.

Soon after the 1977 municipal elections, a group of Communist Party economists produced a fresh interpretation of the Common Programme based on massive wage increases and predicated on an implausible growth rate of 6% per annum once the Union of the Left had taken over. The figures were published just before Mitterrand was due to take part in a television debate with the French Prime Minister Raymond Barre, who was able to throw Mitterrand on to the defensive by attacking him using the unrealistic economic projections announced by the Communist Party as their version of how the Common Programme would work out. So when Mitterrand and Marchais met together with Robert Fabre, the leader of the Left Radicals, in May 1977 to discuss the future of the Common Programme, Mitterrand startled everyone by announcing that there was nothing to renegotiate. The Common Programme signed in 1972 would stand. They could enter into discussion about minor refinements in order to take into consideration new facts since 1972 but there would be no major revisions or additions.

Mitterrand told the Socialist Party Congress in Nantes in June 1977: 'We shall go into the elections with the Common Programme, we shall go into government with the Common Programme.' The debate over the Common Programme was a reflection of the power struggle going on inside the Socialist Party itself. Mitterrand was not the object of the struggle, as he now had almost complete domination of the Party; journalists covering the Congress noted how 'dominant and secure of himself' he appeared. The fight centred on a major effort by the CERES group to regain influence over policy and fight its way back into holding some of the top leadership positions. Their bid was backed by Pierre Mauroy; not that Mauroy had much sympathy with the CERES political perspectives but as the man who put party unity and organization above all else, he acknowledged the influx of members into the CERES group at the base and wanted to avoid a discontented faction at odds with the leadership and the official party line in the run-up to the elections.

Mitterrand rejected the idea of rehabilitating CERES. He suspected, with reason, that CERES was too willing to accept Communist positions on a good number of policy questions and would act as a stalking horse for the Communist Party if re-admitted to the National Secretariat. He refused to support the return of CERES and his opposition decided the matter. Instead the Congress was a triumph for Michel Rocard, by now one of the Socialist Party's National Secretaries. Rocard made an impressive speech outlining what he saw as the twin tracks of Socialist development, one leading to *autogestion,* the other to collectivism. It was a dazzling display of dialectical skill. On the major economic question of public ownership, Rocard stood firmly on the right, opposed to widespread nationalization, proclaiming the virtue of private ownership and the market and openly questioning the Common Programme. But this was balanced by his imaginative interpretation of *autogestion,* a process of self-discovery and self-enrichment that would transform workplace, community, social, cultural and just about any other relationship the bewitched listener felt unhappy about. Rocard emerged from the Nantes Congress with his position as the Socialist Party official responsible for renegotiating the economic sections of the Common Programme confirmed.

In the meantime, the Communist Party came forward with some sweeping proposed changes to the Common Programme. Eight new major companies were to be added to the list of those to be nationalized and the 800 subsidiaries of those already on the list were to be definitely included in the state takeover. They wanted a major rise in the minimum wage. They wanted trade union-nominated directors to be placed on the boards of companies, a policy which, given the dominance of the Communist CGT in manufacturing industry, would have placed Communists or Communist sympathizers in key positions throughout French industry.

202

Another issue was that of defence, where the Communists now wanted to drop the Common Programme policy of shedding France's nuclear strike force. The sudden conversion to support for nuclear weapons was announced by the Political Bureau without any debate inside the Party. The sudden announcement shocked all France as the Communists had been strongly opposed to nuclear weapons for thirty years. Mitterrand said he would stick by the Common Programme's disavowal of nuclear weapons. Marchais went on to television to announce in his picaresque way: 'When I heard François Mitterrand refuse to support a system of independent national defence, I said to my wife, "pack the cases, we're going back to Paris, Mitterrand has decided to break the Union of the Left".' It was an astonishing outburst, all the more absurd as Mitterrand had made reservations about the outright suppression of the French nuclear forces proposed by the Communists in 1972. Now Marchais was appearing more militaristic than Mitterrand.

The Communists also said that the disposition of ministries would have to be reorganized and the Communists guaranteed ministries proportional to the votes they received. Finally, they returned to a demand they had tried to secure when the Common Programme was negotiated in 1972, the automatic dissolution of the government when one of the parties forming it chose to leave the Union: this would give the Communists the power to bring down the government of the Left at their own convenience.

Mitterrand was ready to discuss some additions to the list of the companies due to be nationalized but on other issues, and especially those aimed at permanently consolidating Communist power inside ministries and industry he was against accepting any substantial modification. While the Communists tried to present Mitterrand as hell-bent on breaking up the Union of the Left, he refused to be drawn into counter-attacks. Marchais even went so far as to compare him with de Gaulle, while *L'Humanité*'s cartoonist drew a picture of Giscard patting Mitterrand on the head. Altogether it was strange behaviour between partners poised, according to the summer opinion polls, to win the elections in a few months' time. The polls may have predicted an election victory for the Union of the Left, but the worry for the Communists was that they also showed the continuation of a

10% Socialist lead over the Communists. In August 1977, Mitterrand appealed for an end 'to these artificial differences . . . which are being swollen up to feed a quarrel that has become fractious and much resented by the people of France'. At the beginning of September, a few days before the final negotiations were due to take place, he defined his position as: 'Yes to the Common Programme, no to a Communist Programme.'

The first meeting between the party leaders to discuss what had been achieved or not achieved by the lower level negotiators got nowhere. Mitterrand went on television to appeal to the Communists. He acknowledged the different philosophy of the two parties but went on 'We represent the same workers, the same oppressed people, the same exploited people and I am sure that popular unity will weigh heavily upon both of us and little by little we will reach some agreement. That, at any rate, is what I want and am working for.' He said that the Common Programme should be a series of successive contracts. 'Now it is for five years. If it works, let's extend it to ten years. If it doesn't work, that poses some problems. But it has worked so far. Let us continue with it.'

His appeal fell on deaf ears. On 23 September 1977, the three parties met. Pierre Mauroy, breaking Mitterrand's rule of not engaging in polemic with the Communists, had accused them of putting the Socialist Party 'on trial'. Marchais railed at this but the angry words did not obscure the main point, which was the list of changes in the Common Programme which Mitterrand was not prepared to accept. Crisis meetings of the French Left always seem to end in the small hours of the morning and this was no different. The three leaders left the Socialist Party headquarters to tell hundreds of journalists that there had been no agreement. They would meet at some unspecified date in the future. It was the end of the Union of the Left.

One day perhaps the minutes of the Political Bureau of the French Communist Party will be available for researchers who will be able to piece together the analysis and arguments that led the Communists from the first attacks on the Socialist Party following the by-elections in September 1974 to the rupture of the Union of the Left exactly three years later. The period, which includes the dropping by the Communist Party of the 'dictatorship of the proletariat' and its embracing of nuclear weapons is one of the most strange in the modern history of the Left in West Europe. In a book (*Here and Now*) published in 1980, Mitterrand outlined what he considered to be four reasons for the rupture. Firstly, the Communist Party did not want to win in the 1978 elections and have to take responsibility for managing the crisis. Secondly, they reacted angrily to no longer being the party with the biggest support on the Left. Thirdly, Mitterrand claimed that the French Communist Party's tone hardened in response to a change in policy by the Communist Party of the Soviet Union. From January 1977 onwards, Mitterrand argued, Soviet Party theoreticians had began to be hostile to unity between Communist and other left-wing parties. Fourthly, was the Russian fear of a successful Union of the Left and the example to the world of a country where 'Socialism, human rights and national independence' could co-exist and develop. It would set a worrying example to the East European countries under Russian domination.

The suggestion that the Kremlin could play a decisive or even an influential role in determining the French Communist Party's domestic politics would not have been one that Mitterrand would have dared to advance in 1977. By the end of 1980, Marchais and the French Communists were so patently following the Soviet Union's line on Afghanistan, Poland, and the treatment of dissidents inside Russia that Mitterrand's explanation for the break-up of the Union of the Left was no longer so outlandish.

After the rupture, abuse was heaped upon Mitterrand. Marchais told his Central Committee in November 1977 that the Socialists aimed 'to manage the social crisis in the interests of big capital, and to continue to impose austerity upon the workers'. A week later, Mitterrand recorded no less than fifteen separate attacks on the Socialist Party in *L'Humanité*. In January 1978, Marchais accused the Socialist Party of 'complicity' with the government.

Yet on the ground the rupture came as a total shock and activists in both parties were dismayed. Only a few months after Socialists and Communists had won power in so many municipalities here were their leaders throwing away the unity that had achieved such a great victory. An opinion poll carried out soon after the rupture showed 90% of the Communist Party members and 70% of the Socialist Party members hoped the disagreement could be resolved. It was not to be. When, early in 1978, Mitterand offered to accept the Communist proposal for a 37% rise in the minimum wage (against the advice of his right-wing economic advisers who were horrified at the inflationary consequences) Marchais spurned the olive branch. 'Mitterrand and Barre,' said Marchais, 'are birds of a feather.'

The opinion polls were holding up reasonably well for a Left victory in the March National Assembly elections but the campaign opened with two different sets of tactics from the former partners in the Union of the Left. For Mitterrand, 'The Left must aim for victory with the programme that it has and not a programme that becomes, by successive touches, a Communist programme.' The Communist Party meanwhile campaigned under the slogans of 'Make the Rich Pay' and 'Communist ministers in a government of the Left'. Mitterrand rushed though several meetings a day tirelessly proclaiming his themes of the two Frances, the richness of the rich and the poverty of the poor, the need for a Socialist revolution that would enhance individual lives. The Socialist Party sent out six million postcards to voters asking them to write in with comments on party policy.

For the Right, the campaign came down to one question, the menace of Communist ministers in the government. Giscard had already taken out one insurance policy with a new regulation permitting French citizens living overseas to vote in a constituency of their choice in mainland France, votes that the efficient right-wing political machines, helped by friendly embassies, could channel to marginal seats. In the first round, the Left did well but not well enough. Overall they obtained more votes than the Right, and the Socialist Party obtained 22.8% of the vote to the Communists' 20.6%.

In between the two rounds, the Socialists and Communists met, agreed to abide by republican discipline, and went forward on the basis of an unamended Common Programme. But the agreement was unconvincing. Either it could have been reached months before and spared left-wing supporters the sight of the two parties attacking each other or it was a piece of cynical electoralism devoid of principle and unworthy of support.

The Right kept harping on the terrors to be unleashed once Communists were in government. Giscard, while promising to respect the voters' choice, said that if the Left were elected France would become enfeebled while a Left government would assure 'at a stroke the economic and monetary preponderance of West Germany'.

The Right won comfortably, gaining nearly a million more votes than the Left. Many people only voted in the second round in order to prevent a Union of the Left government. Both the Socialists and Communists gained some seats but the overall right-wing majority in the new National Assembly was 290 aganst 201. Again, Mitterrand had failed to win power, though this time it could be fairly said that the Communists had helped snatch a defeat for the Left from the jaws of victory. But having someone else to blame was scant comfort. The political strategy he had developed and fought for since 1965 – an alliance with the Communist Party – lay in ruins. Once again, as in 1958 and 1968, there was another desert to cross.

15
The Last Years in Opposition

I am here to restore Socialism to France and France to Socialism.

The aftermath of the 1978 election was not happy for Mitterrand. Very soon, calls from inside the Socialist Party, at first muted and then more strident, were made for his replacement. Everyone agreed that the Left had done well since the Congress of Epinay. Yet, when it came to the ballot box under Mitterrand's leadership, it kept losing. With the presidential contest only three years away, would it not be better to choose a new candidate? Mitterrand would be sixty-four years old at the end of the 1981 presidential election. He had made his mark on history in reconstructing the French Left but not as an election winner. There was a younger and equally popular Socialist leader available in Michel Rocard who had been a constant critic of the close alliance with the Communists and of the Common Programme's emphasis on nationalization. The alliance with the Communists had collapsed and the Common Programme, on which Mitterrand had fought the 1978 elections, had failed. To rub home the point the *Nouvel Observateur*, hitherto the journal that had always supported Mitterrand, published a photograph of Rocard on the front page of its post-election issue. The editor had gone to see Mitterrand and asked him if he would be upset if they put Rocard on the front page, and Mitterrand had answered they could put who they liked, but he was known to be upset all the same. Here was one of his oldest, and in terms of its 400,000 circulation mainly in left-wing circles, one of his most influential supporters none too gently hinting that his time was up.

Those who wanted to replace him underestimated him. Defeat was nothing new to Mitterrand. In the war he had been twice recaptured before succeeding in his escape bid. He had been removed from a Cabinet post at the age of thirty-five. He had been humiliated in the 1958 elections and by the 'Observatory' affair. He had had to creep away after announcing his willingness to form a government in 1968. He had survived the disappointment of 1974 and the attacks from the Communist Party after 1975. But from all those past defeats and disappointments, he had come back to fresh successes both for himself and the Left.

As in the past, he retreated from Paris. Not only did he travel abroad, he spent more time enlarging his home in the south-west of France. There he went for walks with his labradors in the pine forest, and looked after his beehives and donkeys, Maron and Noisette. When Jean-Pierre Chevènement arrived to stay and could not tell the male from the female donkey, Mitterrand chided him: 'You will never learn to know people unless first you learn to understand animals.' He pruned his roses. His wife, sons, grandchildren, sister and close family friends would stay; they were ever ready to welcome a colleague in the Socialist Party leadership or even a passing Socialist Party member wanting to shake hands with Mitterrand. His weekends were spent in his constituency, a hectic Friday to Monday round of meetings and dealing with the problems of the 150 communes in the Nièvre. He stayed in a small, sparsely furnished room in a local hotel, eating like any passing salesman in the hotel dining room.

There from the local people he could hear the grumbles about Giscard's France. Because the 1978 election, comforting as it was to those in France who had believed the opinion polls' steady prediction, right up to the last moment, of victory for the Left, had resolved nothing. France had the same government, which had no new answers and exactly the same problems. Giscard endeavoured to capitalize on the Left's defeat by projecting himself as a President of all of France who was governing from the Centre, not the representative of the Right. He invited Mitterrand and Marchais and other party leaders to the Elysée and also received the leaders of the trade-union confederations. He included Socialist representatives in France's United Nations delegation but his most successful stroke was to persuade Robert Fabre, the leader of the Left Radicals, the third and most junior of the partners in the Union of the Left, to work for the government as chairman of a special commission on unemployment. Fabre's defection angered his own party and provided the Communists with useful propaganda ammunition in the campaign to paint Mitterrand and the Socialists on the point of following Fabre into the Giscard orbit.

Giscard's attempt to open the Elysée to opposition currents reflected the period immediately following his election in 1974. Then he had quickly initiated certain reforms, bringing the voting age down to eighteen, legalizing abortion (though on the most restrictive terms in Europe), and setting up a Ministry for Women. In a book, *French Democracy*, he defined his vision of France as 'a modern democratic society, liberal by the pluralist structure of all its powers, advanced by the high degree of its economic performance, social unification and cultural development'. But the Giscard vision never matched up to the performance. The reforms he was so proud of in 1975 were commonplace elsewhere in Europe's liberal democracies. All he was doing was catching up with what has been introduced in Britain and West Germany in the 1960s and Scandinavia in the 1950s. Other reforms, such as breaking up the monopoly state broadcasting corporation into three television channels and four radio networks, all separately run, appeared to be progressive, but the head of each channel was carefully vetted by the government and unsurprisingly often turned out to be a Giscardian associate. The hand of the President was felt right down to the appointment of interviewers and reporters. Giscard dispensed with the old French model of a minister acting as a kind of editor-in-chief and adopted the more modern corporate method of appointing media chiefs whose political outlook and past record could be relied upon not to shake the establishment. Certainly none of the journalists purged by de Gaulle in 1968 got back their jobs and the 1974 reorganization of broadcasting provided the opportunity to sack or consign to some broadcasting ghetto those remaining journalists whose allegiance to the Giscard state was open to question. On one important issue, the death penalty, where liberal reformers in other countries had stood by their abolitionist principles in face of a hostile public opinion, Giscard, despite announcing himself to be in favour of doing away with the guillotine, gave way to the Right's implacable support for France's gruesome form of execution. Several people were decapitated during Giscard's presidency, some of them after highly dubious convictions. Another reform Giscard proposed, an extremely modest tax on capital, was emasculated by right-wing deputies against whom the government dared not fight.

Underneath the patina of reform and Giscard's liberal, modernist verbiage, France remained a country run in the interest of the conservatives who had swept back with de Gaulle in 1958 and held on to power ever since. They had some reservations about Giscard, even though they had united around him as the best candidate to beat Mitterrand in 1974. In exchange for that support, Giscard had to accept the ambitious young Gaullist, Jacques Chirac, as his Prime Minister. Chirac tried to develop an executive authority of his own from inside the Prime Minister's office, but Giscard was determined to maintain the Fifth Republic conception of the President as the dominant power in government. The two kept clashing until Giscard dispensed with Chirac in 1976, reassuring the conservatives by appointing Raymond Barre, a right-wing economics professor, as Prime Minister. In addition to his academic post, Barre had been a European civil servant. He did not have a seat in the National Assembly and his appointment underlined Giscard's indifference to the processes of parliamentary democracy. Barre believed in the virtues of an unrestrained market – one of his early acts was to demolish long-established price controls on staple foods which pushed up the price of that essential part of every French meal, the long, thin loaf of bread called a *baguette*. These price rises meant a lot to the millions of French poor. And there were plenty of them. In 1979, in addition to 1.6 million unemployed there were 6 million workers still paid only the minimum legal wage. To Barre's favourite audiences of business-men and executives, the price liberalization was proof that they had a Prime Minister who understood the need for profit and where it should come from. The gap between the rich and the poor remained as wide as ever. One survey in 1980 showed that the highest-paid Frenchman earned thirty times as much as the lowest-paid. A 30–1 ratio was unknown in any other Western country. Barre showed himself indifferent to democratic or parliamentary procedures: when leading opposition speakers would go to the rostrum he would pointedly leave the Assembly saying he had more important things to do. In a television debate Mitterrand said to Barre: 'You don't believe in the alternation of power, do you?' Barre replied: 'Yes, I do, but not with anybody.'

Giscard had replaced one right-wing Prime Minister, Chirac, with another, Barre, but the energetic and ruthlessly ambitious Chirac was not going to be pushed into eclipse. In December 1976, he founded a new Gaullist movement, the Republican Rally. Launched at a stadium packed with 50,000 cheering supporters, the Republican Rally, its very title chosen to echo de Gaulle's Rally of the French People, swept into its orbit the old and still efficiently implanted Gaullist machine. In 1977, Chirac won a bitterly fought contest to become Mayor of Paris – one of the Giscardian reforms had been to restore Paris's mayoralty, which had been kept suppressed since 1871 by successive govern-ments fearful that a Mayor of Paris would set himself up as an alternative power centre; which is precisely what Chirac did. New projects were initiated; Paris street signs suddenly had the Mayor's name on them; he received foreign visitors like a head of state and started all sorts of quarrels with the government in order to assert his difference and independence.

The governing majority was therefore split and Giscard could not stray too far from the Right for fear of handing yet more ammunition to Chirac who was ever willing to denounce any deviation as a sign that Giscard was turning into the social democratic Schmidt of France. For workers the squabbling between Giscard and Chirac was an argument between Tweedledum and Tweedledee. First Chirac, then Barre, and reigning over both, Giscard, were prepared relentlessly to sacri-fice jobs and hold down wages in order to safeguard the profits of those sections of French capital deemed to have a secure future. Unemployment tripled between 1974 and 1980, rising to 1.8 million at the end of the Giscard presidency. Industries such as textiles and steel were allowed to run down and the regions where the steel plants and cotton factories were based were hard hit. Strikes, occupations and demonstrations were violently suppressed by the CRS riot-police. Mitterrand would rush from strike meeting to occupied factory speaking to workers, and the Socialist Party put forward several plans for saving the industries selected for rundown. Despite the rupture of the Union of the Left, and the French Communist Party's desire to be the sole defender of the industrial working class, Mitterrand made sure that he and the Socialist Party were to be seen fighting on the proletariat's terrain. To this end Mitterrand encouraged the setting up of workplace branches of the Socialist Party; by the end of 1978, more than 1,200 had been formed.

In the National Assembly, where his debating skill had made him one of the speakers that deputies would stay in the hemicycle to hear, Mitterrand delighted deputies with set-piece orations on the unscrupulous practices of the police and judicial system under Giscard. There were plenty of examples to chose from. Sometimes it was a question of blatant executive interference with judicial processes. When Abu Daoud, the leader of the terrorist group involved in the Israeli athletes' massacre at the Munich Olympics was arrested in Paris, the government ignored extradition demands from both West Germany and Israel and bundled him on to a plane destined for an Arab country. On the other hand, when a left-wing West German lawyer, Klaus Croissant, who had defended the Baader-Meinhof gang was picked up in Paris, he was handed over to the German authorities even before the proper extradition procedures had been gone through.

Independent magistrates came under pressure. One who remanded in custody a factory owner in whose factory a worker had been killed by unsafe machinery, was suspended from the magistracy despite having acted within the limits of his judicial powers. Leading journalists like Simon Malley, editor of a magazine specializing in French African relations, or Roger Delpey, who promised to reveal all about the diamonds Giscard had been given by the tyrannical 'Emperor' Bokassa, were detained on administrative orders.

Mitterrand himself, together with other Socialist Party leaders, was charged with an illegal act after they had broadcast on a pirate radio station set up by Socialist militants. The spread of 'free' radio stations was a gesture of defiance against the Giscardian official radio networks. They were helped by the new, very cheap radio transmitter technology that meant one could produce limited radio broadcasts at little expense; by 1981 there were more than 300 of those stations. The government decision to break into the Socialist Party station and charge Mitterrand was one of pure spite that greatly embarrassed the examining magistrate that had to hear the case. French security forces placed bugs in the offices of the *Canard Enchainé*. Giscard, in the final months of his presidency, even launched a libel suit against *Le Monde*, a paper which more than any in the world has the justified reputation for getting its facts right and avoiding sensation.

Amongst those hardest hit by the repression of the Giscardian state were immigrants. Like other advanced industrial countries in Europe, France had encouraged immigrant workers in the boom years to settle in the country in order to carry out the dirty, exhausting or low-paid jobs that the indigenous population were unwilling to perform. By the middle 1970s, there were an estimated 4 million immigrants, mainly North Africans, Spaniards and Yugoslavs in France. Thirty-one per cent of the construction industry workforce and 26% of the automobile industry workforce were immigrants. One of Giscard's first steps in 1974 was to prevent both further immigration and immigrant families joining their breadwinner in France. In 1977, the government tried to bribe immigrants with an offer of 10,000 francs (£1,000) to individuals willing to be repatriated. Few took up the offer despite the appalling circumstances in which many lived. There were shanty towns outside all the main industrial cities. One in four immigrants was living in derelict warehouses or huts with just a cold water tap in the yard as the only plumbing. Racist attacks were common and police harassment frequent, so much so that the ambassadors of Morocco and Algeria in Paris had to beg the French government to protect immigrants from assaults. In 1979 the government introduced new anti-immigrant measures which provoked protests from Mitterrand and the Socialists. A new law gave the government the right to expel immigrants if they were picked up without papers, without a job or could show no means of support. The expulsions could be ordered administratively and while awaiting expulsion, the hapless individuals could be detained in special internment camps. Internment and administrative expulsions were too much for a France which was still sensitized to similar Nazi procedures in the war and, after vigorous protests from the opposition, the proposed law was considerably modified. But it showed how authoritarian the supposedly liberal regime had become.

Mitterrand reacted angrily against a new law called 'Liberty and Security' which was put forward by Giscard's Justice Minister in 1980. The law substantially increased sentences for a range of crimes and reduced the accused's right of protection or appeal. Considerable new powers were given to courts to dispense summary justice without the traditional rights of defence. Mitterrand attacked the proposed law in the National Assembly as giving the state more power in the dispensation of justice than even Napoleon had wanted. One would have to go back to the worst edicts of the Vichy regime to find an equivalent conception of justice. On the issue of personal liberty and the balance of power and rights between the individual and the state Mitterrand made long, rolling yet pointed speeches full of historical and literary allusions. One senses that he regretted not having been able to stand beside Zola and Jaurès to defend Dreyfus.

France's university structure was brought back more tightly under state control with a dismantling of the democratic structure squeezed out of the authorities following 1968. Research was channelled into money-making areas and funds for 'nonprofitable' pure research were withdrawn.

Giscard himself was involved in a bizarre set of scandals. He was accused of receiving a valuable collection of diamonds from Bokassa and of accepting a plot of land in Greece from the Greek colonels. His passion for big-game hunting in Africa or hunting bear on estates reserved for the Communist elite in Gierek's Poland aroused comment. The accessible, informal Giscard projected by his public relations advisers in 1974 gave way to an aloof, unapproachable Giscard who insisted on being served first off gold plate at state banquets even when there were women present. A special presidential crest was invented and various relatives appeared to benefit rather more from state patronage than their individual talent might otherwise have merited.

The trade unions were able to do little to oppose Giscard's programme. Following the break-up of the Union of the Left, the leaders of the two main confederations had pulled apart despite the strong calls from the rank and file of both organizations for unity of action, at least, at the base. In 1979, the CGT announced a week of action in September. Two days before the announcement was made, the CGT leader had met with his opposite number in the CFDT but had not mentioned the week of action. When the independently minded CFDT refused automatically to fall in behind the CGT campaign, they were accused of not being willing to struggle against Giscardian oppression! From 1978 onwards, although there were some impressive mass demonstrations, trade union activities were uncoordinated.

The unions also found themselves directly attacked by government and employers. According to French law, union representatives cannot be dismissed without permission of the local work inspector, a government-appointed official. Unions recorded numerous incidents in the 1970s when permission to sack a local union leader was refused by the work inspector, but the decision was overturned when the company appealed to the Ministry of Labour in Paris. French industrial tribunals started to hand down massive fines against unions accused of damaging a firm's profits because of strike action. Big firms increased the size of their personnel departments in order to supervise each worker individually and discourage union activity. There was a widespread introduction of employment on temporary or fixed-term contracts with the threat of non-renewal if workers became active in the union. In February 1980, a union activist in a Peugeot factory killed himself after explaining that he could not stand the anti-union pressure directed against him in the factory.

By the late 1970s, union membership was falling. Edmond Maire, the CFDT leader, angry at the failure of the political Left to compose their differences, argued that French unions should distance themselves more from politics and try and develop better organization inside workplaces and aim for a more institutionalized system of collective bargaining with the employers in the British or American tradition. He saw the Giscard years stretching ahead into the 1980s. In December 1979, Maire said: 'We are not primarily concerned about joining battle to see who will be beaten by Giscard in 1981 . . . in current circumstances, whoever is the Left's candidate will lose.'

Maire's judgement was shared by many who watched with concern the fighting inside the Socialist Party and the non-stop attacks by the Communist Party on their erstwhile partners. As soon as the National Assembly elections were over, Michel Rocard had launched a campaign to project himself as the Socialist's presidential candidate in 1981. As he said on television on the night of the second round: 'At least it's only three years to 1981.'

Rocard benefited from a double-sided political profile. He was the former militant leader of the almost ultra-left Unified Socialist Party and at the same time he was the reformist, even right-wing social democrat on many economic questions. One side of his profile attracted the young Socialist Party activists while the other side reassured those who had always had their doubts about the Common Programme. He was very popular with the media and enjoyed the support of the *Nouvel Observateur* and the new left-wing daily paper, *Le Matin*, which was launched in 1977 and quickly achieved the difficult feat for France, indeed for Europe, of establishing itself as a serious, readable, progressive morning newspaper with a decent circulation. Rocard had his own group of associates who worked with him on political questions – when he was appointed a National Secretary of the Socialist Party he had refused to move into the Party headquarters, preferring to maintain his own suite of offices as an independent power centre within the party. He had advisers who chose his clothes, hairstyle, even his tie: that Rocard intended some day to run for President was not in doubt to the whole of France.

Mitterrand watched the rise of Rocard with some bitterness. An opinion poll carried out in September 1978 revealed that only 31% saw Mitterrand as a future President. The same month Rocard had given a radio interview in which he said that 'a certain political style, a certain archaism stands condemned'. The attack on Mitterrand was obvious. Rocard had been touring the country speaking to local Socialist groups in order to build up his power base. It was all reminiscent of Mitterrand's behaviour in the 1960s when he had used the Convention of Republican Institutions and provincial tours to make up for the absence of a solid regional base behind him.

Not just the left-wing media were behind Rocard. In a three-week period in the autumn of 1978 he appeared seventeen times on television and radio. In the same period, Mitterrand, who was after all still the Socialist leader and who had just published a new book, appeared only twice. 'There has never been a politician who has benefited from such support by the media, most of it initiated by those in power,' commented an angry Mitterrand. In December 1978, opinion polls showed that 40% thought Rocard would be the best presidential candidate for the Socialist Party and only 27% backed Mitterrand.

Most Socialist leaders in democratic countries have to learn to live with a hostile media and discomfiting opinion polls. Mitterrand ignored them, saying: 'It took Léon Blum fifteen years to lead his party to power after the split [between Socialists and Communists] at Tours in 1920. So far I have only had seven years and I am ready to answer for them.' He insisted that he would stick by the broad policy lines laid down in the Common Programme though at the same time he set up dozens of new working groups on policy. Keeping the party busy might take its mind off the internal feuding. It was no good. The 1978 election failure meant that the divisions inside the Socialist Party which had been shoved into the background during the period of growth and vote-gathering following the Epinay Congress would now have to come into the open and they would have to be resolved.

The Socialist Party's Congress held at Metz in April 1979 was where Mitterrand turned the tables on Rocard and secured his own position in the party. Rocard had made an alliance with Pierre Mauroy who refused to accept Mitterrand's wish that Rocard be removed from the party leadership. Mauroy, as always, was the conciliator looking for some compromise to keep the party together. As the question of Mitterrand's future began continually to be raised after March 1978, Mauroy also was a possible runner in the fight for succession. Whoever the candidate was he would be chosen by delegates at a special Party Congress and it was in the grass roots of the party that Mauroy knew his way and felt at home. Mauroy had also become irritated by some of Mitterrand's high-handed behaviour and his insistence on packing the party headquarters with young officials personally loyal to the leader. Some of these had tried to circulate an anti-Rocard statement and gather signatures, including Mauroy's, for it. Such overt arm-twisting offended Mauroy's sensibility about party unity. There were also rumours that in order to forge a successful alliance against Rocard, Mitterrand was prepared to welcome back the CERES group whose outlook, according to Mauroy, was far too close to that of the Communist Party.

Mitterrand was preparing to do precisely that. In his speeches he continued to proclaim his belief that the Left could only win by basing its strategy on a Union of the Left. He still spoke of the need for a 'rupture' with capitalism. In June 1978 he proclaimed: 'I am here to restore Socialism to France and France to Socialism.' He still called for meetings with the Communist Party to try to work out a new pact after the 1977 break, though by now the Communists were making it clear they were not interested in re-creating the Union of the Left. Mitterrand was determined to keep the Socialist Party on a steady left-wing course, despite the Rocardian winds trying to blow the party towards an anti-Communist Centre. The alliance with CERES made political as well as tactical sense.

Mitterrand had another important ally in Gaston Deferre, who objected to Rocard's attempts at wooing away Socialist Party activists in Marseilles and the surrounding region. One in twelve party members came from that area so Rocard had very little choice, if he wanted to quarry votes, but to tread on Deferre's toes. Rocard, said Deferre, was 'neither a new man, nor a young man'. The alliance between the two Fourth Republic veterans, Mitterrand and Deferre, and the left-wing CERES group was enough to see off Rocard and Mauroy. Mitterrand pleased the CERES delegates at the Congress when he said: 'I recognize Marx and Marxism as perhaps the most profound sources which have produced the great current of Socialism on which we float today.' In his keynote speech, Mitterrand went on to elaborate the need for a synthesis between Marxist collectivism and the need for individual liberty and personal development. It was clear before the Congress that Mitterrand would defeat Rocard but the result – 62% for Mitterrand and his allies and 38% for Rocard and Mauroy – was larger than expected. All the Paris-generated excitement in the media or the unfavourable opinion polls had not hurt Mitterrand inside the Socialist Party itself. His support was particularly strong from the provinces where the local party workers recognized his achievements in rebuilding the party. Some Paris-oriented Socialist leaders might be frustrated at not holding government office but under Mitterrand the Socialists had captured power in scores of town halls and there were hundreds of mayors and councillors whose loyalty was to the man who spent every weekend tending his local municipality.

A few weeks previously the Socialists had maintained their vote in the departmental elections. Republican discipline had worked well with Socialist and Communist candidates standing down to let the best-placed candidate through. At the base, therefore, no matter how noisy the row at the top, it was apparent that the Mitterrand strategy of searching for unity on the left and his emphasis on the need for mutual electoral support with the Communists was the only one that could bring victory.

His victory at Metz gave Mitterrand a secure hold over the party. He brought in more young intellectuals to work for him. His aim, he said, was to ensure that whatever happened in the 1981 presidential election the Socialist Party would be in good shape in the 1980s. A year after Metz he was able to boast that thirty-six of the Socialist deputies elected in the previous four years were younger than forty. Thirteen of the nineteen National Secretaries were also under forty. The average age of the provincial secretaries was thirty-nine while in his own constituency the local party officers had an average age of thirty-six. The Socialist Party headquarters was transferred to an elegant nineteenth-century building with its own courtyard in which receptions were held. The party stepped up its output of books and decided to launch its own evening newspaper. Mikis Theodorakis composed a special theme-tune for the Party but there was no denying that the feeling of excitement and achievement that had characterized the party from Epinay up to the break-up of the Union of the Left and the failure in the 1978 elections was no longer there. Membership was static rather than growing and much as Mitterrand had control of the party, Rocard would not give up his candidature and the opinion polls in 1979 and 1980 continued to say he would be a more popular presidential candidate than Mitterrand. In the elections for the European parliament in June 1979, the Socialists experienced their first fall in electoral popularity since 1973. Their vote went down by 1.1% compared with 1978 and they were only just ahead of the Communists.

For Georges Marchais, the European results confirmed his belief that the anti-Socialist Party line he had taken since 1977 was correct and that the distance taken up by the French Communist Party would pay electoral dividends. The Communist Party had also been through a period of well-publicized internal disputes after the 1978 defeat. Liberal intellectuals in the Communist Party had wanted to continue the policy of opening up debate and admitting past mistakes. This contrasted with the hard-liners in the leadership, who could normally put together a majority, who wanted to return the Party to its base in the industrial working class and who wished to repel all who tried to encroach on that base, especially the Socialist Party. That party, together with other West European Socialist parties, was now declared to be 'an active participator in the strategic counter-offensive of the forces of capital'. Emphasis was to be placed on building up the factory cells and the Communist Party was to support any group of workers who were on strike anywhere for any reason – a degree of workerism that irritated even the Communist-dominated CGT. After an initial period of opening up, the hatches were battened down and Communist dissidents inside the Party began to feel the pinch. Although Marchais promised in 1978 that there would be no more expulsions, by the end of 1980 several leading dissidents had been forced out of party posts or had simply not had their membership renewed at the end of the year. It was not quite expulsion but if you were not issued with a party card it was difficult to tell the difference.

As with Czechoslovakia and Portugal, foreign problems

completely soured whatever chances there might have been of reviving the Union of the Left. The Soviet intervention in Afghanistan in the last days of 1979 and the arrival of Solidarity in Poland in August 1980 were two major events on which Socialists and Communists completely diverged. The Communists supported the Soviet intervention in Afghanistan – Marchais announced his endorsement in a television broadcast from Moscow, his first visit there since 1973, and were lukewarm about Solidarity – *L'Humanité* described the Polish strikes in July 1980 as 'workplace discussion sessions', so reluctant was the paper to admit that workers might strike against a Communist government. Mitterrand vigorously condemned the Soviet invasion of Afghanistan and offered his unqualified support to the Polish workers. Marchais now appeared as the arch-defender of the Soviet Union while Mitterrand now appeared to treat Russia as the greatest threat to liberty in the world. A delighted Giscard opened up the airwaves to Marchais – the Communist leader made 150 television and radio appearances in 1980 – because Giscard judged correctly that Marchais would use much of the airtime to insult and criticize Mitterrand.

Autumn 1980 was the time for presidential candidates to declare themselves. Despite the continually increasing unemployment, an inflation rate of 12%, a growth in extreme right-wing attacks aimed at immigrant and Jewish targets, and the seemingly endless series of scandals which showed an unsavoury and often legally dubious side to the behaviour of government ministers as well as all the stories coming from the Elysée about the imperial style of the presidency, the opinion polls still gave Giscard victory in May 1981. Most commentators saw Giscard in power for a further seven years and Mitterrand, if the Socialist Party did finally choose him and not Rocard, would go down in history as a third-time loser.

16
Presidential Candidate – 1981

*The presidency is neither the beginning nor the
end. My ambition is to spread my ideas.*

Mitterrand and the Socialist Party moved towards 1981 and the
presidential contest with a strong left-wing profile. The return of
the CERES group to the National Secretariat in 1979 had led,
early in 1980, to the publication of the *Socialist Plan for France in
the Eighties*. This 400-page paperback set out the traditional
left-wing programme that had been developed in 1972, jointly
agreed with the Communists in the Common Programme and
enriched with the *autogestion* theories debated at the Socialist
Assizes in 1975. By Anglo-Saxon standards of political manifestos, plain lists of tasks to be accomplished, the *Socialist Plan
for France in the Eighties* is an elaborate document starting from
a philosophical defence of democratic Socialism with quotations
from Marx, Brecht, Marcuse, Gramsci and Chomsky to a
detailed critique of economic and political relationships in the
Soviet Union and then a consideration of the variations in the
application of industrial democracy to differing workplaces. The
book made clear that, despite the break of the Union of the Left,
there was to be no retracing of the fundamental policy decisions
concerning nationalization, decentralization, a loosening of

economic ties and dependence on the United States and an extension of rights for women, immigrants, and other oppressed groups in French society.

A new and urgent call in the book was for a return to full employment. With unemployment heading for 2 million, this prime failure of Giscard's seven years was to develop into a major campaign theme for Mitterrand. Unemployment could be contained, argued the *Socialist Plan*, by introducing the thirty-five-hour working week, making it far more difficult for employers to lay off workers and introducing local labour market councils (an idea, borrowed without acknowledgement, from Sweden) which would try to ensure, on the basis of tripartite discussions that no worker lost a job unless he or she had a replacement one to go to.

With the return of politicians from their summer holidays in September 1980, there was an outbreak of candidatures for the presidency. The Communist Party had already announced that Georges Marchais would run in 1981. Having been absent in the 1965 and 1974 presidential elections, the Communists were not going to allow Mitterrand a clear run this time. Marchais presented himself as the only authentic 'anti-Giscard' candidate. Marchais had an extraordinarily dominant personality like a burly, no-nonsense shop-steward always ready to lay into the bosses. In fact, it was more than thirty years since he had worked as a mechanic but despite the elegance of his suits he brought the spirit of proletarian France to the television screen. He was compulsive viewing, ready to insult Giscard, Mitterrand or the television interviewers. He enjoyed his tough, aggressive image but his rollicking style, often tripping over into vulgar bombast, seemed somewhat removed from what would be expected of even a Communist President. Marchais spent as much time attacking Mitterrand as Giscard and, as we shall see, his choice of tactics, if anything, helped the Socialist candidate. The left Radicals put up their leader, Michel Crépeau, as a candidate. There were also candidates from the Unified Socialist Party and a Trotskyist candidate.

On the Right, Giscard faced unwelcome competition in the shape of Jacques Chirac, who, as leader of the Republican Rally, laid claim to the Gaullist inheritance, even if that was disputed by two other right-wing candidates. What Chirac had was an excellent political machine and the advantage of a head start on Giscard who could not begin officially campaigning until the spring – the first round of the election was due to be held on 26 April, 1981, and the second round on 10 May 1981. All the opinion polls argued that Giscard would go through to the second round but he nevertheless could hardly look forward to fighting off a heavyweight attack by Chirac on his right and Mitterrand coming in from the opposite flank.

The unknown quantity in the election would be the ecologists, whose young leader, Brice Lalonde, was to be seen on television and in magazine photographs bicycling in his long woolly scarf around villages in search of the five hundred signatures of local notables necessary to be a presidential candidate. The ecologists had done well in the 1979 European elections, taking 4% of the votes, a margin greater than that which had decided the 1974 election. Their popularity had zoomed in a France that had become worried about the environmental impact of the motorways and office block developments of the Pompidou and de Gaulle period. Giscard had made some concessions, stopping the building of skyscrapers in Paris but on the ecologists' main issue, nuclear power, he refused all compromise. France's nuclear industry is the most developed in the world and Giscard's aim was that half of France's electricity should come from nuclear power stations by 1985. This involved a large construction programme and in the second half of the 1970s there were several major, and often bloody, demonstrations on nuclear sites. The temperature was raised by the incident at Three Mile Island as France used the same kind of nuclear reactors. Giscard was not alone in his pro-nuclear policy. The Communist Party also endorsed the nuclear programme and although the Socialists talked about slowing down the rate of new construction and investing more in solar, wind- and water-generated electricity, they, too, accepted the central thesis that France should move toward greater self-sufficiency in energy supply. The ecologist campaign and candidate therefore would play an important role in keeping the nuclear and environment issues in front of the public and might be decisive when advising their voters on whom to support in the second round.

At least one of Mitterrand's closest associates, the journalist Claude Estier, believes that Mitterrand was undecided about running right up to the last moment. In September, opinion polls only gave him 18% of the vote to Giscard's 33%. Michel Rocard had already announced his candidature and was being strongly supported by *Le Matin* and the *Nouvel Observateur*. According to Estier it was Rocard's pushiness that finally tipped Mitterrand over the edge and into announcing his candidature.

The picture as painted by the pro-Mitterrand Estier is one of the great man, humbly poised between anxiety and duty. But after so much effort in rebuilding the Socialist Party, so many years waiting to return to power, and having never manifested a lack of ambition at key moments earlier in his life, it would be absurd to suppose that Mitterrand would now make way for Rocard. On 8 November 1981, two weeks after his sixty-fourth birthday, he announced his candidature and Rocard withdrew his own.

As so often in the past, Mitterrand brought out a book to coincide with a major political contest. Called *Here and Now*, the book reviews the development of French society and the Socialist Party since 1977. One of the strongest chapters is the attack on the Giscardian state. A few days before the book appeared, there had been a bomb explosion outside a Paris synagogue killing four people. Despite his fervent pronouncements in favour of law and order, it appeared that Giscard could not control the growth in extreme right-wing attacks of which this appeared to be the latest and worst example. A leader of the police union said that one in five French policemen had fascist sympathies. Mitterrand's attacks on the manipulation of justice by Giscard coupled with the growth of unemployment and declining help for the underprivileged struck a chord in a France shocked by the synagogue bomb blasts and by a succession of murders and suicides which had political links.

In the chapter on foreign policy, there is a long attack on the Soviet Union's Afghanistan intervention and praise for the Polish workers who had just formed their own union, Solidarity. The underlining of the distance between Mitterrand's vision of Socialism and Communism could not have been made more distinct.

After announcing his candidature, Mitterrand stayed in the background, making no speeches and refusing interviews, until the beginning of 1981. He went to Madrid and Israel on Socialist International business and in December 1980 was in Washington DC alongside Tony Benn and Olof Palme for a seminar on the challenging, if unusual, theme of the possibility of the arrival of Socialism in the United States.

The opinion polls continued to rate him well below Giscard but elections for the Senate in September and six National Assembly by-elections in November showed strong gains in the Left vote. The Senatorial elections had been marked by the refusal of the Communist Party to withdraw their candidates in the second round: Marchais even went so far as to declare the tradition of republican discipline 'out-dated'.

Mitterrand used the last months of 1980 to make minute preparations for his campaign. Two main campaign slogans were used on the scores of thousands of posters, leaflets and stickers. One simply read *Mitterrand: President* while the main catchphrase was *La Force Tranquille* – the calm strength. Most left-wing parties campaigning on how they will bring change to the society they are asking to govern choose aggressive action-invoking verbs in their election slogans. Against his own inclinations, Mitterrand's media advisers settled on this soft, reassuring yet comfortably solid slogan. It was almost as if the radical change proposed in the Socialist Party's programme would bring order and stability to the troubled France of Giscard. The slogan was backed up by the poster which showed Mitterrand against a kind of red, white and blue rainbow through which the sun's rays could be seen rising to illuminate a village complete with church and steeple. It was a far cry from the lurid orange posters of the 1965 presidential bid with his slogan of 'A young President for a modern France'.

To run his campaign, Mitterrand brought in all the leading Socialist Party figures including Pierre Mauroy, Michel Rocard, Gaston Deferre and Jean-Pierre Chevènement. All worked loyally and hard for his success.

Their first job was to take the great mass of Socialist Party policy and knock it into a campaign manifesto. This became Mitterrand's 110 propositions for France. (See Appendix for full details.) The 110 propositions were true to the policy proposals developed in the previous decade. Nothing important was left out. The commitment to controversial policies such as nationalization, a wealth tax, an increase in the minimum wage, a shorter working week, workers on the board of publicly owned companies were all included. On nuclear energy it was proposed to continue with those sites where work had already begun but not to start any new nuclear power station until after a referendum on the issue had been held. French nuclear weapons, now re-termed an 'autonomous dissuasion strategy' would be maintained. There were brickbats for the Soviet Union which was told to get its troops out of Afghanistan, and for the United States, whose aid to Latin American 'dictatorships' was condemned. Two hundred thousand new public service jobs would be created and the state retirement age reduced to sixty for men and fifty-five for women.

One policy which few commented upon was the reintroduction of proportional representation in national and local elections. Proportional representation had long been a demand of the Communist Party who considered de Gaulle's abolition of it in 1958 an act aimed principally at reducing their presence in national and local assemblies. With a vote that usually hovered around the 20% mark, the Communists felt entitled to at least one fifth of whatever seats were going. Under the Fifth Republic's first past the post system, albeit split over two ballots, they often found their representation proportionately well below their actual vote. On Communist insistence the policy had been included in the Common Programme and Mitterrand had kept it in his 110 propositions. (He made little reference to it in his campaign and it will be interesting to see if the French Socialist government does, in fact, bring back proportional representation.)

The death penalty would be abolished, the State Security Court wound up and the President would no longer appoint all judges. His term of office would be reduced to five years, renewable once, or limited to a single term of office lasting seven years. The EEC would be enlarged with Spain and Portugal joining while the Brussels commission should develop a stronger social policy and should be prepared to protect European industry against Japanese and American imports. There would be more help for small businessmen and farmers. Contraception would be free and paternity as well as maternity leave introduced.

A cynic might say that there was something for everybody in Mitterrand's 110 propositions. It is in the nature of election manifestos to be catch-all. But Mitterrand's list of easy-to-read points represented things that many in France had been waiting to see put right for more than twenty years. What was on offer were specific proposed laws, and detailed new rights; as a reading of the 110 propositions shows there is little verbal padding and Mitterrand knew that he was providing a check-list against which the public could measure his actions once he had won.

At the special party Congress held in January 1981 to endorse officially his candidature, Mitterrand returned to his favourite theme when he told the cheering delegates:

> Since first we set off on this road together I have never stopped appealing to a union of popular forces beyond party rivalry. . . I appeal to our people to provide a massive support for the Socialist candidate, who by the nature of things is the only one capable of beating Giscard d'Estaing and with him the Right, the privileged and big capital!

It was the last time that Mitterrand was to express himself in such language of class.

At the Congress, Mitterrand stepped down as First Secretary. In his place was elected Lionel Jospin whom Mitterrand had groomed for the post. The announcement of Jospin's succession included a reference to the fact that he was the 'interim' First Secretary. Mitterrand was heard to exclaim, 'Why interim?' Whatever happened in May Mitterrand would not return as party leader. The decade spent since Epinay in building the Socialist Party would now join the decade spent as a Fourth Republic minister and the decade spent opposing de Gaulle. Others would lead the Socialist Party for the rest of the century and beyond. If Mitterrand failed in May, his political life would be over.

Mitterrand spent two weeks in February touring China. The trip provided plenty of opportunities for photographs without his having to issue any statements. Mitterrand the international statesman was on display. At the beginning of March it was

Mitterrand the resistance leader and determined wartime escaper who was offered for public consumption as he retraced, in the company of Willy Brandt, his escape-route from the German prisoner-of-war camp in which he had been held forty years previously. In his earlier political life, Mitterrand could claim no exclusivity about his wartime courage. Plenty of his opponents, Gaullists, Communists or Christian Democrats had equally distinguished resistance or Free French records. By 1981 however, Mitterrand was the last of a vanishing breed, the only major candidate who could claim a distinguished war record from 1939 to 1945.

To a France still haunted and fascinated by what went on during the war – the previous summer had seen widespread celebrations, in the media and through publicly organized events, of the fortieth anniversary of General de Gaulle's appeal to the French people to resist the German occupier – Mitterrand's often repeated invocation of his time spent as a soldier and in the resistance struck the appropriate patriotic chords. All the more so as a news magazine had recently revealed that Georges Marchais' war record was murky at the very least; he had apparently been obliged as a teenager to go and work for a Messerschmitt factory in Germany, and had voluntarily agreed to sign on for another year's work. Although he claimed to have returned to France in 1944 Marchais could not account for his activities in the closing stages of the war: whatever he had been doing, the period remained a shadowy part of his life.

This differentiation between Mitterrand and Marchais was important for the Socialist candidate's campaign. Anti-Communist smear tactics had been central to the Right's attacks on Mitterrand since the signing of the Common Programme and the formation of the Union of the Left. In 1978, right-wing politicians made great play of what kind of police force a Communist Minister of the Interior would install.

In 1981, those cards were no longer there to be played. The estrangement between the Socialists and the Communists had been worsened by the treatment of the leading Soviet nuclear physicist and oppositionist, Andrei Sakharov and the continuing denunciation by Moscow and other East European capitals of Poland's new independent trade union, Solidarity. At the beginning of 1981, there had been an extraordinary scandal when the Communist Mayor of Vitry near Paris had ordered municipal bulldozers to demolish a hostel being used by immigrant workers. The Mayor claimed that the hostel did not conform to the required health and safety standards, and that the government and Chirac's Paris administration were combining to dump immigrants in Communist municipalities. There was something in both charges, but most of the French Left were shocked at the crude and brutal response of bulldozing the workers' hostel. Instead of condemning the Mayor's activities, Marchais came to his defence with remarks about immigrants that bordered on the racist. The Communist Party's anti-immigrant campaign was heightened when Communist councillors in another Paris working-class suburb demonstrated in front of an apartment block where several Moroccan families lived in order, so they said, to protest against the drug-dealing which they claimed was centred there. A local Communist official even named the family which he said was involved.

Again, the anti-immigrant tone of these Communist prounce-ments caused a sensation while the naming of individuals seemed reminiscent of the behaviour of wartime informers. One of the Communist Party's leading intellectuals, Etienne Balibar, wrote an article comparing the Communists' support for Algerians during the Algerian war to their harassment of North Africans today. He was expelled from the Party for his pains.

At the same time Marchais kept up his attacks on Mitterrand whom he repeatedly declared to be no different from Giscard. In March, the Communist candidate stated on television: 'The real danger would be to see François Mitterrand, if his hands are free, in power and governing with the Right in order to continue and exacerbate present policies.' In Moscow *Pravda* also accused Mitterrand of sliding to the right and praised Giscard as a 'prudent and stable politician' with a sensible foreign policy. It was little wonder then that Mitterrand talked of an 'objective alliance between the Right and the Communists': whether in France or in the Soviet Union, the Communist message was that a Socialist victory was the last thing that sensible people could desire.

These insults that Marchais aimed at Mitterrand, and the

widening gap between the Socialists and the Communists, as if the Union of the Left had never existed, undoubtedly helped Mitterrand. For no one could now convincingly argue that after the election he would be a prisoner of the Communists, nor that in electing Mitterrand the voters would also have to swallow the policies and personalities of what in recent months had become to many a repellent and unsavoury Communist Party. People looked at Mitterrand and what the Communists were saying about him, and judged that the incantations of the Right about Trojan horses and introducing Communist collectivism into France no longer rang true. It seemed to be another of those delicious ironies by which Mitterrand, having worked so hard and staked his political career on bringing the Communists out of their political ghetto in the 1960s and having kept the Socialist Party leaning firmly leftwards, despite the Rocardian push in the opposite direction in the 1970s, was now facing the most virulent opposition from those he had helped and with whom he had forged a programmatic alliance.

The advantage lay with Mitterrand, however. In addition to those voters of the Centre or the Left who were content to know that he would have no obligations to the Communists after the election was over were the millions of Communist voters themselves who were not Party members but who loyally voted Communist as the Party best expressed the need to defend working peoples' interests as well as hold out the possibility of change. They all knew that despite Georges Marchais' vigorous, punchy campaign there was no way he could be elected. Even, if by some miracle, he was to be one of the two candidates to make it to the second round, the bulk of the non-Communist Left would simply not vote for him. But in the first round his candidature could pose problems for Mitterrand. Assuming the Communists would not fall below the 1978 vote of 21% and with ecologists and other left-wing candidates, as well as Chirac and the other Gaullists dissipating the combined anti-Giscard vote, there was a faint possibility that something might go horribly wrong and the second round would either be between Giscard and Chirac or be between Marchais and Giscard. Either way Giscard would be in power until 1988. It was from calculations like this that the idea of the 'useful' vote was born, that is, someone who normally votes Communist plumping for Mitterrand in the first round to ensure the presence of an effective Left candidate in the second round. If anything then, the Communist decision to run a candidate in the 1981 election and their strong hostility to Mitterrand during the campaign period as well as the months before acted in Mitterrand's favour.

Giscard's other great anti-Mitterrand ploy in the 1974 election, that the Socialist candidate was a man of the past, was also a card whose value had been reduced to nothing. You had to be middle-aged for the reference to being a Fourth Republic politician to have any pejorative value. Mitterrand came over as a man with a courageous wartime record who since 1958 had stood against the regime of personal power incarnated by de Gaulle and his successors. He had made Socialism acceptable in France and embodied the traditions of Jaurès and Blum. The policy put foward by the Socialist Party since 1971 and the progamme contained in his 110 propositions could be qualified as adventurous, risky or untried but by no means could they be described as the policies of the past. As so often happens it falls to a relatively older person to represent the political hope and dynamic energy of the young within his party. For the hundreds of thousands who had flocked to the Socialist banner since 1968, Mitterrand, despite being only six months away from pensionable age, was the man through whom that youthful hope and energy seemed to flow.

Now it was Mitterrand's turn to base his campaign on Giscard's past record and looking back over the seven years he had plenty to choose from. Giscard himself had been forced to drop his Olympian style once the campaign got going in March. From having played the role of the President, unable with his heavy national and international responsibilities to participate in the politicking going on at ground level, he suddenly became very much the candidate lashing out at Mitterrand and Chirac in turn. Chirac, in particular, ran an extremely dynamic campaign and was often more extreme in his denunciations of Giscard than Mitterrand.

Mitterrand, however, enjoyed the fight, saying of Giscard: 'It is difficult to be such a good candidate and such a bad President. He has one speciality, which is to have plenty of compassion for two months every seven years.' The reference to compassion was a revenge for Giscard's wounding remark – 'You do not have a monopoly of compassion, M Mitterrand' – during the 1974 television face-to-face debate. In denouncing Giscard's foreign policy which he said was too complaisant towards Soviet aggression in Afghanistan, Mitterrand said Giscard had acted as a 'little postboy' for Brezhnev in bringing a message from the Soviet leader to the Venice meeting of the leaders of the industrialized nations. The next day Giscard's Foreign Minister denounced Mitterrand as having used language that was 'an insult to France'. It showed how rattled Giscard was becoming; the majesty of his presidential style began to look very thin indeed.

As Giscard began to look more like a fallible candidate and an unattractive human being, Mitterrand became more grave and talked more and more of uniting all the population:

> When M Giscard d'Estaing or M Chirac say they want to bring together all the people of France they usually mean they want to bring together all the people of France except for the five or six million who vote Communist. Well, I will never say that. I have worked for fifteen years to reunite, without exceptions, all those who can contribute to rebuilding France. There is someone who said and did that before me and that was de Gaulle in 1944 during the war when he needed everybody. Now we are in a crisis and I need everyone.

The references to de Gaulle multiplied as the campaign wore on. Defending his nationalization programme and the need, despite the recent behaviour of Communist Party leaders, to make Communist voters feel part of French political life again, Mitterrand cited de Gaulle as the man who had taken so much into public ownership and who had brought Communist ministers into government:

> I am not renouncing the political struggle I had with de Gaulle in the past. I fought openly, cleanly, honestly and never allowed myself to behave like others in spreading poisonous tittle-tattle or stabbing him in the back. I also acknowledged what he achieved with Socialists and

Communists in nationalizing the major banks and getting planning going again. But what matters today is to assemble Frenchwomen and Frenchmen for the important work of national recovery. This is an appeal to national resistance against the fatality of the crisis, as General de Gaulle appealed in his day in other circumstances that were difficult for the nation.

Mitterrand's television manner had changed, becoming more weighty, even solemn. It was not quite, but almost, as if he was laying claim to the personal, if not the political inheritance of de Gaulle.

The campaign itself focused on Mitterrand and his duel with Giscard. Mitterrand flew around the country in a small jet to speak to ever increasing crowds. Considerable effort was put into the election meetings. A specially made film entitled 'Giscard by himself' which wickedly contrasted presidential promises with what had actually happened in France in the past seven years was shown before Mitterrand arrived. He would walk slowly through the cheering crowd surrounded by local Socialist Party deputies and mayors and at the end of his speech they would group round him holding up their red roses and singing the *Internationale*. More and more, Mitterrand emphasized unemployment as the key failure of the Giscard era. He had mentioned the subject almost in passing in a speech early on in the campaign and found the issue provoked an immediate crowd response.

He therefore returned to the rise in unemployment and drew considerable support with his promise to bring in the thirty-five-hour week and to create 200,000 public sector jobs. As head of his official campaign support committee he chose an unemployed, middle-aged mother of two whose personal descriptions of what life under Giscard meant at the sharp end contrasted with Mitterrand's more traditional oratory.

As 26 April 1981, the day of the first round, grew nearer, Socialist Party speakers emphasized the need for a big vote for Mitterrand in order to send him into the second round from as strong a base as possible. He underlined the point in his eve-of-poll television broadcast:

I am the Socialist candidate but you also know very well that I am the only candidate of the Left who can win through. Votes given to other candidates, worthy as they may be, will compromise that victory. The stronger I am in the first round, the more chances I shall have to be elected to bring about the desired changes.

It was almost a tactical dissertation rather than a political appeal. But it worked. When the results were announced, Giscard had obtained 28.31% of the votes cast; Mitterrand 25.84%; Chirac 17.99%; Marchais 15.34%.

Never before in the history of France had the Socialist Party received such a high score; for the Communists it was a disaster. They had to go back fifty years to find an election in which so few French people had voted Communist.

Nevertheless, it was the Communist bogey that Giscard invoked at the very beginning of the second round. 'Liberty would be in danger' with the Socialists in power. Possessions, second homes, land, small businesses would vanish in the wave of leftist expropriation and ruinous taxation following a Mitterrand victory. Mitterrand's rebuttal was more dignified than the attack. Giscard, he stated, 'wants us to forget about unemployment, the high cost of living, the inequalities and the exclusion of young people from society. My choice of society is simple: it is based on jobs. His is based on unemployment.'

Both the public and private opinion polls placed Mitterrand ahead and the campaign had a slightly unreal air as people other than the two candidates made statements with a view to establishing positions after the final count. Chirac said that he would personally vote for Giscard but left to his voters their own decision. It was a lot less than an enthusiastic endorsement and indicated how far apart the two main wings of the Right now were.

The Communist Party leadership called for a Mitterrand vote. They posed no conditions and did not even ask for talks with the Socialist Party. Marchais' humiliation at the polls had had a chastening effect. The Ecologist Party did not tell their supporters how to vote but between Giscard and Mitterrand the latter was the lesser of two pro-nuclear evils.

The key word in France had become 'change'. With some variations in personnel and ideology, the Right had now been in power in France for twenty-three years. The Fifth Republic had been shaped to produce a strong executive President but how democratic could France be said to be if there was never any alternation between the two broad political forces in the country? None of the other major Western democracies – the United States, West Germany, or Great Britain had gone so long without an alternation in governments. The one big country that had kept the same political group in power for as long, in fact longer than France, was Italy and no one wanted to hold up Italy as an example to follow. In addition the idea of Giscard in power for a further seven years, particularly the arrogant, imperial Giscard who had been increasingly on show in recent years was hard for many French people to take. Perhaps one of de Gaulle's fundamental mistakes in drawing up the Fifth Republic consti-tution was to give the President a seven-year term. It may be a good idea in providing a longer period of office to effect change than in other countries but it would require a rare and special individual who would win a second term. De Gaulle managed it but it is a very unusual democracy that is prepared to live with the same ruler for fourteen consecutive years. The call for a 'change' became more noticeable in the closing stages of the campaign and was supported by many who may not have been convinced by Mitterrand but who, above all, wanted rid of Giscard.

Mitterrand promised change but at a reasonable pace. As he told the magazine *Le Point*:

> The presidency is neither the beginning nor the end. My ambition is to spread my ideas rather than gain personal position . . . Ideas ripen like fruit and like men. They have to be given time. You cannot sow one day and reap the next and history is not made as fast as newspapers . . . We will not overcome the crisis by issuing decrees or by purely technical measures . . . How can we give back to our people enthusiasm and high spirits and thus the desire to overcome the crisis if we do not overturn our present system of values and replace policies based on the profit of a small group by policies based on human respect? The Socialism of freedom

is above all else a cultural idea, a choice of life and survival, or rather a choice of civilization. I am asking all French people to join with me in inventing a culture, a way of life, in short a French model of civilization.

In another interview with the *Nouvel Observateur* Mitterrand stressed the need to 'change economic structures . . . the reproach made against social democrats is not to have attacked capitalist society at the heart of its power over economic decision. The result is that when the conservatives regain power they can knock down structures that had not been properly built up.' But Mitterrand stressed that the only nationalizations he would carry out would be those listed in this manifesto. Any new public takeovers would have to be after another election.

His face-to-face television debate with Giscard did not have the same dramatic impact as the 1974 confrontation. Mitterrand's television performance, thanks to tuition and practice had improved while conversely, Giscard, the master television practitioner of 1974, had become less competent during the seven years of the presidency. Each of his interviews had been so well orchestrated with hand-picked interviewers posing soft, unchallenging questions, that he had lost the touch that only comes when a politician regularly faces tough questioning. Even his 1974 trick of suddenly posing a detailed technical question to Mitterrand failed to work. When Giscard asked Mitterrand if he knew the exchange rate for the German mark, Mitterrand replied that he was not in the studio to pass an examination, and then promptly gave the correct figure.

In his final television address Mitterrand offered France five objectives: to conquer unemployment, re-launch the economy, construct a just society that was more free and more responsible, restore French strength and independence and promote world peace. 'Elected President of France I will be the man of reconciliation, of dialogue, of uniting our people.'

On Sunday 10 May 1981, François Mitterrand received 15,700,000 votes (51.76%) against Valéry Giscard d'Estaing's 14,600,000 votes (48.24%). The first part of the odyssey was over.

17
President Mitterrand

I am no longer the candidate of the Socialists.
I am the President of all France.

Mitterrand's first act as President was to appoint Pierre Mauroy as Prime Minister. It was a reassuring appointment. Mauroy had a record of competence as Mayor of Lille and his bulky, friendly figure gave notice to French people that there would be no sudden upheavals upon the arrival of the Socialists in power. He was also loyal to Mitterrand. Lille was particularly touched by unemployment and the presence of Mauroy in the Matignon would underline the importance of the fight against unemployment. It was, after all, one of Mitterrand's chief campaign weapons against Giscard. Unemployment figures continued to mount – they reached 2 million by the end of 1981, nor was there an appreciable drop in the rate of inflation. The two issues with which the Socialists had flayed the previous administration continued to haunt them.

Mitterrand also immediately dissolved the National Assembly. Everyone expected a victory for the Left but in the elections held in June 1981 the Socialist Party secured a victory as great, if not greater, than Mitterrand's presidential triumph. The number of Socialist deputies increased from 107 to 270, an absolute majority in the 491-strong Assembly. The Communists

239

went down from eighty-six seats to forty-three. The twin presidential-legislative electoral triumph meant that there was a complete Socialist dominance of political power that would last until 1986 when new National Assembly elections would have to be held. No one echoed the famous 1945 Labour Party refrain, 'We are the masters now,' but the triumphant spirit was in the air. Hardly anyone noticed a gloomy Jean-Pierre Chevènement speaking on television in the small hours following the night of the legislative elections victory. 'We may have political power but we still do not have economic power,' he said.

Chevènement moved into the government as a senior minister charged with research. Other Socialist leaders left their town halls and Paris offices to take over ministries. Mitterrand and Mauroy balanced the Cabinet carefully. No one was left out. Rocard became Minister of Planning. Deferre was made Minister of the Interior – the Mayor of Marseilles could now set about his life-long ambition of trying to transfer some real power from Paris to the regions. Jacques Delors became Minister of Finance and Economics, an appointment that was designed to placate the business and financial community. Claude Cheysson became Minister of External Relations, the change of title in his ministry from Foreign Affairs to External Relations was meant to symbolize a new French approach to foreign policy and its relationship with other countries though no one ever explained what the terminological difference really meant. Jean-Pierre Cot, another of Mitterrand's left-wing intellectual protégés became Minister of Overseas Development and Co-operation while Charles Hernu, a Mitterrand associate whose connection dated back to the 1950s, became Minister of Defence. Pierre Dreyfus, a seventy-five-year-old former head of the nationalized (and highly successful) Renault automobile firm, was installed as Industry Minister. Renault was held up as an example of how France's publicly owned firms could successfully compete in the world market and Dreyfus was there to indicate that Mitterrand's nationalization proposals would aim at efficient, well-managed enterprises rather than the bureaucratic corporations depicted by the Right.

Mitterrand's most dramatic step was to offer four ministerial posts to Communists. Charles Fiterman, number two to Georges

Marchais in the Communist Party hierarchy, became Transport Minister; three other Communists were appointed Health, Civil Service and Vocational Training ministers. For the first time since 1947 Communist ministers entered the Cabinet. Mitterrand even symbolically placed Fiterman at his left-hand side for the first post-election meeting of ministers.

The new government set to work. A budget was formulated providing for a 27% increase in public spending in 1982, designed to achieve a 3% growth in GNP. Although this meant the public sector deficit doubled, the government could still point out it would be less than that of West Germany. A quarter of a million new public housing starts were promised. Civil research spending went up by 29%. Five key industrial holding groups, Rhône-Poulenc (chemicals and textiles), CGE (electrical), St Gobain (glass and electronics), Thomson (electronics), and Pechiney (metals and chemicals) were taken into public owner-ship. Only the parent groups were nationalized; subsidiaries would continue to have private shareholders. But the newly nationalized firms were to work within a planning framework agreed with the government. Broad objectives would be laid down in a national plan and the companies would be free to develop production and marketing strategies according to how the market and economic environment changed. Industry Minister Pierre Dreyfus said: 'We are nationalizing them so that they can take a longer and broader view of coherent industrial development. They can take more risks than are usually taken in France by private enterprise . . . But business will stay business even for nationalized firms.' Mitterrand put it more dramatically when he declared: 'I am doing with nationalization what de Gaulle did for nuclear defence. I am giving France its economic strike force.' Rhetoric apart, Mitterrand appointed proven and successful managers to head the nationalized enterprises and in two cases – St Gobain and Rhône-Poulenc – he left the previous chairmen in place.

Thirty-nine banks, some with world famous names like Rothschild, were taken into public ownership. But one should not exaggerate the bank takeovers. The main French banks with over 70% of the country's deposits had been state-owned since 1945. Now 95% of funds were under state control. The French government had always kept a guiding hand on institutional financial policy and the increase in state ownership rationalized an existing trend in the French banking system.

Two crucial areas in which critics would have to be pacified were unemployment and inflation. On employment, Mitterrand again held to his election promise and announced the creation of 65,000 public sector jobs with the promise of more. But this could not offset the growth in unemployment throughout 1981, nor did surveys of firms indicate that many were expecting to engage workers in the forseeable future. The arrival of new technology meant that most firms, in France, as in other countries, would expand output by introducing automated machinery rather than by hiring new labour.

Unemployment was supposed to be eased by the introduction of shorter working time though to begin with the employers' federation would concede nothing to the unions' claim. When Prime Minister Mauroy said he was ready to legislate, the employers came forward with the offer of a thirty-nine-hour week and fifth week's annual holiday, though there were numerous disputes over the precise terms of its introduction. Mauroy has made clear he wants the thirty-five-hour week brought in by 1985. On inflation, Finance Minister Delors established a kind of voluntary price freeze with the distant threat of statutory price control.

Gaston Deferre forged ahead with his decentralization measures. The awesome power of the Paris-appointed prefects was to be broken, though they would remain in place to co-ordinate spending and provide an information link with Paris. Local and regional councils would be given increased powers and everyone waited to see if the French, after two hundred years of centralized control, could handle democratic local administration.

On defence, there was no real change. In fact, Mitterrand's defence budget was slightly larger than Giscard's. An atom bomb was tested underground in the French Pacific and Mitterrand authorized work on a French neutron bomb. The great nuclear disarmament wave that produced crowds of several hundred thousand to demonstrate against nuclear weapons in Britain, West Germany, the Netherlands and Italy in the autumn of 1981 barely touched France. Mitterrand was photographed on board a nuclear submarine and French television extolled the value of the French arms exporting industry. As we have seen, de Gaulle's decision to remove France from NATO's military command and the removal of foreign bases and troops from French soil had changed French attitudes on national defence. Also at the back of Mitterrand's mind was the need to keep the French army reasonably content and ensure that it would have no grumbles that could be exploited by those who might be tempted to remove the government by extra-constitutional means.

The death penalty was abolished and the guillotine consigned to the museum despite opinion polls showing that two thirds of the population wanted it retained. De Gaulle's state security court, his own special star chamber set up for political offences and last used in 1975 by Giscard against Corsican nationalists, was abolished. On nuclear energy Mitterrand did no more nor less than his manifesto. Work continued on the nuclear stations already under construction but those that were only on the drawing board were scrapped.

The television and radio stations came under immediate government action. The heads of networks and new channels plus some of the more notoriously pro-Giscard interviewers either resigned or were asked to go. At first there were attempts to set up internal editorial committees but these quickly fell apart as Socialist, Communist, Gaullist and Giscardian journalists were unable ever to arrive at a common policy. Instead the government appointed broadcasting professionals to replace the Giscard appointees. The new people might be broadly sympathetic to Mitterrand but had solid professional reputations behind them. Unlike the arrival of Giscard in 1974 when 270 journalists were forced to leave broadcasting jobs, there has been no witch-hunt. Only about ten journalists below the executive level left. The journalists' unions were trying to secure a new law that would guarantee them some editorial independence irrespective of the person appointed by the government to run the channel.

Foreign policy soon bore Mitterrand's stamp. On one hand he became the strongest European critic of the Soviet Union and in particular the Russian installation of SS20 nuclear missiles targeted on West Europe. He strongly supported the American decision to place Cruise and Pershing missiles on European soil to counter the Soviet weapons. But this was an easy enough demand to make as the American missiles would not be stationed on French territory. The criticism of Russian policy in Afghanistan and on its Euromissiles had been gathering momentum since the beginning of 1980.

But he was equally critical of United States policy in Central America and angered Washington when together with Mexico, France issued a statement recognizing the left-wing forces in El Salvador, currently struggling against the American-backed regime, as a 'legitimate representative force'. This initiative was followed up by the sale of weapons to Nicaragua which the Reagan administration had been depicting as little better than a Russian colony bent on overthrowing United States domination in the region.

He also upset Reagan with his call for more help from the industrialized world to developing countries and he upset Mrs Thatcher when he told her that Europe's first priority should be to conquer unemployment rather than follow monetarist policies aimed at reducing inflation. Yet he kept his lines of communication open with the White House, meeting Reagan four times within the first ten months of the presidency, including one visit in March 1982 when he took the Concorde from Paris for a three-hour meeting with the American President and then flew straight home again!

Mitterand became the first important Western head of state to visit Israel when he went there in March 1982. Much as his visit was proclaimed by the Israelis they were less pleased when Mitterrand bluntly told the Knesset (Israel's parliament) that the Palestinians had a right to a homeland and a state. His acknowledgement of the Palestinian cause was emphasized when he ordered his External Relations Minister, Claude Cheysson, to have an official meeting with the PLO leader, Yassar Arafat. Mitterrand's penchant for spelling out uncomfortable truths was further underlined when he told an Arab audience in Algiers that they should recognize the right of Israel to exist behind secure borders.

For millions of French people the arrival of Mitterrand did mean a positive improvement in their lives. Family and social allowances went up and the minimum wage was increased. Harassment of immigrants was eased. Thousands of petty criminals were amnestied and released from prison. Basic food prices were controlled and family-planning services improved. Mitterrand gave several women important posts in government service and put his authority behind pro-women reforms. Inside workplaces, employers and managers were more conciliatory to union representatives, agreeing to negotiate and consult with them instead of issuing the traditional unilateral *diktat*. But all this is in comparison with the meanness of the Giscard state. By comparison with, say, the conditions of life in countries like Sweden, Denmark or West Germany where a Social Democratic Party had reigned or was reigning, or even by the standards of the last Labour government in Britain, there was little that could accurately be described as a distinctively Socialist breakthrough. And what had been gained could easily be eroded by inflation or unemployment.

A Socialist transformation of social and economic relations would require time. Waiting, patience, biding time are amongst Mitterrand's supreme qualities and he has until 1988 to translate the promises and rhetoric detailed earlier into permanent change. Central to the question of the possibilities and obstacles of the coming period will be the balance of political forces in France.

His handling of political relationships with allies and opponents will be crucial in the next few years. The French Right is badly divided. Giscard blames Chirac for his defeat and it is difficult to see how the two could ever be reconciled. Despite its success in holding on to power for such long periods, the French bourgeoisie is far from homogeneous and at the political level its rule has been based on a series of coalitions and shifting alliances whose contradictions may be contained in office but would be difficult to control in opposition. Each wing has different concepts of what French conservatism should be and its political leaders have unlimited personal ambition. There is no sign of a right-wing equivalent of Mitterrand, ready to devote his political life to forging a Union of the Right.

After its shock at being defeated, the French Right, particularly the populist wing headed by Jacques Chirac began using extreme language to denounce Mitterrand. A continual butt for their rhetoric was the presence of Communist ministers in the government or the occasional Communist Party member who was appointed to a position on the nomination of the government. This aggression of the Right is likely to worsen. While Chirac is firmly committed to parliamentary democracy, one cannot help but recall the many recent examples of extremist groups in France who have been ready to use violence to pressure the state. Potential pressure-points are easy to identify. The latent racism that could be ignited against France's four million immigrants. The small farmers who have seen a steady drop in income during the 1970s and who have been ready to attack lorries containing imported vegetables from Spain or boats with wine coming from Italy. The various French police services, which have been accustomed to function almost as a parallel state under previous administrations, have a noted capacity for political mischief-making which they can easily put into effect should their powers and operational methods be put under effective challenge. Separatist movements in Corsica and in the overseas territories are likely to press their demands as are the ecologists, who are extremely disappointed with Mitterrand's pro-nuclear programme. The French franc can easily be made vulnerable by international speculation. Some factory owners faced with strikes and workplace occupations may turn to physical force as a way of resolving a conflict. The atmosphere created by Chirac and other right-wing politicians will be important in determining whether at a lower level those who would use violence or other forms of behaviour they would not consider using under a right-wing government would feel their actions justified.

The divided political opposition and the guaranteed long life-span of the Socialist administration has, at least provisionally, tempered employers' hostility. A new President of the French Employers' Association opened 1982 with a visit to Mitterrand in the Elysée, something his virulently anti-Socialist predecessor had refused to do, and a vague statement that the employers' aims were the same as the government's was issued. It seemed a long way from the 'rupture with capitalism' proclaimed by Mitterrand only two years previously.

The trade unions sensed this as well, though as usual their ideological differences prevented a common analysis. Those who had predicted, prior to May 1981, a repeat of 1936 if Mitterrand won were disappointed. There were no wholesale strikes or occupations. Instead union leaders opted for wage restraint in exchange for the government package on working time and the rise in the minimum and social wages.

The CFDT complained that the government had made no real suggestions about moving towards *autogestion*. The government replied that it wanted to get the nationalization over first and then it would see. The unwritten social contract between government and workers is based on three components; the rise in wages and social protection for poorer workers; the commitment to increasing employment and job security; the promise of greater power for unions and workers in the workplace. Already there have been differences between the CFDT and CGT. The Communist CGT has urged the government directly to compel employers to make concessions on the shorter working week and in other areas. The CFDT has argued that workers must try and negotiate themselves for these rights and if necessary, strike to obtain them. The difference between the CGT version of the state as the source of benefits for the workers and the scourge of recalcitrant employers is very different from the CFDT who want to see workers take more independent control of their destiny. One of the most important aspects of the Mitterrand government will be whether or not there are significant advances in the direction of some of the ideas contained within the *autogestion* concepts so eagerly held up during the years after 1968 as the keys that open the way to new workplace relationships.

As has been noted, both wage rises and job-security could be wiped out by rising inflation and unemployment, and there were clear indications at the beginning of 1982 that the government would put more emphasis on 'business confidence' than on *autogestion*. In any case, *autogestion* is not an important priority for the Communist Party. Mitterrand's relationship with the Communist Party will be of great importance. It has four ministers in government and on many issues Mitterrand has faithfully followed the policies outlined in the 1972 Common Programme.

But there have been tensions. Predictably it was a foreign issue, the repression of the trade union Solidarity in Poland, that caused early trouble. While Mitterrand, the Socialist Party and the non-Communist French Left strongly condemned the Jaruzelski crackdown and bitterly criticized the Soviet Communist philosophy that underpinned it, the French Communist Party and the CGT blandly said it was all for the best and supported the official Warsaw-Moscow line that the *coup d'état* was necessary to prevent a Solidarity-inspired civil war. This time, to the delight of the French right-wing press, it was the Socialists' turn to vilify the Communists. The Socialist Party's number two, Jean Poperen, accused the Communists of trying to 'Finlandize' France, that is to turn the country into a neutral state dependent on Soviet goodwill. It was a silly accusation and Mitterrand rebuked him. But it showed how close to the surface lay an almost SFIO style anti-Communism in the Socialist Party. The abuse heaped by Georges Marchais and the Communist Party on Mitterrand and the Socialists between 1977 and 1981 was not easily forgotten nor, despite the government alliance, forgiven by many Socialists.

The Communist Party found itself in its traditional dilemma. Having tried to assert its separate, independent and more class-conscious identity by breaking the Union of the Left in 1977 it found that its new role drove voters into Mitterrand's arms. In ten years the Socialist Party had overtaken it in terms of popular vote. There were now six times as many Socialist as Communist deputies in the National Assembly. Its working-class support had declined. In Paris, where there had been massive purges of liberal Communist Party members, its vote went from 18.6% in 1969 to 9.2% in 1981. In Stockholm, the tiny, fringe Swedish Communist Party obtains a higher vote.

Was the nightmare of the French Communist Party – to see itself fade into the fringe in the face of a growing Socialist Party, such as had happened in most north European countries after 1947 – about to come true? It is too soon to say; Marchais' vote may have gone down to 16% but that is still 4.5 million people. Amongst youth he was the most popular candidate. Among people aged between eighteen and twenty-four, Marchais took 24% of the vote, Giscard 23% and Mitterrand 22%.

The CGT, despite the careful cosmetic dressing of a few Socialists in its leadership, remained firmly under Communist influence. Its new General Secretary, Henri Krasucki, was a notorious Stalinist who had always been on the hard-liners' side in the internal debates over Czechoslovakia, Party liberalization, the treatment of intellectuals and the rupture of the Union of the Left. The CGT remained France's dominant union, especially in key industrial areas, in transport and in printing. The moment the CGT chooses to cut up rough, either because its members feel that the Socialist government is not delivering enough or because the Communist Party decides it has more to gain outside of government causing trouble than staying inside the government supporting Mitterrand, then the Socialist government is in trouble.

Both Mitterrand and Marchais know this. In 1972, Mitterrand stated that he wanted to build a great Socialist Party that would occupy political terrain currently held by the Communists and peel away a good percentage of the Communist vote. This he has achieved. Mitterrand has based the last two decades of his political life on building a Union of the Left, either directly with the Communist Party, or at least with Communist voters. It is reasonable to suppose that he would not be unhappy to see the Communist Party lose more of its influence but only if the Socialist Party can gain the support of hitherto Communist voters.

He has always rejected the siren calls to move to the Centre. To repeat 1947 and expel the Communists from government, even if there were Communist provocations to justify such a move, could so split the Left that it would again lose power for more than a generation. Such a move would halt the changes in French society that Mitterrand hopes will earn him his place in history.

On the other hand, the whole tradition of French Communism militates against a more supporting role for a Socialist government and Communist leaders do not see it as their job to ensure Mitterrand's greatness in the future video-cassette accounts of French history. What can they do? If they break out of government the whole weight of public, Socialist and right-wing opinion can be turned upon them. There would be little international support. The Italian and Spanish Communist Parties keenly hope that Mitterrand's incorporation of the French Communists is shown to work so as to open the way for other Communist Parties to participate in government. Unlike 1947, when the French Communists could hold up the Soviet Union as a contrast to pre-war capitalism and fascism, the misery and exploitation of workers in present-day Russia combined with the corruption of the Soviet *nomenklatura,* means that the example of Russia or East European Communist states holds little attraction.

A Communist Party that walked out of government and then organized industrial resistance to Mitterrand would have to shoulder the blame for the consequent economic or social dislocation. Finally, a Communist Party that splits the Left vote in the 1986 or 1988 polls is likely to see its own vote reduced, the Left defeated overall and the Right back in power for another long period.

Set against that is the vision of an ever declining Communist vote. Sixteen per cent in 1981. How much in 1986 – 10%? Seven per cent in 1988? There is also a growing concern that the working class and other minority groups might turn to the ultra-Left for leadership and defence if Mitterrand's policies do not succeed in helping the exploited half of French society.

Nor should one underestimate the individual, personal ambition of those Communist leaders anxious to displace Marchais. A common mechanism for either advancement or self-protection in a left-wing political party is to ensure that one is not outflanked on one's left. If one way to maintain leadership and internal coherence is to break with Mitterrand, then Marchais or whoever succeeds him could consider that sufficient reason. At the beginning of 1982 Marchais looked to be reasonably in control. His five-hour speech to the Twenty-fourth Party Congress held in February 1982 was well received. In it he pledged continued support for the government. At the same Congress Krasucki was critical of the government's lack of pressure on employers to introduce the shorter working week without loss of pay. The Communist Party and the CGT appeared

to have divided up their roles. The Party would remain support-
ive of the government while the union would be critical and the
staunch defender of workers' rights. After the municipal elections in 1983 the tactics might be revised depending on how well,
or badly, the Communists did at the polls. A poor Communist
showing in the 1982 departmental council elections (the Left lost
votes overall but the Communists did far worse than the
Socialists) may hasten this re-evaluation.

Unless Mitterrand is completely convinced that the French
Communist Party is poised on the edge of collapse, and the
evidence does not support this, he will try to keep them inside the
government. Their presence is a necessary reminder of the need
to maintain the policies calling for a transfer of wealth and power
to France's working people and the reorganization of social and
economic practices that may make this possible. For both tactical
reasons and in order to have a political force inside the government that reminds ministers and civil servants of the policies and
principles enunciated by Mitterrand since 1971 it is likely that
Mitterrand will try to retain the Communist ministers.

One tactic the Communist Party could try is to withdraw their
ministers but continue to offer critical support, rather like the
relationship between the Communist Party and Léon Blum's
Popular Front government in 1936. Mitterrand is unlikely to
accept this, nor will he give way to blackmail should the
Communists threaten withdrawal unless a specific measure is
passed. They will have to be with him all the way and take the
consequences, or leave the government and take the consequences. The French Communist Party is finding out that, as
Pierre Mendès-France said in quite a different context: 'To
govern is to choose.'

This digression on the French Communists is necessary
because it is on their calculation and strategy that the possible
fate of the Socialist government hinges. The Socialist Party, as
distinct from government, will also be playing a role. At one level
of course the Socialist Party simply slipped into government.
National secretaries, Mitterrand's Socialist Party advisers,
emptied their desks in the Rue Solferino headquarters of the
party and installed themselves in the various ministries dotted
around Paris. Lesser party officials and researchers entered the

ministerial private offices where they would play a decisive political role in formulating and applying policy. Inside the National Assembly the 270 Socialist deputies each had a research assistant and the Socialist group of deputies had its own offices and staff. One hundred and thirty-eight of the Socialist deputies were former teachers and only two were manual workers. In fact the handover from the Giscard to the Mitterrand government seemed like one set of intellectuals giving way to another set. One looked at Rocard, Chevènement, Cot, Joxe, Cheysson and Delors, and the rule of the brilliant technocrat remained unchallenged. Many of them were old boys of the prestigious National Administration School just as Giscard and Chirac were. Cheysson and Delors had worked under Pompidou and Giscard. The Socialist victory meant new faces, new policies but the educational and career background of many of those now in power was identical to their predecessors'.

Mitterrand began distancing himself from the Socialist Party as soon as he won the presidency. He met his deputies and senators in a Paris hotel saying that as President he could no longer be on the partisan territory of the Socialist Party head-quarters. 'I am no longer the candidate of the Socialists. I am not their President. I am President of all the French.' Party politics, as Mitterrand knows, cannot be washed away as easily as all that. In the first months after victory the internal differences of the Socialist Party were buried. A single motion was presented at the Party Congress in Valence in October 1981, the Rocardians having at the last moment withdrawn their own motion in favour of a majority one. Lionel Jospin now sits as First Secretary in Mitterrand's old seat facing serious difficulties. Since 1971, the Socialist Party has lived from election to election culminating in 1981. Its electoral strategy has succeeded but now Jospin has to construct a new set of political relations that will be as engaging for the rank and file member when his or her party is in power as it was exciting when the party was leading the struggle against Giscardism. Four by-election defeats and an indifferent showing in the departmental council elections for the Socialists early in 1982 suggested that this would indeed be a problem.

The Socialist Party enjoyed a wave of new recruits after May 1981 bringing its membership to 200,000 at the beginning of

252

1982. That is still only one third of the Communist Party's membership. As Jospin himself has observed:

> The French Communist Party is still stronger than us in many respects, by its links with the working class, its organization, its finances, the power of its full-time officials, all of which play a concrete role in political and social struggle. The French Socialist Party is not in the same position as the Labour Party, the West German Social Democratic Party or the Swedish Social Democratic Party.

The Socialists may be sitting in the Elysée and the ministries but the Communists retain power within the working class and its communities through their party organization. Mitterrand unified and rebuilt the Socialist Party: Jospin has the equally difficult, some would say more difficult, task of making it permanently the dominant party of the Left, and in the Left.

Jospin enjoys privileged access to Mitterrand and it is inconceivable that Mitterrand is not conscious of the need to shape his policies over the next few years in such a way as to help Jospin and the Socialist Party emerge victorious in the 1986 and 1988 elections. There will be little honour in Mitterrand's presidency if, at the end of it, the Socialist Party is weak, divided, and beginning to resemble the SFIO of thirty years ago. The future development of the Socialist Party is therefore an important question to which Mitterrand must address himself.

One problem in writing this concluding chapter on Mitterrand is that he had not, by the beginning of 1982, had to face any major problems. In a curious religious metaphor, the period following Mitterrand's election was known as the 'state of grace'. This implies a potential, indeed a probable, fallibility and as Lionel Jospin pointed out early in 1982 'neither euphoria nor a state of grace is the normal condition of a democracy'. There was a contrast between the quite dramatic structural changes in the French economy and the soothing speeches of the ministers carrying them out. The state share of industry by turnover went up from 18% to 32% but what was interesting was the qualitatively different type of firms nationalized. Unlike the wave of post-war nationalizations when basic service industries such as transport and energy supply were taken over, the Mitterrand nationalizations involved firms at the sharp end of modern manufacturing whose products were amongst the most advanced to be found on the world market. The French state now has a stake in the latest developments in bio-technology, informatics, and micro-circuit production. If it works it could mean the beginning of a new era of economic relationships in a modern industrial democracy.

None of that was evident in many of the speeches of Socialist leaders in the first months after May 1981. Prime Minister Mauroy, Finance Minister Delors and Industry Minister Dreyfus were to be seen touring the country trying to maintain that fragile and ill-defined concept called 'business confidence'. The word 'reform' replaced 'rupture' while Mitterrand himself spoke of the 'slow ways of history'. It was almost as if well-meant ministerial directives and reassuring speeches would convince French managers and businessmen that nothing very dramatic was happening to them. Mauroy has tried to encourage what are termed 'solidarity contracts' between government, unions and individual employers. In return for certain tax advantages firms would guarantee jobs and engage unemployed youngsters. The use of the word 'solidarity' (Mitterrand also named his minister for social affairs, Nicole Questiaux, the Minister for National Solidarity) was a shameless steal from Poland.

But the appeal to 'solidarity' was also an appeal to change attitudes, to accept the arrival of Mitterrand and the Socialists as the occasion for change just as the post-liberation government brought about immense changes between 1944 and 1947.

A big difference between then and now is the internationalization of capital and manufacturing and the arrival of new technology. In 1970, 27.5% of the household goods sold in France were imported; by 1981, that figure had risen to 51.7%. Imported capital goods had risen, in the same period, from 25% to 37.3%. French exports were earning good money overseas, though some of the chief foreign exchange earners were politically sensitive exports like arms or nuclear technology, but the re-launch of the French economy depended on international factors and was no longer something completely under the control of whosoever sat in the Elysée or the Matignon.

On new technology, the change was even greater. One international trade-union study predicted that by the year 2010, the goods produced by the Western world's manufacturing industry could be made using only 10% of the current blue-collar work-force. The thirty-nine-hour or even the thirty-five-hour week and bringing retirement down to the age of sixty will hardly dent the potential that new technology has to wipe out jobs.

To a certain extent Mitterrand has begun addressing that problem by placing more emphasis on the so-called North-South dialogue than his fellow Western leaders. He understands that an increase in demand, sufficient to maintain let alone extend living standards in the North must be partly based on an increase in purchasing power and demand in the South. It is in that context that Mitterrand has constantly urged his co-Presidents, Prime Ministers and Chancellors to re-launch their economies, cut interest rates and make employment and an increase in demand a major international economic priority. So far he has been ignored but he will still be in office long after the next round of elections in the United States, Great Britain and West Germany and if his policies are successful, even on a limited scale inside France, then his message will carry greater conviction in the rest of the world.

He seems uncertain about what kind of presidential style to develop. To begin with there was a grandeur and an aloofness that reminded many of de Gaulle. He transferred the presidential office to de Gaulle's old study in the Elysée. As the *Financial Times* reported from Mitterrand's first presidential press conference in September 1981: 'There was a Socialist President sitting in the same Salle des Fêtes at the Elysée that President de Gaulle used to make his major pronouncements, looking pontifical and serene, and pulling out of the hat the same Gaullist stage props about France's place in Europe and the world that the French Right used to consider their own.' It did not last. As more and more rows developed inside the government Mitterrand had to act as the referee and become involved in relatively detailed policy making. He announced, for example, that he would oversee in person the development of the newly nationalized concerns. Above all, that was a policy he wanted to make work.

In 1975, Mitterrand recorded in his diary a conversation

between Gaston Deferre and a journalist in which Deferre was asked when Socialism would arrive. 'In my opinion,' said Deferre, 'it will take fifteen to twenty, probably twenty-five years before we reach a truly Socialist society.' Mitterrand observed: 'It seems to me that it was a trick question. Socialism is not an objective. It is a journey.' Is France now becoming a more Socialist country or are we simply seeing an alternative set of social and economic managers for what will remain an unchanged capitalist state? Mitterrand would probably agree with Ignazio Silone when he wrote:

> I cannot conceive of Socialism tied to any particular theory, only to a faith. The more Socialist theories claim to be 'scientific', the more transitory they are. But Socialist values are permanent. The distinction between theories and values is clearly enough understood by those who ponder the problems, but it is fundamental. A school of a system of propaganda may be founded on a collection of theories. But only a system of values can construct a culture, a civilization, a new way of living together as men.

Despite the study of political and economic theory that he had undertaken prior to entering office there is no indication that Mitterrand has a conclusively worked out and interlocking set of theories about the state, capital and labour, or the relations between men and women or nation and nation. After forty years of political life he is no doctrinaire. The libertarian streak in him is strong and has kept coming up through the various vicissitudes in his career. Individual personal rights and how to protect and defend them have been at the centre of his political life. In his two volumes of diaries published in the 1970s, he will break off an entry about some abstruse political theory to record his anger about some hapless individual being maltreated by the state. It is this concern for personal liberty that conditions his attitude to the Soviet Union. The expropriation of the means of production by the Bolsheviks bothers him hardly at all; at least there is no evidence in his writings that this is so, but the stamping out of constitutional rights and human freedoms by Lenin, Stalin and their successors is the reason why, in his view, Soviet Communism is to be completely rejected. Again his dislike of

American support for Latin American dictatorships is not based on whether or not capitalist relations should be maintained, but because the price of preserving American hegemony is paid for by the removal of political freedoms in the region. The question of liberty, Mitterrand told a seminar early in 1981: 'is the great problem on the road towards Socialism. If Socialism is a better way of putting liberty into practice we cannot claim to be building Socialism by getting rid of those liberties that already exist in order to move along more quickly.'

Since 1945, West Europe has seen several attempts at government by parties that call themselves Socialist, or Social Democratic or Labour. If we look at the problems of West Europe – unemployment, social unrest, great poverty co-existing alongside excessive, vulgar wealth – we might reasonably believe that whatever their achievements the post-war governments of the Left in West Europe have not succeeded in bringing about the changes that open the way to new forms of economic, social, and cultural relations that will permit material security for society as a whole coupled with personal satisfactions. Mitterrand has had twenty-three long years of opposition to consider these questions and has until 1988 to show if he can fashion, in France, a form of democratic Socialist society which works.

Of his own commitment to Socialism there can be no doubt. His arrival at what might be called a Socialist culture was slow, winding and tortuous. Some of his left-wing detractors in France have given the impression that he put his career before his politics, that he was a kind of St Augustine of the Left – 'Lord, let me be a Socialist, but not yet.' This is not fair. The middle years of his life were spent in opposition. From the age of forty to sixty-four, he held no office and enjoyed none of the fruits that politics brings its servants. It required a certain belief to stay that course; belief in an ideal of a Socialism that was democratic and libertarian, which involved the breaking of existing patterns of capitalist control but yet not placing collectivist economic reorganization above broader political questions, particularly those concerned with the need to enable French citizens to control their own destinies.

The successes of François Mitterrand have been supremely those of a leader of the opposition who brought himself, the

Socialist Party and the French Left to the conquest of political power in France. He, and they now have to show that they can use that power, and more importantly, share it with their fellow-citizens.

Appendix

François Mitterrand's 110 Propositions for France

I. *Peace: France open to the world*

Protection of human rights and solidarity with struggling peoples

1. Demand the withdrawal of Soviet troops from Afghanistan.
2. Condemn US support of Latin American dictatorships.
3. Confirm the right of Polish workers to their liberties and respect of trade-union independence.
4. Peace in the Middle East by ensuring the security of Israel's established and recognized borders, the right of the Palestinians to a united Lebanon.
5. The independence of Chad. Respect of the sovereign rights of Cambodia. Support of the right of self-determination in Eritrea and the western Sahara.

Disarmament and collective security

6. Progressive and simultaneous disarmament to abolish military blocs maintaining a balance of stationed troops.
7. Reinforced international action against the proliferation of nuclear arms and for stricter inspection of nuclear power stations.
8. The opening of negotiations on joint security in Europe

following the conference on the reduction of armed forces and tension, proposed by the French Socialists. Withdrawal of the Soviet SS20 missiles along with the cancellation of the installation of American Pershing missiles on European soil.

New world economic order

9. Priority for the North–South dialogue in implementing a new world economic order. Public aid to the Third World raised to 0.7% of the GNP of each developed country.

10. Definition of a new world monetary system through the reform of the International Monetary Fund, of the World Bank and 'monetary basket'; a moratorium and increased cash possibilities for the poor nations of the Third World.

A strong France within an independent Europe

11. Strict enforcement of the Treaty of Rome. Common Market: encouragement of the democratization of its institutions and putting to use its social provisions. Defence of European employment by the development of communal industrial policies, by the protection of those sectors threatened by the import of certain products from Japan and the United States, by the elaboration of a community regulation on the activities of multinational companies.

Thorough reform of the agricultural policy and regional policy

12. Before Spain and Portugal are admitted to the EEC, four preliminary conditions must be respected (agricultural, industrial, regional and fishing policy), in conformance with the Socialist Party resolution adopted in Montpellier in September 1978.

13. Creation of a Council of the Mediterranean Nations.

II. Employment: Social growth through control of the economy

Re-launching the economy

14. A programme for re-launching the economy will set,

following the next legislative session, the first orientations: employment, prices, technological development, living conditions.

15. Industrial improvements will be made in the fields of electronics, energy, durable goods, transport and the automobile, chemical and bio-chemical industry, steel industry and agriculture in order to strengthen the market within France and stimulate employment.

16. A programme of public works, construction of community housing and facilities (nurseries, school restaurants, kindergartens) will be set up during the second half of 1981.

17. Research will be stimulated in order to reach 2.5% of the GNP by 1985. For small companies, financial aid will be facilitated and creativity encouraged.

18. 150,000 jobs will be created in public works and social services to improve working conditions and public facilities (health, education, post and telecommunications, etc.). 60,000 jobs of public utility will be placed at the disposition of local groups and associations.

19. This programme, democratized and decentralized, will strengthen economic development. Social growth will depend on the dynamism of the public sector, investment incentives, raising low income levels and improving working conditions.

20. The franc will be protected from speculation. Industrial and agricultural development and economizing energy will make growth less dependent upon imports. By 1990, the percentage of foreign trade in the gross interior product will be reduced to less than 20%.

21. The public sector will be extended by the nationalization of the nine industrial groups mentioned in the Common Programme and Socialist Programme as well as of steel works, and the aerospace and arms industries which are financed through public funds. Certain banks and insurance companies will also be nationalized.

22. Working contracts for an unlimited period will again become the basis of working relationships; the possibilities for trade unions to mediate with their companies will be extended and strengthened through aid and protection of elected representatives and time devoted to information and free expression

for all employees.

23. The working week will gradually be shortened to thirty-five hours after negotiations between social groups. Shifts will be made shorter for heavy manual labour. The fifth week of paid vacation will become effective.

24. The national employment agency will be democratized. It will be transformed into a public service for employment (co-ordination of information, education and changes in profession, temporary work).

25. A law will set the conditions for increases in rent and utilities. Furthermore, special provisions will be made in favour of tenants in low-income housing.

26. Saving will be encouraged. Family savings books will be index-linked. Interest rates on other deposits will be increased. The reform of the financial system will enable the French people to invest their savings in those areas considered most important in re-launching the economy.

27. Interest bonuses or fiscal advantages will be offered on a contractual basis in order to contribute to the realization of the objectives of the economic and social policy, in particular to the manual industries.

28. The price of products for which there is no competition will be checked. Distribution will be reformed, the voice of the consumer reinforced.

29. Artists and small businesses will see their social and cultural role recognized and protected. A fiscal salary will be set up for non-salaried workers.

30. The basis of the employers' share of social security will be modified so as not to penalize factories taking on workers.

Social justice

31. The minimum wage will be raised. This level will be fixed after negotiations with trade-union organizations. The new scale of salaries noted in the social conventions will be respected. Benefits for the handicapped and the minimum old-age pension will be raised to the level of two thirds of the average income. Family benefits will be increased by 50% in two steps. Unemployment compensation will be greatly increased.

32. The rate of value-added tax will be brought back to zero for items of necessity.

33. New family benefits will progressively replace the system based on the number of children. The latter system will no longer allow for further increases.

34. A tax on wealth, on a progressive scale, will be instituted. Inheritance taxes will be reformed to decrease the burden of smaller inheritances (for direct or indirect heirs) and to increase the taxes on larger inheritances. The capital gains of companies will be taxed on the basis of re-evaluated net assets.

35. Income taxes will be decreased for low-income tax-payers, increased for those with greater earnings in order to reduce the tax range.

36. The ruling on disputed claims regarding veterans of war, return to proportional veterans' pensions below 100%, a special card for veterans of Algeria.

37. New law on indemnities for repatriated persons, providing for the reconstruction of family ties, more limited for the wealthy.

Energy

38. The energy supply of the country will be diversified. The nuclear programme will be limited to those power plants already under construction, until the French people are informed in greater detail about this programme and can express their wishes by referendum. Aid in favour of new energy resources or new techniques for exploiting traditional forms of energy (coal) will be increased considerably.

39. An extensive programme of investments, designed to economize energy, will be set up. Energy-saving groups organized by state-educated personnel will provide household advice. A new policy will encourage the production of machines, products or materials which will reduce energy consumption.

40. A framework law will guarantee that the voice of the people and elected officials is taken into consideration in all decisions, especially security in nuclear matters.

Agriculture

41. The government will propose to the members of the EEC,

to return to the spirit of the Treaty of Rome, the reform of the Community's agricultural policy. This policy should take into account the necessity of doing away with all inequities of revenue between farmers, salaried wage-earners and all other labourers. Special measures will be initiated for animal husbandry, vine growing and the cultivation of fruits and vegetables, as these areas were not greatly encouraged up to the present time. Markets will be organized by regional bureaux for specific products or groups of products, in order to establish fixed prices in consideration with the cost of production and with a limited quantity per farmer. This policy will take into account the needs of the consumer.

42. A full-time working status will be granted to wives of farmers. The introduction of young people to farming and especially providing access to land will be strongly emphasized. Farming in mountainous regions will receive special aid.

43. The working tool – the land – will be protected against speculation and an excess of exploitation by the creation of county land offices where the representatives of the agricultural profession will have a majority.

44. A fishing policy will be established, including the reorganization of markets, the improvement of working conditions, compensation for workers at sea, investment assistance, etc. On the European level, the government will propose the institution of a Community fishing policy, based on guaranteed access to resources, the rational management of stocks, the organization and protection of the Community market and the harmony of social systems.

III. Liberty: responsible women and men

A respected democracy

45. The presidential term of office will be reduced to five years, with the possibility of re-election for one more term, or limited to one term of seven years without the possibility of re-election.

46. The parliament will recover its constitutional rights. The use of the blocked vote will be limited.

47. Proportional representation will be instituted for National

Assembly elections, regional assemblies and municipal councils for communities of 9,000 inhabitants or more. Each list will contain a minimum of 30% women.

48. The parliamentary representation (deputies and senators) of French people living abroad will be assured by mechanisms of a guaranteed democratic character.

49. Public life will be regulated: candidates for the presidency, ministers, deputies and senators will declare their wealth and income before and after taking up office.

50. The full light of justice will be shone on affairs involving public personalities.

An independent justice

51. The independence of judges will be assured by the reorganization of the board of discipline for municipal officers.

52. The abolition of exceptional procedures (security court, military tribunals in times of peace), of the anti-vandal and Peyrefitte laws. The fundamental principle of innocence until proved guilty will be reaffirmed.

53. Abolition of the death penalty.

Organized counter-powers; a decentralized state

54. The decentralization of the state will be a priority. The regional councils will be elected by popular vote and their direction assured by a president and a bureau. Corsica will have a special status. A department for the Basque Provinces will be created. The authoritative function of the prefects in the administration of local collectives will be revoked. The administration of the department will be handled by the president and bureau of the General Council. The reform of local finances will also be undertaken. The tutelage of the state over the decisions of local collectives will be abolished.

55. Administrative secrecy will be limited and the authorities compelled to justify their actions and to execute judicial decisions.

56. The promotion of regional identities will be encouraged, and the languages and cultures of minory groups respected and taught.

57. Communities, departments, regions will benefit from a more just distribution of public funds between the state and local collectives. These organizations will be responsible for decisions related to the improvement of the living environment: the rapid development of community transport, improvement of the roads, social services, and parks. Such ameliorations will encourage a more animated social life and more active and widespread community projects.

58. For the peoples of French territories overseas who desire a true change, this will mark the beginning of a period of planning and dialogue on the recognition of their identity and their rights to realize their ambitions. Among other changes, in overseas departments, the institution of a departmental council, elected proportionally and responsible for the local affairs of each department with mandatory consultation before any international agreements are made which affect their region of the world. The law drawn up on this subject by the Socialist parliamentary group will be submitted at the next legislative session of the parliament.

59. The draft law on associations will also be submitted to the parliament at its next session. Social representatives will have a recognized status. Organizations associated with this plan for the amelioration of living conditions will have increased benefits and financial means at their disposal.

Economic democracy
New rights for workers

60. The works council of each company will have at its disposal all necessary information concerning the running of the business. For hiring and laying off workers, the organization of work, training, new production techniques, the council has the right of veto with appeal under a new working jurisdiction.

61. The health and safety board will have the authority to close down a workshop or construction area for safety reasons.

62. The management of the public sector will be decentralized to a large extent. Company management will either be tripartite (public collectives, workers, users of the companies' goods or services), or formed by a co-existing management council elected

by the workers and a supervisory council. The greatest possible number of representatives of the workers will be elected directly and through proportional representation. Unit and workshop councils elected by the workers will be set up. A social economy based on mutual co-operation will experiment with new forms of labour organization.

63. The active participation of trained personnel will be guaranteed and their role recognized in those companies representing salaried staff in general: on the boards of companies and holding companies, in private law firms, tripartite administrative councils, public unit and workshop councils.

Equal rights for women

64. Equal employment rights will be guaranteed through co-educational training in all professions (minimum quotas). Loans will be available for further education in relation to the number and sex of those employed by the company in each category. The law will no longer permit the use of sex as a legitimate reason to refuse a woman a job.

65. An equal pay scale for men and women will be guaranteed and applied following negotiations on the collective agreements in each industry.

66. The status of full-time female workers will be accorded to wives of farmers, shop owners and artists, considered up to the present time as persons without professions.

67. Information on sexuality and contraception will be distributed through schools, businesses, municipal offices, health and pre-natal clinics and the media. Contraceptives will be free of charge and the conditions for obtaining legal abortions will be revised.

68. The dignity of women will be respected, especially through the image presented in school books, advertisements and on television. Organizations for the defence of women's rights will be able to bring civil action against parties in case of discrimination.

69. A guarantee fund for the recovery of food pensions will aid divorced women heads of household. Alimony will be equal for husband and wife. An allocation will be made to widows and

divorced women during a minimum of two years, provided they register with the National Employment Agency or in a professional training course.

The family and child

70. Parental leave, half for the father and half for the mother, with compensation and job re-integration guaranteed, will be granted to parents of children under two years of age.

71. A single family allocation will be paid when a pregnancy is announced and when the first child is born.

72. Equal employment for women will require an extensive programme of community facilities: nurseries for 300,000 children will be created as a first priority.

73. An institute for families and children will be set up with the participation of representatives of parliament, trade unions, family and youth associations, the medical profession and teachers.

The right for young persons to be themselves

74. Young people will be eligible to vote in political elections from the age of eighteen and for workplace elections at sixteen.

75. The freedom to call meetings in all schools will be guaranteed to the parents of students, as well as for students in secondary education and vocational schools. Class representatives will participate in class councils and in the management of socio-educational groups without restrictions of their rights.

76. Individuals called up for military service will have the right to assemble and call meetings. Conscientious objection will be respected within the terms of the law.

77. Technical instruction of all kinds will receive the personnel and material means necessary to ensure that no young woman or man will enter the workforce without adequate professional qualifications.

78. The special tax for motorcycles will no longer be required.

New rights for immigrants

79. Discrimination against immigrant workers will be checked.

Any refusal to issue a residence permit will require a valid reason.

80. Equal rights will be assured for immigrant and national workers (work, social protection and aid, unemployment benefits, updated training). The right to vote in municipal elections after five years of presence on French territory. The right of immigrants to assemble will be recognzied.

81. The Programme will set the annual number of foreign workers admitted in France. The National Immigration Bureau will be democratized. Measures against illegal immigration will be reinforced.

A unified society

82. Men will be eligible for retirement with full benefits at the age of sixty years or over and women from fifty-five years of age. Retired persons will have the right to be heard in matters of social security and pension funds. Social security deductions for retired persons will be abolished. A law will be drawn up defining the rights of retired and elderly persons in housing, health and culture, and will assure their participation in the community.

83. The handicapped will be duly integrated in society: possibilities for work, education, housing, transport, leisure activities and access to culture will be adapted to their particular needs.

84. A national system of social potection with equal benefits for all will be instituted progressively. The state will reimburse unfair expenses and will make available those financial resources necessary for expenses in the public interest. The system for insured individuals paying a portion of the cost of treatment will be abolished.

Health protection

85. A community health service will be created for the development of preventive medicine, a third-party scheme will gradually be applied, the creation of integral health centres to which each medical doctor could belong if desired. A new agreement will be negotiated. The Council of Medical Doctors will be abolished.

86. The respective aims of hospitals and private clinics will be clearly defined. A new medical card will be adopted. Medical

equipment will be designated by region and the financing of such facilities redistributed (the daily rate will be done away with).

87. A new medical policy will be created with the help of large nationalized industries where medical and pharmaceutical research will be intensified.

The right of every person to housing

88. A community housing policy will be drawn up in order to provide every household with adequate lodging within the proximity of essential social services (nurseries, day care centres, mass transport facilities). Special facilities catering for young people will also be created (the construction of one- and two-room apartments).

89. The reform of public intervention instruments. The proper use of urban land by local collectivities by the imposition of a property tax, of the right of pre-emption and state-credited loans.

Quality education

90. A unified, lay public service will be instituted for national education. The setting up of this group will be negotiated without monopoly. Associated contracts of private establishments, drawn up by communities, will be honoured. Democratic management councils will be created at the different levels.

91. Schools will be open to everyone. Teaching methods will be extended and the physical well-being of the individual stressed. The teaching of history and philosophy will be developed. Regardless of the branch of study, all persons at the end of their studies should have a certain level of general and professional education. Classes will contain a maximum of twenty-five students.

92. The Seguin-Rufenacht law on the composition of university councils and of the UER will be repealed as well as the decrees modifying the university card.

93. Each worker will dispose of an educational credit worth two years which can be used any time during his or her working life. The managing of the programme for further education will be on a tripartite basis.

Free and pluralist information

94. Television and radio will be decentralized and pluralist. Local radio stations will be able to establish themselves freely as a public service. Their framework of activities will be established by the local authorities. A national audiovisual council will be created, the representatives of the state being in the minority. Creative activities will be encouraged. The rights of citizen-band protagonists will be recognized.

95. The ordinances of 1944 concerning the press will be applied. Those dispositions which assure the independence of journalists and newspapers confronted with the pressures of the authorities, of private groups and of advertisers will be reinforced. The independence of the French Press Agency *vis-à-vis* the State will be guaranteed.

96. All censoring of information, including that in military barracks and prisons, will be forbidden.

Science and culture

97. Fundamental research will be an essential objective: extensive public credit will be granted for its development on the regional and national level. All necessary co-ordination will be assured.

98. The state will encourage and help to finance the implantation throughout the country of centres of creative activity. Outside of France, the active and growing presence of French culture will be encouraged. The teaching of art in schools will be developed and access to cultural centres made easier: longer opening hours in museums, libraries, monuments, and the recruitment of the necessary personnel.

99. Support of the creative arts – cinematography, music, theatre, plastic arts and architecture – will place cultural renaissance in France as one of the first major Socialist ambitions. An international council for science and culture, a European film school and an international music centre will be created.

100. Uncontrolled pricing of books will be stopped.

Natural balances

101. An environmental charter guaranteeing the protection of

natural sites, parks, river zones, forests, waterfalls, holiday and recreation areas will be drawn up and submitted to the parliament, before the end of 1981, after consultation with local authorities and collectivities.

102. The fight against water and air pollution will be intensified. Any association found to be polluting the environment will be penalized.

103. Specifications for the construction of machines and motors dangerous to handle and excessively noisy will be revised and strictly applied.

Sports

104. The independence of the sports movement *vis-à-vis* the state and its financial backers will be guaranteed. Physical and sports education will become an essential part of teaching in national education.

IV. France: a free and respected country

The security and identity of France

105. Development of an autonomous strategy of dissuasion; and new organization of the military service reduced to six months.

106. Concise definition of the extent and content of the Atlantic Alliance. Increased cohesion in Europe.

107. Development of the relations between France and the Soviet Union within the framework of existing treaties.

108. Reinforcement of exchanges with China.

109. Privileged ties with non-aligned countries of the Mediterranean area and the African content, especially Algeria.

110. Establishment of close relations with Quebec. Creation of a French-speaking academy.

Index

Military service 25
Miners 47, 91
Minister of Defence 68
Minister of Information 48–9
Minister of the Interior 59, 61, 68, 69, 165
Minister of Justice 63, 87, 215
Minister of Overseas Territories 53, 66
Minister of War Veterans 43
Mitterrand, Danielle 43
Mitterrand, François
    birth of 15; Brandt W., relations with
    230; Brezhnev, L., relations with 193;
    children 43, 88, 209; colonial issues 51–
    63; Communist Party, relations with 35,
    146–9, 185, 187; constituency 41, 83,
    209; Europe 72, 108, 164, 196; foreign
    policy 117; Gaulle, de, relations with 33,
    98; Kissinger H., relations with 195;
    leader of the opposition 110–12; leader
    of the Socialist Party 142, 182; marriage
    42; Marxist attitudes 132–3, 219;
    ministerial career (see under Ministers);
    nationalization 97, 139, 154–5; nuclear
    weapons 115; oratorical style 78, 106,
    173; Palme, O., relations with 150, 227;
    parents 16; President 239–58;
    presidential candidate 101–109, 167–74,
    227–37; Schmidt, H., relations with 197;
    schooldays 17, 18; socialist beliefs 94,
    133, 138, 257; television performer 105,
    173, 235; travel 53, 88, 192, 209;
    university days 18–24; wartime activities
    25–34; writing 88
Mitterrand, Jacques 26
Mitterrand, Joseph 16
Mitterrand, Yvonne 16
Mollet, G. 8, 46, 59, 71, 81, 90, 95, 122
Monde 68, 94, 214
Monnet, J. 39, 107
Montgomery, General 34
Morocco, 51, 58, 214
Morvan, Le Vieux 3
Mouvement des Radicaux de Gauche see
    Left Radical Movement
Mouvement républicaine populaire see
    Popular Republican Movement
Multinational corporations 154, 197
Municipal parties 177
Mussolini, B. 17, 19

Nantes 189, 201
Napoléon I 215
Napoléon III 9
National Defence Council 68–70
National Liberation Front, of Algeria 61, 71,
    73, 81
Nationalization 39, 97, 117, 147, 156, 238,
    241, 253
NATO 47, 81, 114, 115, 243
Neutron bomb 242
New Caledonia 52
New French Review 22
Newspapers 39
New technology 254
Nicaragua 244
Nice 190

Nickel 52
Nièvre 41, 83
Nixon, R. 103, 152
Nomenklatura 250
North-South dialogue 255
Nouvel Observateur 166, 208
Nuclear power 225, 228, 243
Nuclear submarines 243
Nuclear weapons 115, 148, 199, 228, 242

OAS 104
'Observatory' affair 84–7, 102, 209
Occupation 31–5
OECD (Organization for Economic
    Co-operation and Development) 2, 161
Oil price rises 162, 166
Ostpolitik 152
Overseas Departments 52
Overseas Territories 52, 108, 246

Pact, electoral 111–13, 117
Palais Bourbon 42
Paris 21, 71, 181, 220, 225, 248
Parti Communiste Française see Communist
    Party of France
Parti Socialiste see Socialist Party
Party Socialiste Unifié see Unified Socialist
    Party
Patriotism 7
Peasants 8,
Pesquet, R. 84–7
Pétain, Marshal 11, 27, 28, 33
Peugeot 105, 122, 216
Pflimlin, P. 75
Pharmaceutical industry 155
Plan, the 39
Planning 39, 93, 180
Pleven, R. 53, 66
Poher, A. 131
Poland 205, 222, 230
Police, Paris 67, 226
Pompidou, G. 93, 113, 124, 130, 159, 166,
    183
Popular Front 8, 19, 20, 105
Popular Republican Movement 39, 40, 75,
    91, 103
Portugal 185, 186, 194
Poujadists 71
Pravda 231
Presidential election 1965 101–9; 1969 130–
    2; 1974 166–74; 1981 224–39
Price controls 245
Price rises 46
Prisoners' aid society 31
Prisoners of war 28
Proudhon P. 179
Putsch, of 13 May 1958 75, 122

Questiaux, Nicole 183, 254

Racism 231, 246
Radical Party 19, 40, 57, 59, 112
Radio 48, 210, 214, 243
Railway workers 29
Rally of the French People 74
Ramadier, P. 39, 43

276

DATE DUE

GAYLORD			PRINTED IN U.S.A.